Human Rights and Social Policies for Children and Women:

The Multiple Indicator Cluster Survey (MICS) in Practice

Alberto Minujin
Enrique Delamonica
Marina Komarecki

Editors

New School University
The New School
with support of UNICEF

New School University

The New School

66 West 12th Street
New York, NY 10011

This book is sponsored by New School University
and is published with the support of UNICEF

Human Rights and Social Policies for Children and Women:
The Multiple Indicator Cluster Survey (MICS) in Practice
© New School University and UNICEF 2005

This edition
Published by New School University
Web: http://www.newschool.edu
Telephone: 212 206 3524

Design
  Vesna Petrovic

ISBN: 0-9766252-0-2
Printed in Argentina

Se terminó de imprimir en el mes de abril de 2005
en Altuna Impresores, Doblas 1968 (C1424BMN)
Buenos Aires, Argentina
altunar@uolsinectis.com.ar

Table of Contents

ACKNOWLEDGMENTS

Human Rights and Social Policies for Children and Women: The Multiple Indicator Cluster Survey (MICS) in Practice, is a collaborative product of The New School's Graduate Program in International Affairs (GPIA) and UNICEF. It is with the support and guidance of UNICEF that the GPIA was able to hold the international conference, "Social Policies and Human Rights for Children and Women: Achieving and Monitoring the Millennium Development Goals", in New York in April 2004. The contents of this book present selected papers from the conference.

No book with a scope such as the one presented in this volume would have been possible without the contribution of a large number of individuals. First of all, we would like to thank Elizabeth Gibbons and Trevor Croft from the Division of Global Policy and Planning, and Michael Cohen, the Director of the GPIA, for their active encouragement and extraordinary commitment in getting the conference off the ground.

Edilberto Loaiza and Gaspar Fajth warrant special thanks for the advice on the substantive design of the conference and valuable suggestions on participants. We thank Jeff Madrick, Mushtaque Chowdhury and Stephen Collier for their contribution in helping us select the papers for the conference.

We would like to thank all authors for their presentations at the conference. We also express our gratitude to several others who made significant contributions as conference participants: Arjun Appadurai, Jorge Balan, Carmen Barroso, Virginia Botelho, Jean-Marc Coicaud, Musthaque Chowdhury, Philip Evans, Marianne Fahs, Kul Gautam, Suzanne Grant Lewis, Sheila B. Kamerman, Viviana Mangiaterra, Albert Motivans, Frans Roselaers, Martin Vaessen, and Meg Wirth.

We would also like to recognize the institutional support of the New School, led by its President Bob Kerrey and Dean Ann-Louise Shapiro, and of UNICEF led by Deputy Executive Director Kul Gautam. Logistical support was provided by a tenacious team: Robin Williams, Kristi Allen, George Calderaro, and Susan Sawyer. Philip Akre provided unfailing support during different stages of the conference planning, and copy-edited the papers. This book was produced in Buenos Aires, with graphic design work from Vesna Petrovic.

The Editors
New York
November, 2004

FOREWORD

We are pleased to present a book that is the result of fruitful collaboration between The New School's Graduate Program in International Affairs (GPIA) and the Global Policy and Strategic Information sections in UNICEF's Division of Policy and Planning. The papers selected for this book were first presented in April 2004 at the international conference "Social Policies and Human Rights for Children and Women: Monitoring and Achieving the Millennium Development Goals", organized in partnership by both institutions.

The increased global visibility of children, greater awareness of their rights at the national level, as well as breakthroughs in medicine and health technology, have all contributed to the improved well-being of children. Children are now more likely to survive and have more opportunities to develop to their full potential than in earlier decades. Tremendous progress has been made in reducing child mortality, improving child health, and expanding primary school education.

Efforts towards more rigorous data collection and data monitoring systems during the past decade have also contributed to these improvements. Newly available data provide a better understanding of the situation of women and children in some of the least developed regions of world and allow for better planning and implementation of programs and policies. The Multiple Indicator Cluster Surveys (MICS) have been a crucial part of these efforts.

MICS were originally conceived as a tool to measure a set of indicators for assessing progress towards the goals of the World Summit for Children set in 1990. Subsequently, the surveys have become an instrument to monitor the Millennium Declaration and its goals. MICS can be useful in determining how many children have and do not have their rights fulfilled.

In late 2003, UNICEF and The New School University announced a call for papers asking for analytical and policy-related research using MICS data on children and women. The aim of the conference was to present analytical and policy papers on the progressive realization of human rights and issues of children's, women's, and family well-being based on the use of household data. In particular, the conference sought to promote the use of Multiple Indicator Cluster Surveys (MICS) among a wide variety of researchers, through special efforts to attract contributions from scholars and practitioners in developing countries.

The response to the call for papers was overwhelming. This enthusiastic response demonstrated the desire, on the part of professionals around the globe, to take part in discussions addressing critical issues of poverty and social development.

The conference offered compelling insights into ways to improve the well-being of women and children. It promoted the achievements of the Millennium Development Goals and addressed how statistical information can be used to change the world for the better.

From the large number of interesting and stimulating papers submitted, an expert committee selected a small group of papers that were presented, commented upon and discussed at the Conference. As difficult as it was to reduce the submissions to a manageable number to be presented at the conference, winnowing them down further proved even more challenging. This volume is the result of that process.

We hope that policy makers, researchers, programmers, statisticians, and advocates will find in this book policy analysis, concrete lessons, and methodological approaches that encourage further research and action in the struggle for the respect, protection, and fulfilment of the rights of children and women.

Elizabeth Gibbons
Chief, Global Policy Section   ·
Division of Policy and Planning

UNICEF

Trevor Croft
Chief, Strategic Information
Division of Policy and Planning

UNICEF

Michael Cohen
Director
Graduate Program in
International Affairs
New School University

INTRODUCTION

Over the past decades, through periods of economic expansion as well as during deepening recessions, through financial crises, economic liberalization, and the harsh demands of structural adjustment programs, the plight of the poor has increasingly drawn attention and has energized global action against poverty.[1] The concept of poverty as one based on insufficient income has been redefined to emphasize multidimensional outcomes.[2] The efforts to reduce poverty now include issues like access to education and health services, as well as social and political participation. Moreover, the 1990s saw an upsurge of extended rights agenda: from basic civil and political rights, the focus has shifted to broader social, economic and cultural rights.

It is in this context that the Multiple Indicator Cluster Survey (MICS) originated, using two important milestones as its founding base: the Child Survival and Development Campaign, initiated by UNICEF, and the adoption in 1989 by the UN General Assembly, of the Convention on the Rights of the Child (CRC). The global action for alleviation of poverty was strengthened in a series of international conferences in the 1990s,[3] all of which shared a common theme of improving the quality of life, particularly of low and middle income nations. Commitment to address poverty increased in momentum, when on 30 September 1990, 71 Heads of State or Government and 88 ministerial delegates adopted a World Declaration on the Survival, Protection and Development of Children and a Plan of Action for its implementation at the World Summit for Children. The same pledge was underlined a decade later in a joint document called *A World Fit for Children*[4] and in the Millennium Declaration. In the latter, commitments on the interlocked issues of peace, human rights, security, democracy and sustainable development were agreed upon by 189 states who also pledged to achieve the Millennium Development Goals (MDGs) by 2015. Most of these goals pertain to child rights, their well-being and gender equality.

The Plan of Action of the WSC specified eight major goals relating to survival, health, nutrition, education and gender equality for fulfillment by the year 2000, and further elaborated twenty supporting goals. Mid-decade goals, to be implemented by 1995 were also adopted. The WSC and its follow up actions have played a significant role in shaping global initiatives and driving the momentum in favor of more vulnerable populations, particularly children and women. The setting of specific time-bound goals by the WSC has helped to focus attention on targets, indicators and results. This gives support to the expansion of child rights by setting quantifiable achievements and deadlines by when they have to be attained.[5]

The Plan of Action that emerged from WSC provided governments and their partners with a framework for integrating human rights into their policy and programmatic efforts. They have embodied political commitments, serving as an important framework to guide national and international initiatives. The WSC has helped to create a partnership between governments, NGOs and the UN agencies; and spurred the drawing up of over 150 National Plans of Action to direct and justify regular and timely data collection, resource allocation, and set out specific targets of achievement on which governments are expected to report publicly. The United Nations was asked to assist countries in achieving those goals and measuring progress, and UNICEF became the lead agency for this effort.

During the 1990s, UNICEF's contribution to measuring the progress was manifested through an annual publication, *The Progress of Nations* that highlighted assessment of achievements and constraints at country and global levels. *The Progress of Nations* showed the existing lack of balance between the measurement of progress and the lack of action. It also noted the dearth of data on the well-being of children, an absence that could be interpreted as insufficient of real commitment to improve their well-being.

The initial assessment of the WSC revealed that some of the critical data on key indicators for assessing progress were missing in a number of countries (e.g. malnutrition and mortality disaggregated by age, etc). To address this issue and help the countries fill in the gaps UNICEF devised the Multiple Indicator Cluster Survey (MICS). Designed as a data-collection tool, MICS is made up of different modules (questionnaires on child health, education, etc) which can be used separately in conjunction with other surveys at the country level or they can all be used together. It uses a cluster sampling framework to obtain nationally and sub-nationally representative estimates. MICS covers issues ranging from immunization, nutrition, school attendance, knowledge about HIV/AIDS, etc. It was developed in collaboration with the World Health Organization (WHO), the United Nations Statistical Division, the London School of Hygiene and Tropical Medicine, and the United States Center for Disease Control and Prevention (CDC). By 1996, 60 developing countries carried out stand-alone MICS, and another 40 had incorporated some of the MICS modules with other surveys; and by 2001, 65 developing countries had carried out MICS 2 studies.

The second version of MICS (the end-decade questionnaire) drew on the experiences of mid-decade MICS evaluation, allowing for modification of the indicators in the initial set, and the incorporation of additional indicators (e.g. child birth, child labor). Assisted by the UNICEF technical and financial resources, National Statistical Offices and Ministries of Health, collected MICS 2 data for 63 Indicators for Monitoring Progress at End-Decade. MICS 2 used nationally representative samples of 4000 to 5000 households. The information was primarily gathered about children and about women of child bearing age (15 and 49), and children under the age of 5. UNICEF in currently preparing a third version of MICS for 2005.

Over the past decade UNICEF has produced several MICS related studies, most of which were concerned with policy-related empirical analysis of the data.[6] Yet, the evidence that the data was being used to enhance capacity in the countries from which it originated, as well as evidence of independent research using MICS data sets was lacking. It is in this context that the international conference, "Promoting Human Rights and Social Policies for Children and Women: Achieving and Monitoring the Millennium Development Goals", was organized. The main themes were structured around measurement and trends of child well-being, poverty, poverty indicators, and policy-making agenda, based on discussing MICS related results.

The authors included in this book bring the diversity of their perspectives as members of academia, NGOs, government agencies, and international development agencies, including UNICEF country offices. Their contributions were selected from a long process which we started with an international call for papers in 2003. The response was overwhelming. We selected 29 papers from 22 countries for the conference.[7] In the light of suggestions by the commentators and the editors, the authors revised their papers. About half of these were selected to be included in this book.

Following the themes outlined in the call for papers (analysis of the situation of children and women using MICS evidence as well as methodological issues related to the surveys), the book is organized in two sections, although for some chapters the designation may be arbitrary as no clear separation between presentation of results and methodological conclusions is possible and entirely justified. The first section revolves around methodological topics, while the second brings out the discussion structured around analytical and policy issues.

The opening chapter describes the background, methodology, goals and stakes in connection to MICS. In chapter 2, Simon Pemberton, David Gordon and Peter Townsend, focus on the relationship between child poverty measurement and child rights, a topic of much recent interest both in academia and in the policy making sphere. The authors bring to light the methodological possibilities for producing poverty measures based on standards arising from international agreements. Montgomery and Hewett, in chapter 3, deal with another important methodological issue related to the analyses of household data, the construction of disparity estimates. They apply an approach to classify households by quintiles according to their characteristics to the Senegal survey.[8]

In chapter 4, Chandra Sekhar and V. Jayachandran from UNICEF, write about the methodological challenges of assessing the level and trends of child immunization coverage in India, especially making compatible the results from various surveys and official data. Chapter 5, by Nicola Jones deals with a similar methodological problem: contrasting the results of different surveys, especially using longitudinal data.

In chapter 6, Marco Segone, from UNICEF, builds upon the multidimensional approaches to poverty and also tackles the comparative analysis of time series from different sources. He proposes an approach to measure income, human and social poverty of children that can be used to track trends. He applies this approach to measuring child poverty in Niger. Enrique Mendizabal and Enrique Vasquez from Peru, in chapter 7 discuss the role of evidence in light of LSMS, DHS and MICS surveys, and identify a methodology that can ensure the inclusion of children within the policy-making process.

Concluding the methodological section, in chapter 8, a group of authors led by Malik Jaffer from The American Red Cross (ARC) and Albanian Red Cross (AlbRC), show how the MICS findings shaped project design and guided selection of technical interventions concerning disadvantaged populations in Albania. MICS results were compared to the project's baseline Knowledge, Practice, and Coverage (KPC) survey findings to identify similarities and differences in use of key services and behaviors in the areas of nutrition, control of diarrhea diseases, acute respiratory infection, and family planning.

The section dealing with policies and results begins with chapter 9 where Seema Mihrshahi discusses the impact of breastfeeding as a strategy to improve the health, nutrition and survival of children in a selection of countries. Continuing with inter-country comparisons related to nutrition, Gina Kennedy analyzes the relationship between chronic malnutrition and poverty in urban and rural areas using data and selected indicators from Kenya and Viet Nam in chapter 10. In chapter 11 an attempt to fill the existing gap in the growing body of literature that reflects on single women households, and the strategies they pursue in coping with vulnerability across a variety of countries is presented. Enrique Delamonica, Asmaa Donahue and Alberto Minujin, analyze the outcomes and experiences of children living in such households, and offer policy recommendations as to how to support the efforts of these mothers in raising healthy, educated children.

Chapters 12 and 13, by Mamdadou Thiam from UNESCO and Robert Jenkins from UNICEF respectively, examine the relationship between education outcomes and the working status of children. The former analyzes the situation in Niger and the latter the conditions in India. Frederick Mugisha uses the MICS data for Kenya to show the extent of inequities in child labor in urban slum, urban non-slum and rural areas in chapter 14. A joint ILO-UNICEF-World Bank effort to analyze the situation of child labor in Bolivia written by Lorenzo Guarcello and Scott Lyon is the subject of chapter 15.

Dr. Abdul Alim from UNICEF's country office in Pakistan ends the collection with a combination of results and methodological observations which also expands the debate. He discusses the political relevance of MICS in chapter 16. The author argues that the kind of response that MICS elicits from the state institutions depends upon the socio-economic conditions and political stability of a government, and also on the position of the survey within the given political landscape.

Alberto Minujin, Enrique Delamonica and Marina Komarecki

NOTES

[1] See, for instance, Cornia (2004), World Bank (1990 and 2000/01), UNDP (1996 and 2003), Townsend and Gordon (2002), Langmore (2000), and Pogge (2002).

[2] Wratten (1995), Boltvinik (1997), Reddy and Pogge(2003), Thorbecke (2004), as well as older classics like Sen (1987) and Streeten et al. (1981).

[3] In 1990, the World Summit for Children (WSC) was held in New York. The same year the World Conference on Education was held in Thailand. In 1992, the Rio Summit addressed the environmental challenges. In 1993, World Conference on Human Rights was held in Vienna. In 1994, Cairo hosted the Population Conference. In 1995, the Social Summit promoted an agenda to fight poverty and social exclusion. In 1995, Beijing hosted the Forth World Conference for Women.

[4] It was signed by the UN and reaffirmed during the Special Session on Children in 2002. The Special Session also endorsed the Millennium Declaration.

[5] Himes (1995) and Alston (1996).

[6] For instance, MICS data were used in WHO-UNICEF (2003a and b), UNICEF-WHO (2004), UNICEF (2003), and UNICEF, UNAIDS, USAID (2004). Also, MICS data were used by Monasch and Boerma (2004), Grassly et al. (2004), Blanc and Wardlaw (forthcoming) and Gibbons, Huebler, and Loaiza (forthcoming).

[7] In particular, cross-country studies by researchers in developing countries were encouraged. See Alatas (2003) on the global division of labor in the social sciences which confines researchers from developing countries to perform only single (own) country case studies.

[8] Their approach can be considered an alternative to the one developed by Filmer and Pritchett (1998 and b) and utilized in Gwatkin et al. (1999) and Minujin and Delamonica (2003 and 2004).

REFERENCES

Alatas, S. (2003). "Comments" (Comments on I. Wallerstein "Anthropology, Sociology and Other Dubious Disciplines"). *Current Anthropology*, Oct. 44, (4).

Alston, P. (1996). "Establishing Accountability: Some Current Challenges in Relation to Human Rights Monitoring". In E. Verhellen (Ed.) *Monitoring Children's Rights*. The Hague: Martinus Nijhoff Publishers.

Blanc, A. and T. Wardlaw (forthcoming) "Monitoring Low Birth Weight: An Evaluation of International estimates and an Update Estimation Procedure". WHO Bulletin.

Boltvinik, J. (1997). "Poverty Measurement methods – an overview". New York: UNDP.

Cornia, A. G. (2004). "Inequality, Growth and Poverty: An Overview of Changes over the Last Two Decades". In A. G. Cornia (Ed.). *Inequality, Growth and Poverty in an Era of Liberalization and Globalization*. Oxford: Oxford University Press.

Filmer, D. and L. Pritchett (1998a). 'Estimating Wealth Effects Without Expenditure Data – or Tears: An Application to Educational Enrollments in States of India'. Washington, D.C.: World Bank Working Paper.

Filmer, D. and L. Pritchett (1998b). "Education Attainment of the Poor (and Rich): DHS Evidence from Around the Globe". Washington, D.C.: World Bank Working Paper.

Gibbons, E., F. Huebler, and E. Loaiza (forthcoming) "Child labour, education and the principle of non-discrimination". In P. Alston and M. Robinson (Eds.). *Human rights and development: Towards mutual reinforcement*. New York: Oxford University Press.

Grassly, Nicholas C.; Lewis, James J. C.; Mahy, Mary; Walker, Neff; Timaeus, Ian M. (2004). "Comparison of household-survey estimates with projections of mortality and orphan numbers in sub-Saharan Africa in the era of HIV/AIDS." *Population Studies,* July, Vol. 58 (2).

Gwatkin, D.R., S. Rutstein, K. Johnson, R. Pande and A. Wagstaff (1999). *Socio-Economic Differences in Health, Nutrition, and Population: Country Notes,* Washington, D.C.

Himes, J. (1995). "Introduction". In Himes. J. (Ed.). *Implementing the Convention of the Rights of the Child; Resource Mobilization in Low-Income Countries*. The Hague: Martinus Nijhoff Publishers.

Langmore, J. (2000). "Reducing Poverty: the implications of the 1995 Copenhagen Agreement for research on poverty". In D. Gordon and P. Townsend (Eds.) *Breadline Europe: The measurement of poverty*. Bristol: The Policy Press.

Minujin, A. and Delamonica, E. (2003). "Mind the Gap! Widening Child Mortality Disparities." *Journal of Human Development,* Vol. 4 (3).

Minujin, A. and Delamonica, E. (2004). "Socio-economic inequalities in mortality and health in the developing world". *Demographic Research,* April, Special Collection Number 2.

Monasch, Roeland, Boerma, J. Ties. (2004). "Orphanhood and childcare patterns in sub-Saharan Africa: an analysis of national surveys from 40 countries". *AIDS,* 18 Supplement.

Pogge, T. (2002). *World Poverty and Human Rights.* Cambridge: Polity.

Reddy, S. and T. Pogge (2003). "Unknown: the extent, distribution, and trend of global income poverty", mimeo, available at <www.socialanalysis.org>.

Sen, A. (1987). *The Standard of living,* Cambridge: Cambridge University Press.

Streeten, P. et al. (1981). *First Things First: Meeting basic human needs in developing countries,* Oxford: Oxford University Press.

Thorbecke, E. (2004). "Conceptual and measurement issues in poverty analysis". UNU WIDER Discussion paper No. 2004/04.

Townsend, P. and D. Gordon (Eds.) (2002). *World Poverty: New policies to defeat an old enemy,* Bristol: The Policy Press, Bristol.

UNDP (1996). *Human Development Report.* New York.

UNDP (2003). *Human Development Report.* New York.

UNICEF (2003). *Africa's Orphaned Generations.* New York.

UNICEF, UNAIDS, USAID (2004). *Children on the Brink.* New York.

UNICEF-World Health Organization (2004). *Meeting the MDG drinking waterand sanitation target: A mid-term assessment of progress.* New York.

World Bank (1990). *World Development Report.* Washington D.C.

World Bank (2000/01). *World Development Report.* Washington D.C.

World Health Organization-UNICEF (2003a). *The Africa Malaria Report 2003.* New York.

World Health Organization-UNICEF (2003b). *Antenatal Care in Developing Countries: Promises, achievements and missed opportunities.* Geneva.

Wratten, E. (1995). "Conceptualizing urban poverty". *Environment and Urbanization,* pp. 12-19.

Chapter 1

Promoting Human Rights And Social Policies For Children And Women: The Role Of Multiple Indicator Cluster Survey (MICS)

Marina Komarecki

HOUSEHOLD SURVEYS

Household surveys are designed to study household welfare, household behavior, and the effects of government policies (Deaton, 1997; Lok-Dessallien, 1997; Grosh & Glewwe, 2000). They are essential instruments to monitor poverty, employment and unemployment, health and nutritional status, earnings, etc. Surveys can provide answers to questions related to the effectiveness of health services, nutritional benefits of food subsidies, or examine links between increased fees for public schools and school enrollment. Moreover, using the data from household surveys governments can determine whether schools, roads, electric power and other basic services are reaching the disadvantaged groups.

Early social surveyors include the Englishmen Reverend David Davies (1795) and Sir Frederick Morton Eden (1797) (Deaton, 1997; Grosh & Glewwe, 2000). Davies and Eden collected the data to bring greater attention to the living conditions of the poor; they used the results to argue in favor of a minimum wage. Something approximating modern form of surveys originated in Britain in the poverty surveys of Charles Booth and Seebohm Rowntree in the late 19th and early 20th centuries and in the early work on probability sampling by A.L. Bowley (Bulmer, 1998). The use of budget data to expose poverty and living standards, to argue for policy reform, and to estimate national aggregates are all topics that are relevant today as they were two centuries ago.

The first national household survey was pioneered in Calcutta in 1950, by the Indian Statistical Institute (Deaton, 1997; Bulmer, 1998). According to Bulmer, the United States is the most surveyed society in the world. Other industrial societies in Western Europe, Australia, East Asia, and elsewhere maintain sizable social survey capacities. In terms of surveys with an international perspective there is an increasing number of programs such as the International Social Survey Programme (ISSP), the Living Standards Measurement Study (LSMS) administered by the World Bank, the World Values Survey, past efforts such as the World Fertility Survey (WFS), and its contemporary successor Demographic and Health Survey (DHS) (Bulmer, 1998). International Food Policy Research Institute, the RAND Corporation, and Cornell University have also carried out household surveys in developing countries (Grosh & Glewee, 2000).

Recent years have seen a marked change in survey practice, in data collection, and in analysis. The number of laggard countries has significantly decreased and many government offices have become more open with their data and have given access to the individual household records (Lok-Dessalien, 1997; Grosh & Glewwe, 1998). Another factor that contributed to more analysis is the reduction of the real cost of computation. Perhaps as important have been changes in the design of surveys, and there is now a much wider range of survey instruments in use than two decades ago.

Household surveys like LSMS, DHS, and MICS have a potential to produce high quality data that can overcome the limitations and fill the gaps of public administration and service data. Different levels of public administration (e.g. the Ministries of Health, Education, Agriculture and Labor), as well as service outlets like the National Statistics Offices are the most common depositories of the information relevant for advocacy, research, policy analysis and poverty monitoring. Lok-Dessallien (1997) points to a number of limitations associated with service record data that have a potential to compromise the quality of gathered information.

Some countries, for example, have a tendency to either underreport or overestimate data. The latter case is often found within the education and immunization data sets, especially in those countries where the allocation of public expenditures is a function of school enrollment, or a number of immunized children. Moreover, the service records often do not disaggregate the data by gender, location, etc. In addition, they often do not provide the information on the most needy and poor, as they sometimes do not have access to public education and health services. Finally, service records data are rarely processed and analyzed in their entirety.

One of the most important advantages of surveys is that they represent the whole population including the rich and the poor, those who use public services and those who do not. Furthermore, the standardized form of surveys allows for the comparison across different countries. In addition to this, surveys can be customized to meet specific country needs. For example, vitamin A, malaria, breastfeeding and mortality modules in the MICS can be tailored specifically to fit the country needs. Similarly, with the DHS in areas with a high prevalence of malaria, questions about the use of bed nets in the household survey can be added. Finally, survey data can be used to examine the links among a variety of topics, such as the effects of education on fertility or HIV/AIDS incidence, or the effects of health status on labor force participation or productivity, or the effects of welfare transfers and consumption behavior (Grosh & Glewwe, 1998).

LSMS and DHS: recent examples of household surveys

At the time when the World Bank initiated Living Standard Measurement Survey (LSMS) in 1979, it became clear that it was impossible to make well-supported statements about world poverty, especially without having the comparable data to back them up. There was no firm basis to assess such fundamental topics as the extent of poverty in the world, which countries were the poorest, or whether the inequality within and between nations was increasing or decreasing. At the time, the World Bank data on poverty could only be offered in 22 of 86 developing countries (Grosh & Glewwe, 2000).

Even within countries, the simple statements about distributional outcomes were difficult. For example, in India, because data on consumer expenditures was only collected every five years, and because rural poverty is so sensitive to fluctuations in the harvest, it was impossible before the mid–1980s to separate trends from fluctuations, or to conclude with certainty that poverty rates were indeed falling. The original aim of LSMS was to remedy this situation by collecting comparable survey data across countries, allowing comparisons of poverty and inequality over time and space (Grosh & Glewwe, 1998; Grosh & Glewwe, 2000).

The World Bank's LSMS was designed as a large, multi-topic household survey with three questionnaires: household, community, and prices (Deaton, 1997; Grosh & Glewwe, 1998; Grosh & Glewwe, 2000). The first covers a long list of the essential information about the household including: a) household roster, b) consumption, c) housing and its characteristics, d) education, e) employment, f) government and NGO transfers, g) the use of social services such as government health facilities, schools, agricultural extension services, and social assistance programs, h) basic information related to the design of the sample and the outcome of the household interview, and i) local prices of food and nonfood goods. In addition to the essential core, it is recommended that five types of information also be collected: anthropometric measurement of household members, the immunization status of children 0-5 years old, basic housing assets such as durable goods, housing, land, and the capital equipment used for agricultural activities, information on interhousehold transfers, and information on rental payments for those households that rent their dwellings.

The community questionnaire, sometimes used only in rural areas, gathers data from local people like village headmen or chiefs, teachers, or medical personnel about local demographics (e.g. population, ethnicity, migration, and religion), and about local economic and service infrastructure (e.g. transportation, marketing, schools, health facilities). The price questionnaire serves to observe food prices on local markets. LSMS uses small nationally representative sample – usually between 2000 and 5000 households. Since 1985, LSMS has been successfully applied in about 30 developing countries.

Demographic and Health Surveys (DHS) use much larger sample size–ranging between 5000 and 30000 households. The standard. questionnaire consists of a household questionnaire and women's questionnaire. The first focuses on indicators related to household living standards (e.g. source of drinking water, toilet facilities, assets of the household), and also to indicators related to nutritional status and anemia. The women's questionnaire collects information on the mother's health, her fertility, the health of the children, as well as the family planning and practices (Lok-Dessallien, 1997; www.measuredhs.com). In some instances, DHS include: a) a service availability questionnaire about health and family planning infrastructure (Hermalin et al., 1996), b) biomarker collection which facilitates a more direct assessment of the health status on certain diseases including syphilis, HIV, chlamydia, hypertension, diabetes or cardiovascular disorders, c) education data, d) geographic data to establish latitude and longitude coordinates for the communities, and e) additional surveys on specific topics like expenditures on health care, and women's empowerment, (www.measuredhs.com).

Despite a number of important advantages, most notably country comparability, both LSMS and DHS invite criticism on several points. First, both incur high cost, and second, they demand long turn around cycles. For example, the cost of LSMS varies between US $200,000 to US $3 million, the median being around US $750,000 (Deaton, 1997; Grosh & Glewwe, 1998), while the estimate of DHS costs is US $500,000 (Kingsbury, D.S. as cited by Unicef, 1999). The total time frame for surveys turnaround, from planning to implementing, and preparing the abstract and public data, lasts from 18 to 36 months in the case of LSMS, with 12 months spent in the field (Grosh, 1998).

Similarly, some of the questionnaires like World Health Survey, used by the World Health Organization have more than 400 pages and require three hours for an interview. Further, as a government funded survey operation, DHS is administered according to the priority list of countries defined by the US government. For example, it does not cover developing countries like Botswana, which by USAID estimate exhibit high living standards, and can administer DHS by their own resources. (High incidence of HIV/AIDS has somewhat changed the perception of needs, stirring the action to extend the list of DHS priority countries, particularly after 2002).

Another disadvantage, particularly of DHS is related to its event-dating, evident in cases of consciously falsified recording by some interviewers (Cleland, 1996). That is particularly noticeable in questions asked about children during the five or three years preceding the survey; interviewers had an incentive to omit recently born children or to shift their dates of birth backward, so that they all fell outside the reference period. Estimates of fertility trends are especially sensitive to these forms of misplacements. Finally, both LSMS and DHS are highly dependent on technical assistance and show limited results with capacity building (Cleland, 1996; Lok-Dessallien).

DHS and MICS: similarities and differences

Because both DHS and MICS represent instruments whose primary focus is on indicators related to maternal and child health and well-being, it is important to contrast some of their features. The data collected by MICS in many aspects complement DHS data, and fill the existing gaps as they cover areas where the DHS has not been recently administered. Planning of a new instrument similar to the MICS has required active cooperation between UNICEF and DHS research teams; this was demonstrated in a number of joint meetings. The cooperative working sessions ensured that the data would meet the same high standards and that the MICS and DHS would pose similar questions as DHS.

One potential limitation of both DHS and MICS surveys is that they lack questions on household income or consumption expenditures. However, several studies have demonstrated that this can be remedied by constructing a wealth index with questions about household assets and housing characteristics (e.g. construction materials, drinking water, toilet facilities, access to the mass media, etc.) (Filmer & Pritchett, 1999; Segone, 2001; Huebler & Loaiza, 2002). In fact, Filmer and Prichett demonstrate that constructed wealth index is a better proxy than consumption expenditures for long-run household wealth in predicting child school enrollment.

When compared to UNESCO's school enrollment data, both DHS and MICS surveys provide a somewhat different picture (Huebler & Loaiza, 2002). UNICEF's study about primary school attendance in Africa that applied DHS and MICS surveys showed an average net attendance rate that was 8 points lower than the average net enrollment rate derived from administrative sources used by UNESCO. Moreover, both instruments overcome a problem of using indicators that are too indirect, in the sense that they apply to households or families as a whole, and not directly to children (Gordon et al., 2003). The MICS is particularly strong in offering a more direct and representative set of data, especially in new sets of modules pertaining to child labor and education.

Getting relevant information in MICS's HIV/AIDS module is a particular challenge. This is one area where the DHS may have some advantage over MICS surveys. The questions about sexual practices in the DHS may be better suited to reveal policy relevant data than the knowledge questions asked in MICS. Overall, however, MICS household surveys have a number of advantages over DHS: they are more time and cost effective, and show considerable benefits in terms of capacity building. A brief look at some figures and features illustrates the comparative advantage of MICS over DHS.

The average total cost of conducting the MICS 1 country study that included UNICEF country staff costs, national and international consultants, and government costs was US $129,000. The country cost ranged between US $14,000 and US $266,000, while the cost to UNICEF was US $80,000 (Unicef, 1999). Unlike DHS that has to send technical experts to the field at a high cost, UNICEF derives multiple benefits from its world-wide country presence. First, the cost is significantly lower because of the local work force. Second, well-established relationships with the local authorities arguably represent a solid base for capacity building.

Moreover, MICS's turnaround cycle is somewhat shorter than in the case of DHS. On average, planing, data collection, analysis and reporting of MICS ranges between 12 and 24 months. The overriding conclusion of MICS' 1999 evaluation was that several aspects of UNICEF's assistance (e.g. financial, technical and administrative support) provided strong incentive in national capacity building. In that respect, the training sessions significantly improved the skills and capacity of local government staff, particularly in using hardware and software relevant for advanced research and policy analysis.

STATISTICAL INFORMATION AND HUMAN RIGHTS

The trend towards extending human rights policies beyond civil and political rights and embracing social and economic rights, including the so-called "right to development" necessitates a new strategy that rests on an evidence-based and science-driven approach (Fukuda-Parr, 2001; Garonna & Balta, 2002). Such a strategy requires the application of all the tools provided, including the development of indicators and benchmarks. Setting specific, time bound benchmarks enables governments and scientific communities to reach an agreement about the amount and pace of adequate progress; and it also allows for the measurement of actual achievements. To this end, building statistical capacity is an essential condition and an integral part of a new approach to measuring and monitoring human rights. In addition, statistical information can be useful in mobilizing resources and implementing policies (Santos-Pais, 1999).

Gathering statistical information about children significantly improved over the past decade, particularly in the area of health, education and gender disparities. Part of this success can be attributed to the MICS. Altogether, with MICS 2 completion 67 countries collected new data on children. Perhaps more importantly, half of them were in Sub Saharan Africa, one of the least developed regions in the world. Before 1995, the year MICS 1 was introduced, only 28 developing countries had data on oral rehydration therapy; the number went up to 63 after the MICS application. A similar trend could be perceived regarding malnutrition: data was improved from 57 to 93 countries, pre and post implementation respectively (Santos-Pais, 1999). Table 1 contrasts MICS 1 and MICS 2.

Despite these advances, it has been noted that accurate data on maternal mortality, data on children above 5 years of age (e.g. as victims of sexual abuse) and data in newly emerging fields of importance like child's participation in decision-making process, are either incomplete or lacking (Santos-Pais, 1999). This points towards a new direction in gathering statistics: information is now needed on indicators that assess protection measures for children, their family environment and alternative care, and their civil rights and freedom (Bellamy, 2000). In addition, the need for direct information on children has been underlined (e.g. questions that are not derived through parental answers (Gordon et al., 2003). Some of the requirements to monitor child rights were met in MICS 2, as several question modules were designed to monitor non-health indicators of child rights. The full list of modules for monitoring Child Rights, Integrated Management of Childhood Illness (IMCI) and HIV/AIDS is included in Table 2.

The human rights approach to children has been officially recognized through the Convention of the Rights of the Child (CRC) in 1989. The CRC is unique, among international and human rights laws, in unifying the human development together with social, cultural, civil and political rights. The model of CRC recognizes that the children's needs are different from those of adults, and suggests a concept of child poverty that can be defined independently of adults (Minujin, 2000; Gordon et al., 2003).

The basic tenets of CRC emphasize children's rights to survive, develop, participate and be protected. It has been suggested that the concept of poverty could be defined in relation to these rights through a consistent set of "organizing principles" such as availability, accessibility or quality (Minujin, 2000; Green, 2001; Gordon et al., 2003). More specifically, poverty could be measured through direct access to food, water, sanitation, education, health care, information, etc.

Survey data collected by DHS or MICS are instrumental in obtaining an accurate picture on the extent children's are rights fulfilled. Indicators such as percent of children with access to safe water and sanitation, percent of immunized children, percent of children with direct access to primary school enrollment, percentage of children and mothers with access to or possession of information mediums, etc., not only reflects the key thematic clusters of the CRC. It also promotes a broader and more comprehensive measure of child poverty that is in line with multidimensional approach to human development.

Two key characteristics are of fundamental importance in relation to human rights measurements. The first is the ability to measure indicators over time in order to allow for progressive realization of socio-economic rights. The principle of "progressive realization" recognizes that time is needed to make the necessary changes to secure rights (Green, 2001; Garonna & Balta, 2002). For example, removing a number of obstacles in achieving universal enrollment to primary school in countries like Burkina Faso, Chad, Ethiopia and Mali where fewer than 4 out of 10 children attend school, and where local traditions against sending girls to school are particularly strong, would require a significant amount of effort, presumably over a longer period of time (Huebler & Loaiza, 2003). Second, human rights require more disaggregated data that will go beyond the "one size fits all" policy advice (Santos-Pais, 1999; Green, 2001).

With regards to disaggregation, one of the four basic principles identified in the CRC– non-discrimination–is particularly relevant. Applying this principle in practice would mean that we have to go beyond general or national averages in order to get a better insight into children's reality. To this end, data need to be disaggregated according to gender, age, national, regional, economic and ethnic origin. Regarding age, it is important to further disaggregate data on early childhood, childhood, and adolescence as each of the periods may be defined by different sets of needs. Moreover, the non-discrimination principle directs attention to the most disadvantaged groups such as girls, disabled children, abused and abandoned children, and children living in remote rural areas (Santos-Pais, 1999; Minujin, 2000). It should be noted, however, that data on disabled, abused and abandoned children cannot be collected with DHS and MICS; and that methodologies other than household surveys may be better suited to gather data in those important areas. Disaggregation has multiple implications for policy design as it has a potential to reveal disparities that exist among different statistical categories, and provide direction on to how to act upon them.

One of the challenges for the future of evidence-based and science-driven approach is paying close attention to how data is analyzed and disseminated (Bellamy, 2000). To this end, effective public communication and advocacy campaigns that would actively engage the media, NGO activists and participating communities deserve more attention.

STATISTICAL INFORMATION AND POLICY DESIGN

Widening the discourse on human rights to include social and economic rights has direct implications for the policy approach. The emphasis today is more on promoting the gradual and progressive improvement of standards and achievements, rather then just expressing concern in how to prevent and punish abuse. In this context issues like the reduction of poverty and inequality, quality of education and health services, better working conditions, and better access to public services merit special attention. The wider scope of problems demands a much more complex approach to analysis and evaluation of trends and policies. The emerging trend also has implications on how people see their leaders and governments: politicians and international organizations are hard pressed to deliver more concrete results and provide facts and evidence (Fukuda-Parr, 2001).

High quality statistics is essential to such approach (Santos-Pais, 1999; Green, 2001). Statistics provide important feedback about present and future trends and it suggests the locus of discrepancies which need further analysis; it is also a fundamental tool for designing, monitoring and evaluating policies (Deaton, 1997). Detailed statistical information about the actual region or country in question is essential for policy design, especially when they are consistent with human rights principles. For example, current poverty research indicates that Sub-Saharan Africa suffers from a combination of shelter and water deprivation, while South Asia's households suffer in large part from shelter and information deprivation. The children in other regions of the world like the Middle East and North Africa are more exposed to shelter and education deprivation (Gordon et al., 2003).

This clearly indicates that paths toward removing deprivation may be different and that anti-poverty policies need to be designed according to these specific needs. In addition, data also permit us to analyze and test relationships between different sets of rights (e.g. health and child labor, health and education, etc.), or between human development and human rights (Green, 2001; Parker & Bachman, 2001). The latter is particularly interesting in cases where adequate government policies are in place (and there is no violation of human rights), but there is no progress on human development indicators (e.g. the resources are insufficient to relieve poverty).

By measuring with facts and figures the state of human rights, analyzing how policies may contribute to their enhancement, looking at the outcomes of implemented programs, the credibility of national and international programs may be restored. But more importantly, perhaps, an evidence-driven approach has the potential to make all relevant players more accountable with respect to their constituencies, public opinion, and the communities whose human rights are at stake (Fukuda-Parr, 2001).

The quality of statistics in the field of human rights has often been questioned. The data is inadequate, lacks accuracy and is not gathered and analyzed by independent institutions. Government institutions sometimes have incentive either to hide, distort, under-report or over-report the real facts. For example, inflated figures of child immunization in Bangladesh are attributed to the fact that health workers are paid for each individual child. By contrast, China underreports figures regarding the sale of children, the abandonment of girl-children, and female infanticide. Furthermore, China never addresses these problems within the context of family planning policy, but rather chooses to blame poverty and persistence of backward thinking as main culprits (Harris-Short, 2003). Reliable statistics can in fact be considered a good indicator of democratic governance (Garonna & Balta, 2002).

At the international level, an important function of the institutions concerned with human development has been to help countries and other actors like NGOs and advocacy groups to set up and operationalize monitoring systems, capable of measuring progress made toward agreed objectives, analyzing trends and gaps, and evaluating policy outcomes (Garonna & Balta, 2002). It is in this context that reference to indicators, benchmarks and statistical data has emerged as a useful tool for making policies more effective.

UNICEF grew as an emergency aid organization and until a decade ago it did not have a strong data gathering and statistical analysis data track. The data, often borrowed from other UN sister agencies like WHO, UNESCO, UNDP or UNPF did not always prove to be satisfying to UNICEF's specific needs. With the adoption of the CRC and the Agenda of the World Summit for Children it became obvious that the more rigorous and more independent data-collecting and data-monitoring system had to be put in place. Since then UNICEF has embarked upon a long-term evidence-driven campaign, which resulted in the design and implementation of two versions of MICS (Santos-Pais, 1999; Unicef, 2000). MICS was originally conceived as a tool with the capacity to measure a set of indicators for assessing progress towards the goals of the World Summit for Children for the year 2000. Subsequently, it became an instrument to monitor Millennium Development Goals (MDGs). At present, national governments are using the survey data to define and set up priorities regarding women and children until year 2005.

One question is of particular relevance in the debate about statistics and policy: why is data on childhood circumstances of vital importance? The answer to this question is especially important in view of recent epidemiological research that puts emphasis on life course perspective on health and well-being (McLoyd, 1998; Daniels et al., 1999; Power, 2002); and the idea that the cycle of poverty can be broken in childhood (Minujin, 2000).

It has been argued that adversity in childhood becomes embodied at an early age, the full impact of which manifests later in adult life. For example, the interplay between biological and social processes could start with complications related to unsupervised labor; this is then followed by the exposure to frequent infections or inadequate diet, all rooted in poorer socioeconomic conditions (McLoyd, 1998). The cumulative effect of such exposures could in turn have lifelong consequences, creating the situations of vulnerability that will pave the way to exclusion (Minujin, 2000).

An extensive body of literature from a multitude of fields (e.g. psychology, nutrition, physiology, education, etc.) continues to accumulate and indicate critical importance of early years. For example, the most rapid period of brain development takes place in the first three years of life, laying the pathways for significant cognitive, emotional, physical, and social functions (Nelson, 1999). Moreover, studies that examined linkages between poverty and health, and between health and school achievement, support a hypothesis that poverty adversely affects children's school achievement in part by decreasing their physical health status; in turn, diminished health status is engendering cognitive deficits. In relation to this, it has been demonstrated that children with low birth weight who suffered various perinatal illnesses as infants experienced greater school failure and missed more days of school (McLoyd, 1998).

Mother's health and well-being also has a critical influence on child's outcome. For example, at least 20 percent of disease among children less than 5 years of age was attributed to conditions associated with poor maternal health, nutrition and quality of obstetrics and newborn care (World Bank document as cited by Parker & Bachman, 2001). Further, women's pre-pregnant weight is a strong predictor of her child's birth weight; in turn, child's low birth weight has been linked to increased risks of coronary heart disease, poorer cardio-respiratory function, and diabetes in life (Daniels et al., 1999; Power, 2002). Recent studies also showed strong relation between mothers education and child labor (Huebler & Loaiza, 2002, p.9), and mother's education and child's school attendance (Huebler & Loaiza, 2003, p.10). Finally, recent MICS data point to the fact that women who were informed about AIDS prevention were more likely to have children who go to school (Unicef, forthcoming).

Presented evidence lends support to the belief that early investment on children, adolescents, and women may lead towards better, more prosperous and healthier society. In addition, the evidence confirms the importance of achieving the Millennium Development Goals, especially those concerning maternal health and education of girls. As Minujin (2000) has argued, childhood is the most auspicious period to acquire skills that will lead towards inclusion in the society and active participation in economy; and it is also an ideal period when the seeds of a more just society, built on human rights values can be sewn.

In relation to this, it is important to emphasize that development of a global and national response has to occur within the context of a combined effort to address the rights of the child and rights of the women simultaneously. For example, efforts to eliminate child labor would have to be considered together with efforts that address social indicators (e.g. female literacy, infant mortality) related to gender inequalities and socio-economic status (Parker & Bachman, 2001). In other words, a central policy implication of this discussion is that the reform approach to improving inequalities has to be intersectoral, (Daniels et al., 1999). Such an approach would recognize the importance of equalizing access to education, medical care, affordable housing, and income security in combination with other anitpoverty strategies like cash transfers and food supplements that would give families incentive to send children to school (Lavinas, 2000; Skoufias & Parker, 2001).

MICS and policy design

Household surveys are a valuable tool for governments and policymakers deciding among many different options. In that respect, three questions can be asked: a) how useful is MICS methodology, b) is improved data leading to better results on specified indicators and delineated goals?, and c) how useful is MICS in reporting on MDGs?

To answer the first question, the available evidence shows that the majority of the countries where MICS was implemented found the instrument useful (e.g. in bringing attention to high levels of malnutrition and low levels of immunization; planning and development of health facilities in provinces and districts; in assessing changes in health indicators, etc.) (Unicef, 1999). It is possible that one of the MICS' features may have particularly contributed to estimated usefulness. MICS is designed as a composite of several modules that can be presented as separate units, and therefore can be either omitted or revised. This gives countries a certain amount of freedom to use the instrument in such a way so that it can more effectively meet their needs. For example, China made revisions of the household module, to include type of building material, and living space; while Lesotho included the age and gender of each household member, and added a separate list with a detailed information about each child a women was responsible for (Unicef, 2000).

Further, UNICEF study from Niger is a good example of how MICS survey proved to be an essential tool in furnishing data instrumental in operationalizing the child poverty. More specifically, the data identified the poorest regions; highlighted the sectors in which the funds should be allocated to narrow the most important gender inequalities (e.g. literacy in the region of Zinder or primary school in the region of Dasso); and identified adequate poverty alleviation strategies for Niger (e.g.

behavioral changes in attacking malnutrition were deemed more useful than increase in the income) (Segone, 2001). This kind of quality data are a clear example of what kind of information is needed for policy design, especially when policies have to be consistent with human rights principles while avoiding the common 'one size fits all' approach.

In a more general context, MICS methodology has also proven to be useful in measurement of child labor (Huebler & Loaiza, 2002). Interesting feature of this study is that it indicated a more complex relationship between child labor and school attendance (e.g. 40 percent of all children in Sub-Saharan Africa work, but this does not necessarily interfere with their school attendance). Another study using MICS data found that the disparity in school attendance between urban and rural areas became statistically insignificant when household wealth was controlled (Huebler & Loaiza, 2003). This study confirms the validity of a theoretical approach that suggests intersectoral approach to poverty alleviation: eradication of severe educational deprivation has to be addressed together with provision of safe drinking water, sanitation and lack of electricity.

The same study about the school attendance in Africa (Huebler & Loaiza, 2003) could serve well in connection to the second question that is asking if the MICS are contributing to producing better results. The study data revealed significant gender differences in school attendance in several African countries; but they were particularly pronounced in Benin, Burkina Faso, Chad, Guinea, Mali and Niger. It is indisputable that MICS significantly contributed in collecting new data in one of the poorest regions of the world (Santos-Pais, 1999). Whether these data yielded better results in terms of producing policies that are producing better outcomes–in this case diminishing gender disparity–is another matter. Several explanations could be considered.

First, there is only limited evidence from some country studies (e.g. Niger) that gender inequalities slightly diminished (Segone, 2001). Based on available evidence–the study did not examine the direct links between MICS and the impact specific program interventions–it is impossible to conclude with certainty if MICS played a role in diminishing gender disparity. Indeed, MICS provides only a baseline and follow-up information from which program impacts could be inferred. As MICS evaluation document stated, the survey does not have the capacity to answer the question as to what program or programs are responsible for these levels or changes in levels (Unicef, 1999). Therefore, collecting data that would establish the links between MICS and different regional or district programs would be of utmost importance in determining how MICS methodology could serve policy planners.

Second, removing obstacles particularly in access to education can prove to be an arduous and long-term task. It is possible that more time is needed to determine if and what kind of changes occurred. Third, one has to consider a situation where data are available and deemed useful, however, they are either not used in practice, of in case they are, there are no studies to report on concrete results. There is some indication that the survey did not result in more action because some of the governments did not accept MICS 1 (Unicef, 1999).

Fourth, research indicates the discrepancy between the commitment given by states to securing the effective implementation of human rights and inability to realize that commitment in practice. Inability to take adequate policy measures has been explained by the absence of human rights culture at a local level, particularly when the rights question impinge upon traditions and practices relating to children and the family.

Acute problems of this kind are particularly evident in the set of earlier mentioned African countries that were found to have great gender disparities. For example, evidence shows how the governments of Chad and Benin report about great difficulty they have with local tribal chiefs who consistently refuse to assist the officials in achieving the necessary reforms in attitudes and practices, particularly in connection with girls school attendance (Harris-Short, 2003). The chiefs are elected by the local population and the government has no influence over them. Moreover, in Guinea, the legislation does not define measures for the protection of the child such as those defined in CRC. All the conditions of protection necessary for the child are assumed by parental authority recognized by the local traditions of the country, including education of the child (Harris-Short, 2003).

The third question asked if MICS methodology is useful in measuring MDGs. If time and cost are considered as criteria against which the progress can be measured on the Millennium development agenda, then it is possible to conclude that in comparison with other similar instruments, MICS has a potential to produce quality reports for less money in a shorter period of time (Unicef, 1999). Other than that, in general, there is little empirical evidence to make accurate estimates about real progress the countries are making on MDGs (Sahn & Stifel, 2003).

For one, according to MICS evaluation, only half of the countries used their data to report on mid-decade goals, one of the reasons being that the data were not available in time for reporting. Two, research indicates that, so far, no independent studies using MICS methodology have been conducted to report on MDGs progress; if such studies exist, the results are not yet publicly available. Three, Sahn and Stifel who used DHS to measure progress on MDGs in African countries, painted a rather grim picture, concluding that the goals will not be reached for most indicators in most countries (Sahn & Stifel, 2003). This ties in with the previously stated problem that highlights the case in which neither the existing sound methodology, nor the explicit commitment to action may be powerful enough to bridge formidable challenges that are in the way of reaching MDGs.

PARTICIPATION AND INFORMATION

Responding effectively, efficiently, and responsibly to the social welfare and economic claims of citizens should be a priority for governments of developing countries. The ability to monitor the impact of economic and social reforms, evaluate the outcomes of public programs and projects, and the capacity to undertake policy-relevant research have been identified as essential components of good governance. Concurrently they constitute what is referred to as the institutional capacity for policy analysis (Grindle, 1997).

Good government has much to do with 1. the quality of human resources, organizations, and institutions in the public sector, 2. their sustained ability to identify important basic and applied problems, and

3. their capacity to collect, process, analyze, and disseminate information that addresses them (Trostle et al., 1997; Garonna & Balta, 2002). A household survey is an important contribution to that endeavor. It is a useful mechanism to direct policymakers to the types of questions that can be answered with empirical data and to stimulate interest in quantitative analysis of policy questions (Blank & Grosh, 1999). Thus, increasing national capacity to gather, analyze and use survey data in developing countries is an important task.

National capacity of developing countries to perform data collection has significantly improved in the past two decades. However, their capacity to undertake complex, multiple methods of inquiry is often weak. The literature identifies several reasons that have a potential to compromise analytical capacity. First, there are problems with the quality of data. In cases where adequate data are collected, because of government restrictions, the researchers are given only limited access (Blank & Grosh, 1999). Second, developing countries often suffer from the lack of trained researchers and appropriate institutional capacities for high-level research (Trostle et al., 1997; Nchinda, 2002). For example, Nchinda quotes UNESCO (1996) data that suggest that 80 percent of working scientists of all disciplines, including health, are concentrated in Western industrialized nations, Japan, and to a much lesser extent, some of the larger Asian countries. Africa, Latin America and the Middle East together have only 13 percent of the world's scientists. Third, the lack of experience hampers the ability of policymakers to frame policy questions, or use the results of final analysis (Blank & Grosh, 1999).

All together, the lack of institutional capacity in developing countries resulted in heavy presence of foreign technical support. The problems related to this are now well documented (Cohen & Wheeler, 1997; Blackburn & Holland, 1998; Mosse, 1998). As a result, in the mid 1980s and 1990s, a concern for capacity building emerged, as both donor agencies and recipient governments became increasingly aware that prior investments in public sector institutions often failed to bring about the intended major improvements in their ability to predict, recognize, prevent, or manage development problems (Grindle, 1997). A number of tools have been instrumental in capacity building/strengthening such as:

training, technical assistance, research apprenticeships (mentoring), and establishing policy analysis unit (Trostle et al., 1997; Blank & Grosh, 1999). I take them in turn.

Research indicates that short-term (at least six weeks) training helps in improving nation's capacity for basic statistical analysis. However, formulating more refined research questions requires more than just workshop participation. In line with Trostle's (1997) idea of "science as a communication", establishing active and more permanent working relationships between existing aid agencies, independent research institutions and government Ministries is necessary for research sustainability (Trostle et al., 1997; Blank & Grosh, 1999; Nchinda, 2002).

Moreover, because technical skills required to analyze survey are common to several disciplines, including economics, sociology, education, public health, and management, it is necessary to assemble multidisciplinary teams. Further, to avoid a common problem in development planning–reluctance of government officials to use the data–policymakers should be included in the training too. Benefits of such approach were evident in Vietnam (Blank & Grosh, 1999). As Blank and Grosh pointed out, joint training with their own computer technicians enabled the policy analysts to pose questions for which the programmers would often generate immediate answers.

More often than not, organizations and human resources, albeit limited, already exist in developing countries. It is more important to understand their present roles and limitations than it is to suggest new organizations and new strategies (Trostle et al., 1997). The capacity can be increased more effectively by reinforcing existing structures than by building new ones. In line with this thinking, it is suggested that the outside consultant participates more as a mentor rather than as a co-investigator. This helps to maintain project control in the hands of the national research team.

Technical assistance and mentorship often overlap and run the gamut of various activities: from access to foreign literature, opportunities to travel to scientific meetings, to assistance in analysis, writing, and dissemination of data (Trsotle et al., 1997; Nchinda, 2002). For example, thanks to a Harvard assisted project that used LSMS survey to strengthen research capacity in Bolivia, the local investigators involved with the project produced a significant body of scientific work within just three years: five books, two research monographs and thirty six working papers.

In a similar effort, the same project improved the quality of publications in some Asian countries where the local incentives for promotion motivated researchers to print and distribute voluminous reports rather than to publish them in national or international scientific journals (Trostle et al., 1997). Over the course of the same project, researchers were also instructed how to write for policy audiences. In addition, the project sponsored separate workshops that brought together policy makers and researchers to discuss the constraints and incentives for using health research in making policy. The advantage of this approach was particularly evident in cases when politically delicate topics to which policy makers could be quite unreceptive were discussed (e.g. ethnic differences and gender disparities).

Finally, local capacity can be enhanced through the establishment of policy development unites or investment in research institutions. For example, the World Bank provided funding to increase Jamaica's analytic capacity of the Planning Institute (Blank & Grosh, 1999). The Survey of Living Conditions (SLC) served as a data collection tool, but also provided a solid base for further research. The Policy Development Unit, which functioned under the auspices of the Planning Institute, produced several policy papers and developed methodology for tracking poverty over time.

UNICEF provided ample resources for MICS administration and implementation and other efforts to collect data. The capacity building efforts consisted both of financial and human resource support, including technical assistance, training, and computer hardware and software to local staff and policy analysis units, research centers, and training programs (Unicef, 1999). According to an evaluation report, MICS 1 participating countries saw some improvement in the organization, management and coordination of surveys, as well as in data processing skills. However, the evaluation pointed out that it was impossible to conclude if the capacity increased as a result of MICS. For example, it was observed that MICS furthered knowledge about health and living conditions; this, however, does not necessarily mean that the capacity in data planning and administration has been improved (Unicef, 1999).

Based on the available, albeit, limited evidence, it is possible that better results in capacity building could have been reached if the training was longer. Six to ten days may have been too short period of time to get a full handle on data processing techniques, particularly in view of the fact that many of the countries reported problems similar to those in the aforementioned section about limited research capacity (e.g. difficulties in processing large data sets, limited expertise available to use the program to conduct data analysis, etc.).

Building on the experience of MICS 1 evaluation, MICS 2 put significant effort into fortifying capacity building process. For example, 4 separate 7-day workshops were conducted in 7 regions on: 1. survey design, 2. data processing, 3. data analysis and reporting, and 4. data use and archiving.

CONCLUSIONS

UNICEF's contribution in setting up more rigorous standards in data gathering in the past ten years is undisputed. The next important stage is to address how other agencies may complement UNICEF's endeavors by putting the data to better use. Providing incentives to both data analysis and dissemination is of utmost importance not only for expanding our knowledge about MICS methodology, but more so for the benefit of the developing countries in their struggle towards poverty reduction.

So far, MICS has improved our knowledge regarding the well-being of women and children, and it continues to do so, as many country reports attest (for example see chapters 4, 8, and 14). For several of the MICS countries, particularly in the Sub-Saharan region, the surveys have replaced an almost total absence of information with some crucial data vital for poverty reduction and sustainable development. Moreover, in comparison with other similar instruments, MICS holds significant advantages in producing estimates on MDG indicators monitoring country progress. MICS approach allows for assembly and data set processing for less money in shorter periods of time.

MICS is also finding its place in policy debates. UNICEF country offices have produced some quality studies, most of which are concerned with policy-related empirical analysis of the data (Segone, 2001; Huebler & Loaiza, 2002; Huebler & Loaiza, 2003). As some of the papers from this volume indicate (for example see chapters 7 and 11) further progress has been made, and there is evidence that the data are being used to enhance capacity in the countries from which they originate.

REFERENCES

Bellamy, C. (2000). "Statistics, Development and Human Rights." UNICEF, internal publication.

Blackburn, J. & Holland, J. (1998). *Who Changes?: Institutionalizing participation in development*. London: Intermediate Technology Publications.

Bulmer, M. (1998). "The Social Survey: A Brief Overview." *American Behavioral Scientist*, Vol. 42, No. 2.

Blank, L. & Grosh, M. (1999). "Using household surveys to build analytic capacity." *The World Bank Observer*, Vol. 14, No. 2.

Cleland, J. (1996). "Demographic Data Collection in Less Developed Countries 1946-1996." *Population Studies*, Vol. 50.

Cohen, J. & Wheeler, J. (1997). "Training and Retention in African Public Sectors: Capacity-Building Lessons from Kenya." In Grindle, M. (ed.), *Getting Good Government: Capacity Building in the Public sectors of Developing Countries*. Boston: Harvard University Press.

Daniels, N., Kennedy, B., & Kawachi, I. (1999). "Why Justice is Good for Our Health: The Social Determinants of Health Inequalities." *Deadalus*, Vol. 128, No. 4.

Deaton, A. (1997). *Household Surveys: A Microeconomic Approach to Development Policy*. Baltimore and London: The John Hopkins University Press.

DHS Surveys. URL (consulted August 2003): <www.measuresdhs.com/aboutsurveys/dhs_surveys.cfm>.

End-Decade Multiple Indicator Survey Manual: Monitoring Progress Toward the Goals of the 1990 World Summit for Children (2000). New York: UNICEF.

Evaluation of Multiple Indicator Cluster Surveys (1999). New York: UNICEF.

Filmer, D. & Prichett, L. (1999). "The Effect of Household Wealth on Educational Attainment: Evidence from 35 countries." *Population and Development Review*, Vol. 25, No. 1.

Fukuda-Parr, S. (2001). "Indicators of Human Development and Human Rights: Overlaps, Differences... And What About the Human Development Index." *Statistical Journal of the UN Economic Commission for Europe*, Vol. 18, No. 2.

Garonna, P. & Balta, E. (2002). "Measuring Human Rights: The Challenges for the Information Society." *Statistical Journal of the UN Economic Commission for Europe*, Vol. 19, No. 4.

Green, M. (2001). "What We Talk About When We Talk About Indicators: Current Approaches to Human Rights Measurement." *Human Rights Quarterly*, Vol. 23.

Grindle, M. (1997). "Introduction." In Grindle, M. (ed.), *Getting Good Government: Capacity Building in the Public sectors of Developing Countries*. Boston: Harvard University Press.

Gordon, D. et al. (2003). "The Distribution of Child Poverty in the Developing World." UNICEF report.

Grosh, M. & Glewwe, P. (2000). *Designing Household Survey Questionnaires for Developing Countries: Lessons from fifteen years of the LSMS*. Washington, DC: The World Bank.

Grosh, M. & Glewwe, P. (1998). "The World Bank's Living Standards Measurement Study Household Surveys." *Journal of Economic Perspectives*, Vol. 12, No. 1.

Gruskin, S. (2001). "A World Fit For Children: Are the World's Leaders Being Passed on the Fast Lane?" *Health and Human Rights*, Vol. 5, No. 2.

Harris-Short, S. (2003). "International human rights law: Imperialist, inept, and ineffective? Cultural relativism and the UN Convention on the Rights of the Child." *Human Rights Quarterly*, Vol. 25, No. 25.

Hermalin, A. (1996). Reweighting DHS data to Serve Multiple Perspectives. *Studies in Family Planning*, Vol. 27, No. 2.

Huebler, F. & Loaiza, E. (2002). "Child Labor and School Attendance in Sub-Saharan Africa: Empirical Evidence from UNICEF's Multiple Indicator Cluster Surveys (MICS)." UNICEF report.

— (2003). "Primary School Attendance in Africa: Empirical Evidence from Recent Household Surveys." UNICEF report.

Lok-Dessalien, R. (1997). "The Data: Where to Find Them." UNDP Technical Support Document. Poverty Reduction, Module 3.

Lavinas, L. (2000). "The Appeal of Minimum Income Programs in Latin America." ILO Document No. 27657.

McLoyd, V. (1998). "Socioeconomic Disadvantage and Child Development." *American Psychologist*, Vol. 53, No. 2.

Minujin, A. (2000). "Making Child Poverty Visible." Presentation on the International Conference on Statistics, Development and Human Rights, Montereux.

Minujin, A., Vandemoortele, J. & Delamonica, E. (2002). "Economic growth, poverty and children." *Environment and Urbanization*, Vol. 14.

Mosse, D. (1998). "Process Oriented Approaches to Development Practice and Social Research." In D. Mosse, J., Farrington, A. Rew (eds.), *Development as Process: Concepts and Methods for Working With Complexity*. London and New York: Routledge.

Nchinda, T. (2002). "Research Capacity Strengthening in the South." *Social Science and Medicine*, Vol. 54, No. 11.

Nelson, C. (1999). "How Important are the First 3 Years of Life?" *Applied Development Science*, Vol. 3, No. 4.

Parker, D. & Bachman, S. (2001). "Economic Exploitation and the Health of Children: Towards a Rights-Oriented Public Health Approach." *Health and Human Rights*, Vol. 5, No. 2.

Power, C. (2002). "Child adversity sill matters for adult health outcomes." *The Lancet*, Vol. 360, No. 9346.

Sahn, D., & Stifel, D. (2003). "Progress Toward the Millennium Development Goals in Africa." *World Development*, Vol. 31, No. 1.

Santos-Pais, M. (1999). "The Challenge of Monitoring the Observance of the Convention on the Rights of the Child." Presentation at the ISI Conference, Helsinki.

Segone, M. (2001). "Child Poverty in Niger." UNICEF report.

Skoufias, E. & Parker, S. (2001). "Conditional Cash Transfers and Their Impact on Child Work and Schooling: Evidence from the Progresa Program in Mexico." *Economia*, Fall.

Trostle, J., Sommerfeld, J. & Simon, J. (1997). "Strengthening Human Resource Capacity in Developing Countries: Who Are the Actors? What are Their Actions?" In Grindle, M. (ed.), *Getting Good Government: Capacity Building in the Public sectors of Developing Countries*. Boston: Harvard University Press.

Table 1.

Mid-Decade MICS **MICS 1**	End-Decade MICS **MICS 2**
Household modules	***Household modules***
Household composition	Household composition
Water and sanitation	Water and sanitation
Salt iodization	Salt iodization
	Literacy
	Alternative care and orphans
Modules for women	***Modules for women***
Tetanus toxid	Tetanus toxid
	Reproductive health
	(antenatal and delivery care)
	Family planning
	Vitamin A
	HIV/AIDS
Modules for children	***Modules for children***
Education	Education
Diarrhoea	Diarrhoea
Vitamin A	Vitamin A
Immunization	Immunization
Child malnutrition	Child malnutrition
	Breastfeeding
	Care of acute respiratory illness
	Child mortality
	Low birthweight
	Birth registration
	Child labor
	Malaria
Optional modules	***Optional modules***
Breastfeeding	Maternal mortality
Care of acute respiratory illness	Child disability
Child mortality	

Table 2. Modules for Monitoring Child Rights, IMCI and HIV/AIDS Initiatives

Key additional indicators for child rights
Birth registration
Children's living arrangements
Orphans living in households
Child labor

Key IMCI indicators at household level
Exclusive breastfeeding
Complementary feeding
Low birthweight
Vaccination coverage
Child malnutrition
Home management of childhood illnesses
Care seeking knowledge
Use of bednets (malaria high-risk areas)
Antimalarial treatment (malaria high-risk areas)

Key indicators for monitoring HIV/AIDS programmes
Knowledge of preventing HIV/AIDS
Knowledge of misconceptions of HIV/AIDS
Knowledge of mother-to child transmission of HIV
Attitudes of people with HIV/AIDS
Women who know where to be tested for HIV
Women who have been tested for HIV

Chapter 2

The Relationship Between Child Poverty and Child Rights: The Role of Indicators

S. Pemberton, D. Gordon, S. Nandy, C. Pantazis and P. Townsend *

INTRODUCTION

In a recent research project conducted for UNICEF by the authors of this chapter, it was found that one billion children in the developing world suffer from severe deprivation and over 650 million suffer from multiple deprivation or absolute poverty (Gordon et al., 2003a). This dire situation appears to contradict some of the basic tenets of the Convention on the Rights of the Child (CRC). Consequently, one of the most pressing issues for social scientists is to detail exactly how child poverty contravenes the CRC. The purpose of this exercise is to gain political accountability and reverse failing macro socio-economic policies that are responsible for these levels of suffering.

This chapter seeks to consolidate existing work on the relationship between child rights and child poverty (Gordon et al., 2003b) by examining the role and potential of indices of child rights and child poverty.

The chapter is in four parts. The first presents a brief overview of the global economic structures that are partly responsible for current levels of poverty, and then considers the role of human rights in this context. The second identifies a number of issues that must be considered when examining the relationship between rights and poverty. The third discusses a number of methodological issues arising from this relationship. The fourth develops methodological issues, with specific attention paid to the role of indicators. This demonstrates the utility of the MICS to the task of quantifying the number of children whose rights

---

* University of Bristol and London School of Economics. This paper is one of three presented by the team in New York. See Gordon, D. et al., "Measuring Child Poverty and Human Rights in the Developing World", and Townsend, P., "Reducing Child Poverty: A review of Tried and Untried Policies in the Developing World".

are infringed because of poverty. This section also considers how indicators using the MICS data might be used to reflect the complexities of right fulfilment.

GLOBAL CAPITAL, NATION STATES AND GROWING INEQUALITIES: THE ROLE OF HUMAN RIGHTS

In June 2002, UNCTAD reported that over the past thirty years the number of people living in extreme poverty in Less Developed Countries (LDCs) had more than doubled –from 138 million in the late 1960s to 307 million in the late 1990s (UNCTAD, 2002a). Furthermore, it was estimated that a further 100 million people in the world's 49 poorest countries may fall below the $1 a day subsistence level by the year 2015. UNCTAD also emphasised that the proposed trend of the developing countries descent into further poverty should be located in the "current form of globalisation" (UNCTAD, 2002b). Thus, to understand these increasing levels of poverty, it is important to understand the global structures that perpetuate the problem. Recognising the role of neo-liberal economics and the policies implemented by this school of thought are key to understanding why the gap between rich and poor has grown substantially over the last 30 years.

The current formation of the global economy owes much to the policies of the so-called neo-liberal "Washington Consensus" (Atkinson, 2002). These policies have sought to minimise the role of the state in the market and include the deregulation of labour markets, legislation that limits the power of trade unions, the privatisation of state utilities and considerable reductions in public expenditure. Two principles underpin the neo-liberal model: the first is that competition allocates resources with the greatest efficiency; the second is that consequential losses experienced by some will be counterbalanced by increased economic growth. We need not dwell on the merits of these arguments, as it is clear that the erosion of basic social services (e.g. the imposition of user fees for health and education, the removal of food subsidies, the reduction in public expenditure onschools and hospitals, etc.) has not improved the lot of vulnerable communities, and has in many countries led to a dramatic decline in their standard of living (Milanovic, 2003).

The extent to which states have adopted the policies of the Washington Consensus has depended on the "strength" of the nation state involved (Chossudovsky, 1997). Developing countries have been encouraged to implement neo-liberal policies as part of conditions attached to structural adjustment loans and programmes from the International Monetary Fund (IMF) and World Bank. Townsend (2002) highlights the deleterious impact of such programmes on developing countries compared to industrialized countries where wage systems are strongly instituted and self-protecting and where long-established social security networks provide a degree of protection from economic instability. He notes that the deregulation and privatisation at the behest of the Bretton-Woods institutions have moved control of markets from these states toward Trans National Corporations (TNCs). At the same time, richer states (where the large TNCs have their headquarters) have acquired greater power to influence global economic developments. This "concentration of hierarchical power" has meant developing countries are forced to sell their products at prices dictated to them, whilst their labour markets provide a low paid and unprotected workforce, both at great social cost.

The current structure of the international economy has clearly been detrimental to the autonomy of developing countries; the same cannot be said for the richer, developed countries. Held (2000) argues that OECD countries, rather than being weakened by the rise of TNCs, have in fact become more powerful. It is important that the claims of governments in the developed world that they are impotent to regulate or control the activities of "footloose global capital" do not go unchallenged. Globalisation is not a "unidirectional" phenomenon, where the state must seek to attract and to accommodate global capital (Hall, 1998). It is simply not true that global capital has trampled over the states of the "north" (Weiss, 1997). To the contrary, TNCs rely on the political and legal systems of states – in particular the national and supra national systems promoted by the "north" – to create and maintain a global apparatus of wealth accumulation. It is these very structures that have facilitated TNCs' growth over the past thirty years. Without the supra-national frameworks of the IMF, World Bank, and World Trade Organisation, corporations would not have been able to operate in developing countries with the impunity they have to date (Chossudovsky, 1997; Townsend, 2002).

It is within this context, that we must evaluate the potential of a human rights perspective. We propose that such an approach offers the possibility of progressive interventions against child poverty in two ways.

The first is the legal obligation human rights place upon a state. If a set of obligations is placed upon the apparatus of wealth accumulation over which the state presides, human rights may have a material effect on these processes. This line of argument is supported by Williams (2003), who argues any social scientist wishing to understand the root causes of poverty cannot ignore the legal structures that create and perpetuate income/wealth imbalances within societies. Thus, human rights arguments might be employed to articulate challenges to the legal discourses (TRIPS, trusts, patents, tax avoidance etc.), which underpin the process of wealth accumulation discussed above.

The second, is the potential that human rights offer as a discursive tool to challenge current macro economic policies. In particular this may be used against supra-national bodies that escape traditional forms of political accountability. These bodies may be called to account by the emergent global civil society. Clearly, social scientists have an important role in initiating and informing debate within global civil society. We propose that an important element of this role is the conduct of objective "audits" of human rights abuses. Thus audits that demonstrate how human rights infringements result from poverty arising from the institutional structure of the global economy may be potentially powerful and persuasive devices. If it can be shown that universally agreed standards of basic human needs remain unmet as a result of the present form of economic and social organisation, then this can only serve to increase the pressure and calls for change arising from global civil society. Such pressure is fundamental to the extraction of commitments from political/economic elites for the realisation of these rights.

HUMAN RIGHTS AND POVERTY: OBSTACLES TO THE REALISATION OF RIGHTS

There are clearly a number of challenges to poverty reduction when adopting a human rights perspective. These are not explored in detail here, although some of the main challenges deserve a mention. First, we acknowledge the considerable literature around the issue of universalism and human rights. We support Sen (1999) and Doyal and Gough's (1991) rebuttal of both the post modernist and Asian Values culturally relativist standpoint. Second, there exists a considerable debate over the subordination of economic, social, and cultural rights to civil and political rights. It would appear that many states are prepared to place civil and political rights in the "justiciable" section of their constitution whilst relegating economic, social and cultural rights to the realm of directive principles. This explains the intention of bodies like UNICEF to remedy this situation by promoting the interdependence and indivisible nature of human rights. The issue of the justiciability of economic, social and cultural rights is critical if these rights are to realised.

It has long been argued that pre-legal "moral" claims contained in human rights conventions are not easily transferred into legal systems. The difficulty posed by translating "ambiguous" or "imprecisely" defined rights into concrete legal decisions has meant that national courts have effectively ignored many rights contained in international conventions. This applies especially to economic, social and cultural rights. As Van Bueren (1999) argues, domestic courts appear adept at making complex decisions in cases relating to civil and political rights, but they have generally avoided the issue of poverty and the non-fulfilment of individual's economic and social rights, citing the impossibility of making these rights justiciable. Admittedly, domestic courts have not been helped much by the lack of international jurisprudence and effective international law. Hence Van Bueren (1999) suggests that both domestic and international judiciaries follow the inventive and progressive approaches of treaty committees and special rapporteurs when addressing the question of justiciability.

In the context of the Convention of the Rights of the Child (CRC) and the economic, social and cultural rights it contains, domestic and international courts could draw inspiration from the following approaches. The Committee for Economic, Social and Cultural Rights (CESCR), in its General Comment No. 3 is clear: a state where a "significant number of individuals are deprived of essential foodstuffs, primary healthcare, of basic shelter and housing, or of the most basic forms of education is, prima facie, failing to discharge its obligations under the covenant". These guidelines recommend that any assessment as to whether a state has discharged its "minimum core obligations" must consider whether the state has used the "maximum" of its "available resources". The Committee on the Rights of the Child General Comment No. 5 states that article 4 of the convention "with regard to economic, social and cultural rights, State Parties shall undertake such measures to the maximum extent of their available resources", should be seen as "complementary" to the CESCRs General Comment No. 3. Consequently, the Committee on the Rights of the Child has on a number of occasions refused to accept the "non-affordability" claims made in the progress reports of states. For instance, Indonesia and Egypt have been requested to justify their failure to make significant progress in implementing the CRC in light of their high expenditure on defence budgets (see Van Bueren, 2003).

These guidelines offer economic, social and cultural rights an increased determinacy and certainty, than exist in the conventions themselves. These assist the further development of both domestic and international jurisprudence and of critical social science. It is the role of critical social science to develop methodological approaches that relate complex social phenomena, such as poverty, to human rights conventions. Furthermore, these methodologies need to be accessible to the "lay" person, to reinforce the chances of speedy implementation.

THE RELATIONSHIP BETWEEN POVERTY AND HUMAN RIGHTS: SOME METHODOLOGICAL ISSUES

So far we have argued that the social scientist has a specific role to play in advancing scientific and political accountability for failing socio-economic policies. This involves developing methodological approaches that have the potential in the long term to develop jurisprudence and in the short term to promote sharp debate within global civil society. This section outlines the mechanics involved in relating the components of poverty to the abuse of specific rights. Our "audit" seeks to measure the levels of non-fulfilment of child rights, which result from child poverty. We present a number of methodological issues and offer a table that links deprivation indices to specific rights. The table provides estimates of the number and proportion of children in selected countries, who because of the deprivations they experience, have some of their most basic rights infringed.

A significant methodological problem is that the CRC does not contain a specific right to freedom from poverty. Hence, to relate rights to the measurement of poverty, a selection process is required to match the rights contained in the CRC to deprivation indices that can be used to measure poverty (Gordon, 2002). The clustering of rights in this way is not to suggest that rights are divisible, as this would contradict our previous arguments. Rather, it makes sense that certain rights in the CRC are relevant to major objectives of a particular kind. Human rights are interrelated, and the fulfilment of certain rights will depend on the prior realisation of others. For example, if 10 million children die from malnutrition and preventable diseases each year before they reach the age of 5, then it makes sense that a child's nutritional and health needs must be realised before other civil and political rights can be secured. A child who dies of malnutrition before she reaches the age of 5 will clearly never realise her right to vote.

Many of the rights, as expressed in the relevant Charters and Conventions, are ambiguous or not sufficiently specific. This is particularly the case in social and economic rights, where human rights confer "imperfect duties" upon others. Formulation of rights may not address issues of how and the extent to which a duty may be discharged.

The distinction between "perfect" and "imperfect" duties helps to clarify the fact that access to some rights is easier to measure. In some cases, rights seem to be normative: a state adheres to them or does not and, consequently, measurement tends to be binary in nature. This is not necessarily useful when attempting to measure a phenomenon such as poverty, particularly when the measurement of deprivation underlying available household resources is viewed as a continuum ranging from "no deprivation" to "extreme deprivation". For instance, a right to health care cannot be partially adhered to. In other words, there cannot be gradations of compliance (even when, admittedly, there are gradations, country by country, in what health care means). Consequently, to avoid these problems we have taken severe deprivation of basic needs as a prima facie violation of the CRC.

A final issue relates to the fit between rights and indicators. As we have demonstrated some rights are more prescriptive than others. The consequence for social scientists when operationalising human rights and relating them to social phenomena, is that some rights and their corresponding indicators represent a better match than others. Hence those rights that confer "perfect" duties – due to their specificity are more likely to find a "direct" match to an existing social indicator (e.g. girls not being allowed to attend school under the Taliban). We think the relationship between rights and indicators should also be viewed as a continuum. Thus, associations of rights and indicators can range from those gathered at the "perfect/direct" point through to those at the "imperfect/indirect" point.

The "perfect/direct" point is characterised by a right that has a prescriptive quality and an indicator that is able to quantify the essence of the duty. This category requires a minimal level of interpretation. An example of a rights/indicator closest to the "perfect/direct" point is that of education. Article 28 establishes "the right of the child to education" and progresses to specify "primary education compulsory and available free to all" and "the development of different forms of secondary education, make them available and accessible to every child...". An indicator of the severe deprivation of education could therefore be the number or proportion of children who are "unable to attend primary or secondary education", which could in turn be used as an indicator of the non-fulfilment of the right to education.

It is of little surprise then that for the more ambiguous articles of the Convention indicators become more indirect. The "imperfect/ indirect" nature of such indicators for rights makes the data difficult to interpret. For instance, Article 24(1) talks of securing the right through facilities "for the treatment of illness and rehabilitation of health" and, similarly, Article 24 (2) (c) describes the need to "combat disease and malnutrition...within the framework of healthcare, through... the application of readily available technology". In order to provide a more comprehensive picture of rights fulfilment in the case of the "imperfect/indirect" end of the continuum, clusters of indicators are required to cover all possible interpretations of these rights.

Table 1 demonstrates the relationship between indicators of severe deprivation and the infringement of specific economic and social rights. These rights are matched with indicators that demonstrate the levels of their non-fulfilment. Alongside these indicators we have designated the nature of the fit between right/indicator; naturally those rights with indirect indicators must be treated with greater care when drawing conclusions from these results. Finally, we have used data from UNICEF's Multiple Indicator Cluster Surveys to illustrate the purpose of this methodological approach. The table contains information from two countries and estimates the number of children whose rights according to the CRC are infringed by poverty.

CHILD POVERTY, MEASURING RIGHT FULFILMENT AND THE ISSUE OF INDICATORS

The "audit" outlined above gives a very specific measure of rights fulfilment. This must be further developed to build a more complex picture. As Green (2001) suggests, methodologies designed to capture the reality of rights fulfilment must provide "information pyramids" to reflect the multifaceted nature of rights and the phenomena to which they relate. The three-tiered approach Green proposes forms the basis of this section. We will deal with each tier in turn.

The first tier contains a few carefully selected statistical indicators, which attempt to quantify levels of rights fulfilment. This tier represents the process described above, whereby indicators are selected to be representative of both poverty and human rights fulfilment. Here, indicators from surveys such as the MICS and the Demographic and Health Surveys (DHS) may be used. We would like to take the opportunity to consider how appropriate these surveys are to the task of measuring rights. This is not a definitive list, rather our remit here is restricted to considering the relative merits of these surveys, in the methodological context of this chapter.

The two surveys are similar in content, although there are some interesting differences between them. The MICS contain a number of modules that are not found in the DHS. These include modules on Child Labour and Vitamin A supplementation. If we take these examples, then

Table 1. The relationship between indicators of severe deprivation and rights contained in the CRC

Deprivation	Severe Deprivation	Indicators	Article/Right Infringed	Rights/Indictors	Sierra Leone% Children deprived/ (number of children)	People's Democratic Republic of Lao% Children deprived/ (number of children)
Food	Malnutrition	Severe Anthropometric failure in children under 5 (severe stunting, underweight, or wasting)	24 (2) (c) HEALTH	Imperfect/Indirect	19% (156,000)	25% (210,000)
Safe drinking water	Long walk to water (>200 meters) which is occasionally polluted	> 15 min to water or surface water (unsafe source)	24 (2) (e) HEALTH	Imperfect/Indirect	43% (967,000)	28% (726,000)
Sanitation facilities	No sanitation facilities in or near dwelling	No sanitation facilities	24 (2) (c) HEALTH	Imperfect/Indirect	16% (349,000)	67% (1,750,000)
Health	Health facilities more than 1 hours travel away. No immunisation against diseases.	No vaccinations or untreated diarrhoea	24 (1)/(2)(c) HEALTH	Imperfect/Indirect	17.0% (379,000)	23% (604,000)
Shelter	No facilities, non-permanent building, no privacy, no flooring, one or two rooms. 5+ per room	Mud flooring or over five people per room (severe overcrowding)	27 (3)STANDARD OF LIVING	Imperfect/Indirect	64% (1,415,000)	8% (207,000)
Education	Unable to attend primary or secondary education	Child of school age (7-18 years) and not in school or not received any education	28 (1) (a)/(b) EDUCATION	Perfect/Direct	50% (596,000)	19% (317,000)
Information	No access to radio, television or books or newspaper.	Combination of (i) Information access - if mother listened to radio in last week or read a newspaper or watched TV.(ii) Information possession - of a TV or radio	13/17INFORMATION	Perfect/Direct	54% (1,02,200)	13% (289,000)

Figures calculated from MICS2 data. Deprivation index taken from Gordon (2002).

both provide "indirect" indicators of the right to education and health respectively. Similarly, the DHS have information that is not contained in the MICS. For instance, as a measure of information deprivation both surveys include an indicator for information possession, however only the DHS contains an indicator for access to information. Thus, the social scientist must draw upon indicators from different surveys, as the clustering of indicators seems to be the most effective approach to quantifying the aspects of rights fulfillment.

A further positive aspect of these surveys is the form of data they provide and this is welcomed for two reasons. First, the data provide a source of comparative indicators between countries and regions. Second, the surveys provide disaggregated data. If we take the example of the MICS, then they provide information that can be broken down according to: region, gender, and urban/rural populations. This obviously informs later stages of methodological work, as a profile begins to emerge of those social groups disproportionately affected by the nonfulfilment of their rights. However, a lacuna in this information is the absence of any profiling on the basis of ethnicity or religion. Again this would aid the later stages of this methodology and would enable a more rounded picture of rights fulfilment. One other shortcoming affecting both the MICS and DHS is the lack of information on the health and nutrition of older children (i.e. over five years old). Older children are too frequently missed by such surveys, and the next round of DHS and MICS should consider collecting such data.

Finally, there are a number of issues about the way these surveys have been carried out. One of the biggest disparities between these surveys is their financial cost; the MICS average cost is $129,000, whereas the DHS average cost is $500,000 (Komarecki, 2003). This disparity exists due to technical experts required for the conduct of the DHS. However, both surveys, when subject to closer scrutiny have highlighted instances of problems in their conduct (see Komarecki, 2003). This should not detract from the utility of these surveys to the social scientist.

The second tier of our "information pyramid", Green (2001) argues, should contain indicators which offer a more detailed understanding of the structures and forces behind the key indicator. Green does not enlarge on the reasons for this, so we have taken this tier to represent a stage where indicators of a more "qualitative" nature may be integrated. As Hammarburg (2000) suggests, rights can never be measured in statistics alone because of their ambiguous nature. Hence, the methodological process must sooner or later involve the use of qualitative indicators. It is commonplace within human rights monitoring to review procedures and policies to assess whether a state has discharged its responsibilities as dictated by a convention. The work of treaty committees, special rapporteurs, and human rights organisations are a potential source of this kind of information.

The work of the Committee on the Rights of the Child provides a number of examples. For instance, in their initial reports states are expected to produce information (including legislative, judicial, administrative etc.) appertaining to a number of rights and their fulfilment. This monitoring is extended in the periodic reports of states to include more detailed questions. On a general level, states are required to provide budgetary details and their provision for children's needs. For example, the committee requires information on "the proportion of the budget devoted to social expenditures for children, including health, welfare and education, at central, regional and local levels..." (see 'General guidelines for periodic reports: 20/11/96'). Other questions relate to specific issues of rights fulfilment. If one takes the example of reporting on healthcare provisions, the Committee requires the submission of information on "children having access to and benefiting from medical assistance and health care, as well as persisting gaps, including by gender, age, ethnic and social origin, and measures adopted to reduce existing disparities" (see 'General guidelines for periodic reports: 20/11/96'). These indicators are important when assessing whether a nation state is taking steps towards the "progressive realisation" of economic, social and cultural rights. Furthermore, a picture is continually being built within the "information pyramid" of whose rights remain unfulfilled.

The third tier of this pyramid is truly qualitative in nature and bears on the causes of non-realisation of rights. This may take the form of case studies upon issues of rights infringements. Examples of this work are regularly carried out by human rights organisations. One such example is the report "The Small Hands of Slavery: Bonded Child Labour in India", conducted by Human Rights Watch (1996). This report, and others like it, are important aspects of the "information pyramid" as they describe human rights abuses, identify their causes, and policies of reform. A vital aspect of such reporting is the identification of international and domestic economic/social policies and the policy makers responsible for the contexts in which these abuses take place.

Up to this point, we have outlined a number of reasons for our three-tiered approach to rights fulfilment, in the context of child poverty. There is a further overarching reason for this model: the issue of political accountability. Here we accept Roth's (2004) arguments that warns human rights organisations, when campaigning upon the issue of economic, social and cultural rights, to refrain from producing lists of human rights infringements for people who are malnourished or do not have access to medical facilities. Roth argues this decontextualises these abuses and removes from the public agenda discussion of culpability and remedy. Consequently, our "audit" through the "information pyramid" would attempt to contextualise our statistical indicators in country specific case studies and distinguish between individual, state and institutional remedy, as well as cause.

Roth (2004) further argues that human rights organisations are usually successful, in terms of shaping public opinion, when they expose "sympathetic" cases and, consequently, are effective politically because of the public shaming they project onto governments. However, the problem with human rights issues relating to poverty is in handling the structural complexities of the phenomena. For Roth (2004) successful human rights messages consist of a simple formula: violation, violator and remedy. Furthermore, he finds that arguments for redistribution and restructuring of macro economic arrangements are equally indigestible. Instead he elects for an approach with a clearly identifiable act and actor. He cites a number of examples, including the South African AIDS/HIV drugs case, where those with the disease were denied access to cheaper generic drugs by the South African government.

While generally sympathetic to the arguments of Roth, he falls foul of reductionism. In producing messages for global civil society and judiciaries, social scientists attempting to produce clear arguments should not decontextualise them. Any audit should contribute messages that contain the violation, violator, and remedy components. However, they have to be related to the global context if the structural causes of child poverty are to be identified and successful remedies promoted.

CONCLUSION

The intention of this chapter has been to demonstrate that an "audit" of child rights fulfilment is plausible in the context of child poverty. In doing so we have demonstrated the role of the MICS within this methodological exercise. We addressed a number of issues that arise from the use of a human rights perspective and sought to recognise a number of contingencies when outlining the relationship between rights and poverty. However, we must add a further caveat to this discussion: it is not our intention that the "audit" we have described should lead to labelling developing countries as the worst human rights abusers. On the contrary, we have taken considerable effort in this chapter to describe the global context of poverty and to provide a methodological approach –"information pyramid"– that identifies these structural causes. Thus, we support the guidance given by the Committee on the Rights of the Child (General Comment No. 5) which specifies that the realisation of child rights are the responsibility of all nation states, be it within their jurisdiction or through international cooperation.

Whilst this methodological approach requires further refinement, we believe it is crucial to the development of jurisprudence and a global civil society that challenges the structures of global poverty so that these rights may move from simple rhetoric to meaningful reality.

REFERENCES

Atkinson, T. (2002). "Is rising income inequality inevitable? A critique of the 'Transatlantic Consensus'," ed. by P. Townsend and D. Gordon in World Poverty: New policies to defeat an old enemy. Bristol: Policy Press.

Chossudovsky, M. (1997). The Globalisation of Poverty: Impacts of IMF and World Bank Reforms. Goa: Other India Press.

Doyal, L., and Gough, I. (1991). A Theory of Human Need. London: Macmillan.

Gordon, D. (2002). "The International Measurement of Poverty and Anti-Poverty Policies", ed by P. Townsend and D. Gordon in *World Poverty: New policies to defeat an old enemy.* Bristol: Policy Press.

Gordon, D., Nandy, S., Pantazis, C., Pemberton, S., and Townsend, P. (2003a). *Child Poverty in the Developing World.* Bristol: Policy Press.

Gordon, D., Nandy, S., Pantazis, C., Pemberton, S., and Townsend, P. (2003b). *The Distribution of Child Poverty in the Developing World.* Bristol: University of Bristol.

Green, M. (2001). "What We Talk About When We Talk About Indicators: Current Approaches to Human Rights Measurement". *Human Rights Quarterly.* Vol 23: 1062-1097.

Hall, S. (1998). "The Great Moving Nowhere Show". *Marxism Today.* Nov/Dec: 9-14.

Hammarberg, T. (2000). "Searching the Truth: The need to Monitor Human Rights with Relevant and Reliable Means". Presentation to the Conference on Statistics, Development and Human Rights, Montreux.

Held, D. (2000). "Regulating Globalization?", ed. by D. Held and A. McGrew in *The Global Transformations Reader: An introduction to the globalisation debate.* Cambridge: Polity.

Human Rights Watch (1996). *The Small Hands of Slavery: Bonded Child Labor in India.* New York: Human Rights Watch.

Komarecki, M. (2003). *Promoting Human Rights and Social Policies for Children and Women: The role of multiple cluster indicator survey (MICS).* (Partly reproduced as chapter 1 of this volume).

Milanovic, B. (2003). "The Two Faces of Globalisation: Against globalisation as we know it". World Development. Vol 31: 667-683.

Roth, K. (2004). "Defending Economic, Social and Cultural Rights: Practical Issues Faced by an International Human Rights Organisation". *Human Rights Quartely.* Vol. 26: 63-73.

Sen, A. (1999). *Development as Freedom.* Oxford: Oxford University Press.

Townsend, P. (2002). "Poverty, Social exclusion and social polarisation: the need to construct an international welfare state", ed. by P. Townsend and D. Gordon in *World Poverty: New policies to defeat an old enemy.* Bristol: Policy Press.

UNCTAD (2002a). *The Least Developed Countries Report 2002.* Geneva: United Nations.

UNCTAD (2002b). Press Release, <http://www.unctad.org/en/pub/ps1ldc02.en.htm>.

Van Bueren, C. (1999). "Combating Child Poverty–Human Rights Approaches". *Human Rights Quarterly.* Vol. 21: 680-706

Weiss, L. (1997). "Globalisation and the Myth of the Powerless State". New Left Review. Vol. 225: 3-27.

Williams, L. (2003). "Introduction", ed by L. Williams, A. Kjonstad and P. Robson in *Law and Poverty: The Legal System and Poverty Reduction.* London: Zed.

Chapter 3

Poverty and Children's Schooling: A Structural Equations Approach Using MICS Data

Mark R. Montgomery and Paul C. Hewett

As developing countries continue to urbanize, national debates about poverty will increasingly need to consider its urban as well as its rural manifestations. To date, the needs of rural areas have occupied policy attention to such an extent that urban poverty has gone unrecognized. Yet as the Panel on Urban Population Dynamics (2003) has shown in its analyses of health, poor urban dwellers often live in conditions that are little better (and are sometimes worse) than found in the countryside. There is reason to wonder whether for the poor, the "urban advantage" in children's schooling might also prove to be elusive. In this paper we take a closer look at the inequalities that can affect children's schooling in urban and rural settings, hoping in this way to better understand the urban–rural differences. Using data from the 2000 Multiple Indicator Cluster Survey (MICS) for Senegal, we focus on three indicators of schooling: whether a child has ever attended school; the completion of at least four grades of primary; and current school enrollment. Of particular interest in the analysis is whether higher household living standards tend to improve educational opportunities for girls.

Despite decades of academic and policy attention to developing-country poverty, surprisingly few data sets give educational researchers much purchase on the concept of living standards. Although exceptions exist –notably the World Bank's Living Standards Measurement Surveys– surveys with detailed information on children's schooling have not often gathered comparably detailed data on household incomes and consumption expenditures. The MICS program is no exception to the rule. Users of the MICS are thus left with little alternative but to fashion an index of living standards from the few proxy variables that are included in these surveys, which range from ownership of consumer durables to crude assessments of the quality of housing.

The past decade has seen a lively debate in the literature on the merits of alternative statistical techniques using such proxies. We explore one of the more promising approaches for distilling the proxies into a living standards index, termed MIMIC models, which are a variant of confirmatory-factor analysis. The MIMIC approach requires that variables serving as *indicators* of living standards be distinguished from those serving as *determinants* of living standards. In this way the method brings a helpful theoretical structure to the estimation of living standards indices and imposes a measure of discipline on the empirical results. We apply the approach separately to the urban and rural households of the Senegalese survey, and from these sector-specific estimates develop urban- and rural-specific rankings of living standards. We then explore whether in each setting, relative living standards make a difference to children's schooling.

The chapter is organized as follows. Section 1 situates our analysis in a wider international debate on how best to gauge progress in children's education. Section 2 describes the MICS data for Senegal, presenting descriptive statistics on the children's schooling measures and the explanatory variables used in the schooling models. In Section 3 we provide an overview of the theories and statistical issues that must be confronted in fashioning defensible measures of living standards from the crude raw materials at hand. Following this, Section 4 presents the multivariate results. The chapter concludes with thoughts on an agenda for further work.

MONITORING PROGRESS IN EDUCATION

Since 1990, when the "World Declaration on Education for All" was signed in Jomtien, Thailand, and the "World Summit for Children (WSC)" was staged in New York, efforts to promote children's educational participation and attainment have been given high priority by many international organizations, donors, and governments. The commitment to children's schooling perceptibly deepened over the decade, and was reaffirmed by the Millennium Development Declaration of 2000, which itself was followed by a burst of activity defining educational goals, quantifying targets, and developing indicators of progress. The two targets for schooling specified in the Millennium Development Goals

(MDGs) are that "by the year 2015, children everywhere, boys and girls alike, will be able to complete a full course of primary schooling and that by 2005 girls and boys will have equal access to all levels of education" (United Nations, 2001).[1] Substantial international research effort is now being directed to this end. The MDG targets single out gender inequities in schooling as meriting special attention; although inequities attributable to poverty are not similarly highlighted, poverty is of course the central organizing theme of the Millennium Development Declaration and the goals and targets associated with it.

There are, broadly speaking, two sources of data available to measure progress toward such schooling targets. UNESCO and UNICEF have long used data collected from national ministries of education, together with the population counts supplied by the United Nations Population Division, to generate gross and net primary enrollment ratios, and estimates of the likelihood that a child enrolled in grade 1 of primary will successfully complete four grades of primary and enter grade 5. These aggregate indicators have been used for cross-national comparisons of schooling levels and trends (UNESCO, 2002; 2003; UNICEF, 2003). As Bruns et al. (2003) have recently shown, further refinements can be made in measures of primary completion.[2]

The quality of the aggregate enrollment data collected from national ministries of education is acknowledged to be uneven.[3] When they are compared with estimates from the main alternative data source –schooling data taken from nationally representative, household-level sample surveys– the aggregate data would appear to be afflicted by systematic biases, with the discrepancies between data sources being particularly significant for countries in sub-Saharan Africa (Lloyd and Hewett, 2003; UNESCO, 2003). Surveys fielded by the Demographic and Health Surveys (DHS) and the Multiple Indicator Surveys (MICS) provide an opportunity to assess school achievement and progress toward universal primary completion. Such surveys gather information on the current educational status of school-age children as well as (limited) retrospective educational histories. These data, and information on adult educational attainment, are usually collected in a household questionnaire in which one informed adult (typically the head of household) answers on behalf of each member.

The survey-based sources have one decided advantage: they permit an exploration of linkages between children's education and household poverty or living standards, an area that cannot be explored with aggregate measures. In principle, if full retrospective schooling histories were gathered for each child, and if these reports were of good quality, household data could be used to form estimates of the primary completion rate and other measures addressed in the Millennium Development Goals. By tracking changes in primary completion rates across age cohorts, an accurate assessment of trends in schooling could be obtained from household data.

The MICS program, which provides the data for our analyses, was specifically developed to monitor the WSC goals. It incorporates more than 75 indicators covering a range of critical statistics for developing countries, including information related to child survival and health, child labor, education and access to basic public services such as potable water and sanitation.[4]

SCHOOLING DATA AND MODEL SPECIFICATION

The Senegalese schooling system is formally structured along the lines seen in much of Francophone West Africa. Primary schooling consists of 6 grades, and students are meant to enroll in primary 1 at the age of seven years. A student who enrolls at this age and advances without repetition or drop-out will complete the full course of primary schooling at age 12. Completion of primary is marked by the award of the CFEE (Certificat de Fin d'Etudes élémentaires). Middle schooling takes one of two forms: a first cycle of secondary training lasting for four grades and ending with the bestowal of the BEPC (Brevet de Fin d'Etudes de Premier Cycle) at age 16; or a three-year program of technical secondary leading to the CAP (Certificat d'Aptitude Professionelle). Vocational programs that entail four grades are also offered in the system. Those students holding a BEPC may proceed to a second cycle of secondary schooling, lasting for three grades and ending at age 19 with the award of a Baccalauréat or Baccalauréat Technique diploma. Alternatively, they may pursue a vocational secondary program, which may involve as few as two or as many as four grades depending on the program chosen. Access to university schooling and similar training (e.g., the Ecole normale supérieure) requires the Baccalauréat or its equivalent.

Schooling measures

The questions that were used to construct our schooling indicators are displayed in Table 1 together with the ages of respondents about whom such information was gathered in the MICS survey. Given that late entry and frequent grade repetition are characteristic of Senegalese primary schooling, children are often found in primary school well beyond age 12, the official age for primary completion. Over 40 percent of children aged 13 to 19 who were enrolled in school were still attending primary school; even among the 18 year olds who were enrolled, 13 percent were attending primary; and the same was true of 6 percent of 19 year olds. Evidently, primary completion rates framed in terms of official age ranges can substantially underestimate the proportion of children who will eventually complete primary.

Table 1. Survey Questions Defining Children's Schooling, Senegal 2000

Measure	Asked of those in age range
Ever attended	
Has (name) ever attended school?	5 and over
Completed 4 or More Years	
What is the highest level of school (name) attended?[a]	5 and over
What is the highest grade completed at this level?	
Current Attendance	
Is (name) currently attending school?	5 to 17

[a] Grades completed in Senegal's informal school system are taken to be equivalent to grades of formal primary.

Mindful of the potential mismatches between children's ages and the official age ranges in Senegal, we define three summary measures of schooling: (1) ever attendance among children 10 to 19 years old at the time of the survey; (2) the completion of 4 or more years of schooling among those who are 15 to 19 years old at survey; and (3) current enrollment among those 7 to 12 years of age.[5] For the "Ever attendance" and "Completed 4 or More Years" measures, we have selected the age ranges with two objectives in mind: the child should be old enough to have had the opportunity to achieve the specified level of schooling, given the likelihood of late entry and repetition; but should not be so old as to render the experience of only historical interest. With the Senegal survey having been fielded in 2000, primary completion rates for those aged 20–24 mainly refer to the educational experiences of students who passed through primary school some 7 to 12 years earlier, that is, in the late 1980s and early 1990s. Such data would shed little light on recent trends.

For the ever attendance measure of schooling, a minimum of 10 years of age seemed to us to be sufficient to take account of late starting ages, and age 15 appeared adequate for the completed 4 or more years measure. Unless life-table methods are applied to handle right-censoring (we have not explored these methods here) a reduction in the minimum age for these indicators would yield underestimates of the percentage of children who eventually attend and complete. Our focus on grade 4 completion is motivated by the importance of basic literacy and numeracy skills, which are probably acquired by that grade, and by the need to provide estimates that are not too far removed from the survey date.

Table 2. Descriptive Statistics for Children's Schooling Outcomes by Age and Residence

	Ever Attended		Completed 4 or More Years		Currently Enrolled	
	Urban	Rural	Urban	Rural	Urban	Rural
Number of children	4966	9083	2262	3547	2796	5281
Age						
7					88.1	86.2
8					87.3	85.4
9					82.4	82.5
10	83.0	51.0			69.1	40.4
11	83.4	58.2			67.8	49.9
12	83.7	51.8			64.6	37.2
13	79.4	52.2				
14	78.7	46.1				
15	77.1	46.2	68.0	29.8		
16	77.8	40.7	67.1	23.4		
17	78.1	36.8	70.3	24.1		
18	74.5	35.0	63.4	21.5		
19	76.5	39.5	69.7	26.5		
All ages	79.4	46.9	67.6	25.0	75.5	56.8

Table 2 provides a descriptive overview of the three indicators by age and place of residence. For the ever-attended measure an upward time trend is evident, with greater percentages of younger than older children having attended school. This trend is more pronounced in rural areas, which have seen nearly twice the improvement in ever-attendance achieved in urban areas. But such recent gains notwithstanding, the gap in attendance between rural and urban areas remains sizable. A wide urban–rural gap is also evident in the percentages completing 4 or more grades, with the urban percentage being more than double the rural. Interestingly, the gap is less evident in the current enrollment figures for children aged 7–9, although it re-emerges for the older children. As can be seen, as age increases the percentage of children enrolled declines more precipitously in rural areas. These patterns hint that retention, rather than access to schooling as such, may now be the critical factor in the urban–rural schooling gap.

Explanatory variables

Table 3 provides weighted means of the explanatory covariates in the estimation sample for each educational outcome, separately for urban and rural areas. Here the education and literacy of adults in the household are of interest. In the urban sample of children, some 60 percent have adult men in the household with at least a primary school education, and 44 percent have adult women. For rural areas, children are at a marked disadvantage with regard to their household human capital, with only 24 percent of children having adult men and 10 percent of children having adult women with a primary education or more. Table 3 also suggests that in urban areas there is greater educational equality by sex within households, with (for example) approximately equal proportions of adult men and women having achieved primary. In rural areas, where adults of both sexes are disadvantaged in terms of educational attainment, the adult women in the sample are far less likely have any schooling than their male counterparts. It is also clear from the table that the proportion of children with literate adults in the household is quite low in rural Senegal, where approximately 70 percent of households lack a literate adult man and 90 percent a literate adult woman. Although higher adult literacy rates are evident in urban areas, particularly for men, even here two-thirds of children live without an literate adult woman in the household.

Table 3. Descriptive Statistics for Explanatory Variables in the Schooling Models

	Ever Attended		Completed 4 or More Years		Currently Enrolled	
	Urban	Rural	Urban	Rural	Urban	Rural
Child characteristics						
Child is female	0.52	0.50	0.54	0.51	0.50	0.48
Child's age	14.30	13.84	16.94	16.77	9.63	9.90
Education of household adults: Proportions						
Adult men with primary	0.29	0.18	0.29	0.18	0.30	0.21
Adult men with middle	0.15	0.04	0.16	0.04	0.16	0.05
Adult men with secondary or higher	0.15	0.04	0.16	0.04	0.16	0.05
Adult men literate	0.59	0.33	0.60	0.32	0.60	0.36
Adult women with primary	0.28	0.09	0.27	0.08	0.28	0.11
Adult women with middle	0.10	0.01	0.11	0.01	0.11	0.01
Adult women with secondary or higher	0.05	0.43^{-2}	0.06	0.38^{-2}	0.05	0.53^{-2}
Adult women literate	0.34	0.08	0.37	0.08	0.34	0.09

STATISTICAL APPROACH: THE MIMIC MODEL

Figure 1. Classifying the Approaches to Measuring Living Standards

	Non-Statistical Approaches	Statistical Approaches
Loosely Structured	Count of all durables owned	Principal components or factor analysis of durables alone
Tightly Structured	Judgment-based weighted indexes durables	MIMIC specifications

It may be useful to preview our MIMIC approach by situating it among the various strategies that have been applied to the problem of measuring living standards with collections of proxy variables. Figure 1 presents one scheme for doing so, in which we distinguish highly-structured and less-structured approaches, and also draw a distinction between approaches that are statistically-based and those that rely solely on the judgment of the investigator. In separating determinants from indicators, the MIMIC approach brings more structure to bear on the problem than do the comparatively unstructured principal components or simple factor-analytic methods. But judgment-based approaches, in which detailed knowledge of local conditions is applied to form weights for each consumer durable or indicator, are also highly structured and they also bring outside information to bear on the problem of defining living standards. We have not seen in the literature a synthesis of the MIMIC and judgment-based approaches, but it may well be possible to draw them together.

The specifications to be explored here take the form of equation systems in which a given schooling variable, denoted by Y, is the main object of interest. As discussed above, in our application Y will represent one of three measures of schooling. For the schooling models, we write the main structural equation in latent variable form as

$$Y^* = W'\,\theta + f\,\delta + \varepsilon \tag{1}$$

with the observed dependent variable $Y=1$ if $Y^* \geq 0$ and $Y=0$ otherwise. The determinants of Y^* include a vector of explanatory variables W and an unobservable factor f that we will take to represent the household's standard of living. Another unobservable, ε, serves as the disturbance term of this structural equation.

We posit a model of the factor f such that

$$f = X'\,\gamma + u, \tag{2}$$

the value of f being determined by a set of exogenous variables X and a disturbance u. Although f is not itself observed, its probable level is signaled through the values taken by $\{Z_k\}$, a set of K indicator variables. The full equation system thus comprises the schooling equation and a set of equations for the living standards indicators. (See Montgomery and Hewett, 2004, for a full statistical description of the MIMIC model.) In setting out the model in this way, with latent factors embedded in structural equations, we follow an approach that has been recommended by several researchers (notably Sahn and Stifel, 2000; McDade and Adair, 2001; Tandon et al., 2002; Ferguson et al., 2003). Filmer and Pritchett (1999, 2001) have developed an alternative approach based on the method of

Table 4. Descriptive Statistics for Household Living Standards Variables.
Unweighted means

Number of households in sample	Urban	Rural
	2185	3885
Indicators		
Car	0.091	0.040
Refrigerator	0.349	0.028
Television	0.522	0.081
Telephone[a]	0.235	
Radio	0.883	0.768
Cooker[a]	0.068	
Motorcycle or bicycle[a]	0.077	
Uncrowded sleeping conditions[b]	0.542	0.532
Finished floor	0.830	0.309
Determinants		
Electricity	0.692	0.087
Home or land	0.727	0.927
Cultivatable land	0.183	0.861
Plow	0.047	0.513
Handcart	0.047	0.417
Sewing machine	0.117	0.037
Head is a woman	0.303	0.092
Age of household head in years	52.58	51.38
No adult man resides in the household	0.114	0.051
Averages years of schooling, adult men in household	4.724	1.327
Proportions literate, adult men[c]		0.301
Averages years of schooling, adult women in household	3.053	0.485
Proportions literate, adult women	0.332	0.072
Dakar	0.422	
Kaolack	0.422	
Saint Louis	0.079	
Thies	0.139	
Ziguinchor	0.122	

[a] Too few households possess the item for it to be includes in the rural specification.
[b] Households members per sleeping room exceeds the (weight) median for sector of residence.
[c] Not included in the urban specification.

principal components. Although useful in descriptive analyses and very easy to apply, this method is perhaps best viewed as a data-reduction procedure whose main virtue is the ease with which the researcher can collapse multiple indicators into a single index. The principal components approach is otherwise rather limited –it does not cleanly separate the determinants of living standards from the indicators of living standards, and it lacks a firm theoretical and statistical foundation. As a result, the method is not readily generalizable to structural, multiple-equation models such as ours (see discussion in Montgomery et al., 2000).

Modeling the living standards factor

With the living standards factor specified as $f = X'\gamma + u$, how should the X variables of this equation be chosen and what relation, if any, should they bear to the W variables that enter the main schooling equation? How are the X variables, posited as determinants of living standards, to be distinguished from the $\{Z_k\}$ variables that serve as indicators of living standards? In Table 4 we present our classification scheme and supply descriptive statistics on the indicators and determinants.

As Montgomery et al. (2000) note, there is little consensus in the literature about how best to define and model the living standards measures found in surveys such as those fielded by the MICS program, which lack data on consumption expenditures and income. With proper consumption data lacking, we think it reasonable to define the set of living standards indicators $\{Z_k\}$ in terms of the consumer durables and housing-quality items for which data are gathered. Using these indicators, we construct what McDade and Adair (2001) have termed a "relative affluence" measure of living standards. The indicators available for Senegal include ownership of a car, refrigerator, television, telephone, and radio; a cooker; a motorcycle or bicycle; and two measures of housing quality: uncrowded sleeping conditions, and having finished (that is, non-dirt) floors. So few households in rural Senegal own cookers, telephones, and either motorcycles or bicycles that it was necessary to exclude these indicators from the rural analysis.

Producer durables are ·deliberately excluded from the $\{Z_k\}$ set of indicators, because while they may help determine final consumption, producer durables are not themselves measures of that consumption. They are a means to an end, or, to put it differently, producer durables are better viewed as inputs in household production functions, rather than as measures of the consumption drawn from household production. By this logic, producer durable variables should be included among the X covariates. These producer durables were included: possession of a house or land, ownership of cultivatable land, and having a plow, handcart, or sewing machine. Some publicly provided services can also be viewed as enabling factors, or inputs, into consumption –notably, the provision of electricity– and we have therefore included electricity in the X living standards determinants. Although city size may be only a distant proxy for the many additional factors that determine consumption –among them, access to multiple income-earning possibilities and heterogeneous labor and product markets– we include dummy variables for Dakar and several other Senegalese cities in the set of determinants to account for such effects.

It is not unreasonable to liken adult education to a producer durable, education being a type of long-lasting trait that produces a lifetime stream of income and consumption; on these grounds we include the age of the household head and measures of educational attainment for all adults in the household in our specification of the X determinants. In doing so, we are mindful of the "dual roles" played by education in demographic behavior (Montgomery et al., 2000). Education is both a determinant of living standards and a conceptually separable influence on behavior via its links to social confidence, to the ability to process information, and to the breadth and nature of individual social networks. In short, education measures belong with the W variables of the schooling equations as well as in the set of X variables that act as determinants of living standards. Model identification is not threatened by variables that are common to both X and W, but we hope to strengthen the empirical basis for estimation by using a summary measure of education (average years) for adult men and women in the living standards model and a more detailed specification, involving levels of adult schooling, in the children's schooling models. The sex of the household head is included among the determinants of living standards, as is a dummy variable indicating whether adult men are present in the household. When no such men are present, the adult education variables for men are "zeroed out." The same approach could have been followed for adult women, but it was so rare for Senegalese households to lack adult women that there was little point in doing so.

Estimates of urban and rural living standards

Table 5 summarizes the estimated β_k factor loadings on the indicators of living standards, and also presents the γ estimates on the determinants. As can be seen in the table, the β_k coefficients are always positive and (with one exception) they are statistically significant. This is encouraging, in that it supports the interpretation of the factor as an expression of the household's standard of living. The table also presents a summary of γ, the effects of the X determinants. These effects are very much in line with expectations. In both urban and rural areas, the provision of electricity is positively associated with living standards, as would be anticipated given its role as a key input. Likewise, the adult education variables are also strongly and positively associated with living standards in urban and rural areas; and, consistent with age profiles of productivity, we find that urban living standards increase with the head's age up to about age 63, and decrease thereafter. No important nonlinearities in age could be detected in the rural models. (Table 5.)

Among the producer durables, ownership of a home or land is positively associated with living standards in the urban model, but does not achieve significance in the rural model. Oddly, however, for rural households possession of cultivatable land is negatively associated with living standards. Almost all rural households in Senegal (some 93 percent) possess either land or a house and almost all have cultivatable land (86 percent). It may be, therefore, that the negative sign on cultivatable land is an indication that non-farm rural households are better off than households directly dependent on agriculture. Further work will be needed to confirm that this is a plausible interpretation.

Other producer durables –possession of a handcart and sewing machine– are positively and significantly associated with living standards in both urban and rural settings. The city-specific dummy variables show weak effects overall, but the estimates suggest that with other things held

Table 5. Estimates of the MIMIC Model of Living Standards

	Urban		Rural	
	Coefficient	$\lvert Z \rvert$ value	Coefficient	$\lvert Z \rvert$ value
Coefficients β_k of the indicators				
Indicators				
Refrigerator	1.948	14.767	2.465	9.137
Television	1.975	14.914	2.683	9.935
Telephone	1.754	14.185		
Radio	0.950	11.579	1.490	8.805
Cooker	2.292	14.712		
Motorcycle or bicycle	2.288	14.217		
Uncrowded	0.353	7.184	0.120	1.771
Finished floor	0.670	10.475	1.827	10.026
Coefficients γ of the Determinants				
Electricity	0.799	13.817	0.701	9.860
Home or land	0.159	5.990	0.029	0.958
Cultivatable land	-0.006	0.221	-0.152	5.578
Plow	-0.026	0.441	0.020	0.934
Handcart	0.216	4.389	0.152	6.052
Sewing machine	0.245	8.240	0.164	3.868
Head is a woman	0.022	0.873	0.076	1.945
Age of head	0.021	5.532	-0.053^{-2}	0.158
Age of head, squared	-0.017^{-2}	5.119	0.001^{-2}	0.433
No adult man in household	0.023	0.597	-0.018	0.357
Averages years of schooling, adult men	0.024	8.376	0.023	5.051
Proportions literate, adult men			0.057	2.633
Averages years of schooling, adult women	0.027	6.069	0.017	2.126
Proportions literate, adult women	0.107	2.926	0.150	2.749
Dakar	0.100	2.890		
Kaolack	-0.044	0.883		
Saint Louis	0.084	1.746		
Thies	0.071	1.684		
Ziguinchor	0.036	0.927		
ρ	0.170	7.595	0.080	5.047

Note: For specification of variables, see text and notes to Table 4.

equal, living standards are generally higher in Dakar by comparison with Senegal's secondary cities. There is no statistically discernible difference between a small city such as Kaolack and Senegal's towns, which serve as the omitted category in this analysis. On the whole, the results presented in Table 5 provide good statistical support for the proposition that the proxy variables collected in the Senegal MICS can be interpreted as indicators of the household's standard of living.

MULTIVARIATE RESULTS FOR CHILDREN'S SCHOOLING

The predicted living standards factor $\hat{f}$ derived from the MIMIC model are grouped into quintiles specific to urban and rural areas, and these quintiles provides the basis for much of the multivariate analysis to follow. Figure 2 depicts the children's school outcomes measures by living standards quintile for urban and rural households, without controls for any other explanatory variables. The bivariate associations shown here

Figure 2. Children who have ever attended school, completed four or more grades, or are currently enrolled, percentages by residence and quintile of household living standards

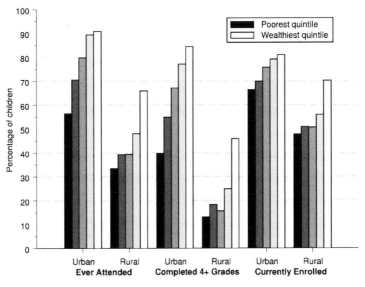

Figure 3. Predicted percentages of ever-attendance, completion of four or more grades, and current enrollment, by residence and quintile of household living standards. Results from Model 1.

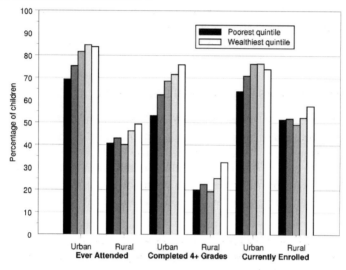

are strongly suggestive of living standards effects on schooling. The urban gradients are especially clear, although in rural areas it seems that the largest differences are those between the households in the uppermost quintile of rural living standards and all other rural households. Is this interpretation sustained when controls are introduced for a host of explanatory variables?

Figure 3 depicts the net association between living standards quintile and schooling outcome, with the predictions based on the estimated models shown in Tables 6 and 7 under the heading of "Model 1," in which living standards quintiles are included but interactions of the quintiles with the sex of the child are not.

The predicted values summarized in the figure were produced by assigning an age to each child (to remove this source of variation) and then, in sequence, assigning each household to a living standards quintile and taking the average of the predicted probabilities (allowing

Table 6. Educational Participation and Attainment, Probit Estimates for Urban Areas

| | Ever Attended School | | | | Completed 4 or More Years | | | | Currently Enrolled | | | |
| | Model 1 | | Model 2 | | Model 1 | | Model 2 | | Model 1 | | Model 2 | |
	Coefficient	|Z|	Coefficient	|Z|	Coefficient	|Z|	Coefficient	|Z|	Coefficient	|Z|	Coefficient	|Z|
Living Standards Quintiles												
Second quintile	0.212	2.006	0.175	1.179	0.269	2.089	0.215	1.324	0.206	1.594	0.130	0.771
Third quintile	0.468	4.858	0.326	2.345	0.459	3.817	0.256	1.535	0.380	2.938	0.086	0.534
Fourth quintile	0.605	5.520	0.450	3.376	0.559	4.535	0.283	2.074	0.384	2.998	0.026	0.168
Fifth quintile	0.565	4.616	0.0501	2.961	0.707	5.406	0.568	3.335	0.303	2.154	0.087	0.522
Second quintile or female			0.073	0.536			0.116	0.649			0.159	0.522
Third quintile or female			0.256	1.883			0.379	1.885			0.585	3.566
Fourth quintile or female			0.291	2.133			0.536	2.825			0.734	3.687
Fifth quintile or female			0.124	0.857			0.268	1.324			0.432	2.685
Other variables												
Child is female	-0.383	8.311	-0.518	6.238	-0.370	5.830	-0.683	4.529	-0.160	3.041	-0.540	4.552
Child's age	-0.037	0.046	-0.075	0.091	15.333	1.015	14.568	0.979	9.330	4.044	9.458	4.070
Child's age, squared	-0.119^{-2}	0.021	0.153^{-2}	0.027	-0.900	1.023	-0.8065	0.985	-1.016	4.180	-1.028	4.196
Child's age, cubed	0.311^{-4}	0.024	-0.321^{-4}	0.024	0.018	1.029	0.017	0.989	0.035	4.215	0.036	4.221
Adult men with primary	0.558	5.926	0.558	5.975	0.456	4.072	0.453	4.125	0.187	1.439	0.198	1.521
Adult men with middle	0.760	5.218	0.755	5.186	0.534	3.349	0.525	3.306	0.344	1.800	0.344	1.793
Adult men with secondary or higher	0.770	5.070	0.765	5.053	0.690	4.362	0.677	4.321	0.406	2.068	0.404	2.062
Adult men literate	-0.104	1.040	-0.102	1.029	0.013	0.119	0.021	0.184	-0.108	0.914	-0.018	0.918
Adult women with primary	0.939	7.182	0.939	7.231	0.572	4.403	0.570	4.416	0.168	1.140	0.170	1.163
Adult women with middle	1.062	5.324	1.066	5.386	1.191	5.032	1.197	5.145	0.313	1.532	0.314	1.526
Adult women with secondary or higher	0.917	3.431	0.920	3.448	0.750	2.730	0.751	2.715	0.117	0.441	0.119	0.442
Adult women literate	-0.041	0.341	-0.149	0.395	-0.125	0.827	-0.130	0.859	-0.003	0.016	-0.017	0.105
Dakar	-0.012	0.105	-0.012	0.102	-0.007	0.57	0.002	0.013	-0.417	3.006	-0.419	3.035
Kaolack	0.255	1.388	0.261	1.419	0.201	0.922	0.215	0.957	0.468	3.151	0.477	3.090
St. Louis	0.051	0.322	0.064	0.341	0.332	1.629	0.350	1.731	0.259	1.713	0.258	1.755
Thies	-0.144	1.001	-0.143	0.993	-0.107	0.604	-0.106	0.592	-0.215	1.320	-0.212	1.306
Ziguinchor	0.459	2.983	0.459	2.989	0.547	3.482	0.551	3.535	0.563	3.923	0.557	3.956
Constant	0.753	0.198	0.998	0.259	-84.756	1.101	-81.556	0.973	-26.639	3.717	26.886	3.724

Table 7. Educational Participation and Attainment, Probit Estimates for Rural Areas

| | Ever Attended School | | | | Completed 4 or More Years | | | | Currently Enrolled | | | |
| | Model 1 | | Model 2 | | Model 1 | | Model 2 | | Model 1 | | Model 2 | |
	Coefficient	|Z|	Coefficient	|Z|	Coefficient	|Z|	Coefficient	|Z|	Coefficient	|Z|	Coefficient	|Z|
Living Standards Quintiles												
Second quintile	0.072	1.103	0.118	1.421	0.101	1.027	0.136	1.060	0.0132	0.150	0.004	0.036
Third quintile	-0.017	-0.2293	-0.080	-0.864	-0.032	-0.313	-0.021	-0.169	-0.060	-0.678	-0.145	-1.475
Fourth quintile	0.168	2.075	0.141	1.436	0.199	1.776	0.284	2.076	0.024	0.264	-0.028	-0.251
Fifth quintile	0.258	2.837	0.240	2.162	0.438	3.346	0.413	2.804	0.166	1.612	0.093	0.772
Second quintile or female			-0.100	-1.026			-0.083	-0.472			0.023	0.169
Third quintile or female			0.132	1.287			-0.023	-0.126			0.179	1.575
Fourth quintile or female			0.057	0.558			-0.185	-0.989			0.111	0.860
Fifth quintile or female			0.039	0.329			0.042	0.244			0.151	1.201
Other variables												
Child is female	-0.434	-11.649	-0.466	-6.031	-0.467	-8.260	-0.418	-3.146	-0.284	-6.982	-0.384	-4.094
Child's age	1.748	3.584	1.745	3.579	-10.494	-0.926	-10.424	-0.914	10.223	5.382	10.221	5.337
Child's age, squared	-0.127	-3.650	-0.127	-3.644	0.596	0.893	0.592	0.881	-1.164	-5.821	-1.165	-5.820
Child's age, cubed	0.289^{-2}	3.567	0.288^{-2}	3.561	-0.011	-0.862	-0.011	-0.850	0.042	6.077	0.0420	6.079
Adult men with primary	0.925	11.230	0.925	11.224	0.812	7.719	0.817	7.980	0.620	5.604	0.620	5.584
Adult men with middle	1.234	7.280	1.230	7.263	1.326	6.818	1.324	6.823	1.081	5.890	1.083	5.896
Adult men with secondary	1.239	5.900	1.239	5.877	1.421	4.843	1.419	4.844	1.519	6.012	1.510	5.981
Adult men literate	0.861	6.258	0.859	6.518	0.460	3.133	0.463	3.174	0.651	3.962	0.649	3.969
Adult women with primary	1.968	4.040	1.969	4.028	1.696	3.211	1.739	3.216	0.449	1.000	0.462	1.029
Adult women with middle	5.801	7.114	5.814	7.024	3.397	4.318	3.933	4.208	-0.116	-0.192	-0.100	-0.164
Adult women with secondary	0.094	1.376	0.092	1.355	0.028	0.300	0.025	0.266	-0.017	-0.215	-0.017	-0.215
Adult women literate	0.124	0.906	0.124	0.909	0.005	0.027	-0.004	-0.020	-0.130	-0.953	-0.130	-0.952
Constant	-7.857	-3.530	-7.827	-3.156	60.424	0.945	60.022	0.933	-27.837	-4.416	-27.773	-4.695

the household's other covariates to vary). Hence, this figure should be viewed as a depiction of the substantive strength of the living standards effects. As can be seen, in urban areas very large effects are evident, with differences on the order of 15 percentage points in attendance, 23 points in the completion of four or more years, and 10 points in current enrollment. In rural areas, however, it is less obvious that differences by living standards quintile are of decisive importance. Apart from the uppermost quintile of "wealthy" rural households, in which children are significantly more likely to attend and complete four or more grades than their counterparts in the lowest quintile of poor rural households, little statistically significant difference emerges. Finally, a comparison of predicted urban and rural schooling across quintiles reveals that an urban advantage exists even for the poorest urban households.

In the attendance and completion of four grades models, adult education exerts a significant positive influence on children's schooling, and the effects are of substantive importance. Curiously, however, the adult education variables make little difference to current enrollments in urban areas, although the education coefficients do have the expected positive sign. In rural areas, the education of adult men is a significant determinant of enrollment. With levels of adult education controlled, adult literacy makes no significant contribution in either urban or rural Senegal. The city-specific variables included in the urban models are difficult to interpret; they suggest that residence in Ziguinchor is associated with a greater likelihood of attendance, completion of four grades, and current enrollment. Finally, as would be expected for much of Francophone West Africa, with other things held constant girls are substantially less likely than boys to attend school, complete four grades of primary, and be currently enrolled.

In the columns of the tables headed by "Model 2," we explore whether educational opportunities for girls are appreciably greater in wealthier households. Some evidence emerges to this effect –it is not always of statistical significance– in urban Senegal, but we see little indication that higher standards of living differentially improve the lot of girls in the rural areas of the country. Figure 4 depicts the multivariate findings in terms of male–female differences in the predicted percentage ever attending school, completing four or more grades, and being currently

Figure 4. Predicted Male–Female Differences in Schooling Outcomes.

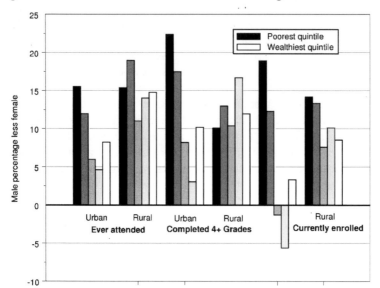

enrolled. For urban Senegal, a reduction in the extent of male advantage can be discerned as we move from lower to higher living standards quintiles, although the highest quintile exhibits a somewhat greater male advantage than the next-highest. The general pattern, however, is one of reduced male advantage. For current enrollment, one even sees greater enrollment levels for urban girls than for boys in two of the quintiles. In the rural areas of Senegal, however, the differences are erratic and, in any case, these differences do not attain statistical significance.

CONCLUSIONS

This chapter has investigated the effects of living standards and relative poverty on children's schooling in the urban and rural areas of Senegal. We have applied a highly structured statistical method –the multiple-indicator, multiple-cause (MIMIC) factor-analytic model– to urban and rural households, using data gathered in Senegal's Multiple Indicator

Cluster Survey. The model performs in a sensible fashion, yielding factor scores that are interpretable as relative measures of living standards, and coefficient estimates for the determinants of living standards that generally have the expected signs and statistical significance.

Do household living standards matter to children's education? We find that living standards have substantial influence on three measures of schooling: whether a child has ever attended school; the completion of at least four grades of primary; and current enrollment. In the urban areas of Senegal, households in the second through fifth quintiles of the living standards distribution are clearly distinguishable from the poorest urban households (those in the first quintile) in these three dimensions of schooling. The estimated effects of urban living standards are large. For example, three-quarters of children in the wealthiest urban quintile are predicted to complete four grades or more of primary school, by comparison with only about half of the children in the poorest quintile. In the rural areas of Senegal, however, the effects are less systematic: only the households in the uppermost (fifth) quintile of living standards can be statistically distinguished from other households. Furthermore, a marked urban advantage in schooling is apparent. When controls are introduced for other explanatory factors, including levels of adult education, the urban children in the poorest urban quintile are found to be much more likely than rural children to have ever attended school, to have completed four years or more of primary, and to be currently enrolled. It seems that where schooling is concerned, a marked urban advantage exists.

But why should household living standards, evidently an important influence on children's schooling in the cities and towns of Senegal, not exert comparable force in the country's rural areas? We cannot give any definitive answer, but wonder whether the result stems from the use of relative rather than absolute measures of living standards. Recall that the MICS data allow us to rank household living standards only in relative terms. Perhaps in rural Senegal, households in the first to fourth quintiles simply lack the discretionary income they would need to support their children's schooling. If this interpretation is correct, then our results would suggest that only the top quintile of rural households are likely have enough of the necessary resources in hand.

The urban advantage in children's schooling also merits comment. No one would be surprised to see a marked urban advantage in secondary or even middle school, because urban households have easier access to these levels of schooling than do most rural households. At the primary level, however, it is not obvious that the urban advantage is explicable in terms of access as such –primary schools are found in or near most Senegalese rural villages. Even so, the absence of middle and secondary schools from rural areas may lead rural parents to conclude that their children will have little real opportunity to progress beyond primary. With the educational horizons of rural parents so limited, they may question whether primary schooling alone can offer a sufficient return to justify significant commitments of parental time and money. Educational ambitions for children may be further undermined by the opportunity costs of schooling in rural settings, that is, by the loss of valuable child labor.

In both the urban and rural areas of Senegal, girls suffer from disadvantages relative to boys in all three of the schooling measures that we have examined. There is a suggestion in the empirical findings that the disadvantages facing girls are somewhat eased in urban households with higher standards of living, but no systematic evidence emerges to this effect in rural Senegal. Even in urban Senegal, however, a male advantage persists in the wealthiest quintile of households.

NOTES

[1] A similarly worded WSC goal for education is to achieve "universal access to basic education and achievement of primary education by at least 80 percent of primary school-age children... with emphasis on reducing the current disparities between boys and girls."

[2] These authors have devised a primary completion rate (PCR), which represents (Bruns et al., 2003:19–20) "the total number of students successfully completing (or graduating from) the last year of primary school in a given year, divided by the total number of children of official graduation age." Unlike the UNESCO indicators, which rely on beginning-of-year enrollment data, the PCR requires end-of-year enrollments. This information is less commonly collected by the national ministries of education; indeed, only 13 of 38 sub-Saharan African countries could provide the necessary data for direct calculation of the PCR. Senegal is one of the 25 countries for which the PCR cannot be calculated. Where the preferred data are lacking, however, a "proxy" primary completion rate can be generated.

[3] The quality of age-specific population data used in these indicators can also be questioned, particularly for countries with no recent or reliable national population census (Bruns et al., 2003:41).

[4] The precise form of the indicators, and survey questions related to them, are determined by the national statistical office of each participating country. Hence, the survey modules included in the MICS vary somewhat from one country to the next.

[5] An additional question in the education module asks "During the current school year, did (name) attend school?" This question is intended to identify students who may have been on vacation or out of school due to illness at the time of interview, but who are nonetheless currently attending. Those responding yes to this question could be classified as currently attending school (UNESCO, 2003:55). However, this approach would mis-classify students who dropped out during the current school year. In the case of Senegal, about 10 percent of children age 7–12 were reported not to be "currently attending" school but had attended at some point during the year. We have chosen not to use the additional question.

REFERENCES

Bruns, B., Mingat, A., and Rakotomalala, R. (2003). *A Chance for Every Child: Achieving Universal Primary Education By 2015*. Washington, D.C.: The World Bank.

Ferguson, B. D., Tandon, A., Gakidou, E., and Murray, C. J. L. (2003). "Estimating permanent income using indicator variables. Global Programme on Evidence for Health Policy", Discussion Paper no. 42. Geneva: World Health Organization.

Filmer, D. and Pritchett, L. (1999). "The effect of household wealth on educational attainment: Evidence from 35 countries". *Population and Development Review*, 25(1):85–120.

Filmer, D. and Pritchett, L. (2001). "Estimating wealth effects without expenditure data –or tears: An application to educational enrollments in states of India". *Demography*, 38(1):115–132.

Lloyd, C. B. and Hewett, P. C. (2003). "Primary schooling in sub-Saharan Africa: Recent trends and current challenges". Policy Research Division Working Paper no. 176, New York: Population Council.

McDade, T. W. and Adair, L. S. (2001). "Defining the 'urban' in urbanization and health: A factor analysis approach". *Social Science and Medicine*, 53(1):55–70.

Montgomery, M. R., Gragnolati, M., Burke, K. A., and Paredes, E. (2000). "Measuring living standards with proxy variables". *Demography*, 37(2):155–174.

Montgomery, M. R. and Hewett, P. C. (2004). "Urban poverty and health in developing countries: Household and neighborhood effects". Policy Research Division Working Paper no. 184, New York: Population Council.

Panel on Urban Population Dynamics (2003). *Cities Transformed: Demographic Change and Its Implications in the Developing World*. Montgomery, M. R., Stren, R., Cohen, B., and Reed, H., editors. Washington, D. C.: National Academies Press.

Sahn, D. E. and Stifel, D. C. (2000). "Poverty comparisons over time and across countries in Africa". *World Development*, 28(12):2123–2155.

Tandon, A., Gakidou, E., Murray, C. J. L., and Ferguson, B. (2002). "Cross-population comparability and PPPs: Using micro-data on indicators of consumer durables". Evidence and Information for Policy Cluster draft paper. Geneva: World Health Organization.

UNESCO (2002). *Education for All: Is the World on Track? EFA Global Monitoring Report 2002.* Paris: UNESCO Publishing.

UNESCO (2003). *Education for All Global Monitoring Report 2003/4: Gender and Education for All: the Leap to Equality.* Paris: UNESCO Publishing.

UNICEF (2003). *The State of the World's Children 2004 – Girls' Education and Development.*

United Nations (2001). *Road Map Towards the Implementation of the United Nations Millennium Declaration. Report of the Secretary-General.* New York: United Nations Department of Public Information.

Chapter 4

Immunization Coverage in India, 1991-2001: Multiple Indicator Surveys vis-à-vis Focused Surveys*

Chandra Sekhar and V. Jayachandran

INTRODUCTION

Immunizing all children against major killer diseases is one of the key goals of United Nations Children's Fund (UNICEF) world wide, and is highlighted in the Millennium Development Goals (MDGs) and in the World Fit For Children (WFFC) documents. This is also a thrust area of World Health Organization (WHO) since 1974, when the WHO Assembly initiated the Expanded Programme on Immunization (EPI). To monitor the progress of immunization program in the developing countries Multiple Indicator Surveys (MICS) were developed. In about 60 countries two or more rounds of MICS were conducted and the data has been made available to researchers and policy makers (visit <www.childinfo.org> to get more information), and is the main source of information for immunization coverage among children for many countries.

The immunization programme in India was formally launched through the Expanded Programme of Immunization (EPI) in 1978 with few antigens. This programme got momentum under the Universal Immunization Programme (UIP) launched in 1985 as a National Technology Mission and became operational in all districts of the country by 1990. UIP became a part of the Child Survival and Safe Motherhood (CSSM) programme in 1992 and the Reproductive and Child Health (RCH) programme in 1997. Under the immunization programme, infants are immunized against tuberculosis, diphtheria, pertussis, poliomyelitis, measles and tetanus. Universal immunization against six Vaccine Preventable Diseases (VPDs) by 2000 was one of the Goals set by the National Health Policy, 1983. This Goal, however, has not been achieved.

* The views expressed in this paper are those of authors and need not reflect that of UNICEF. The authors would like to express appreciation to Robert Jenkins, Chief, Strategic Planning, Monitoring and Evaluation Section, UNICEF, India for his support and guidance.

In India, three nationwide household surveys on immunization were used to review and implement the immunization programme during the last decade in the absence of reliable service statistics. These are, the National Family Health Surveys (NFHS), Multiple Indicator Survey (MICS) and Coverage Evaluation Surveys (CES). Of these, CES are designed and implemented exclusively to obtain child immunization coverage. The other two viz., NFHS[1] and MICS, information on immunization is obtained as a part of multiple indicator questionnaires rather than a focused on immunization as in CES.

Despite wide usage of immunization estimates provided by the multiple indicator surveys (NFHS & MICS) and the focused surveys (CES) in various programme reviews by managers and policy makers, debate over the levels of immunization coverage from these surveys remain alive. A general perception amongst the stakeholders was that immunization modules canvassed as a part of multiple indicator surveys will tend to provide under estimates as they loose focus during canvassing. This perception has inspired us to analyze the immunization trends in India during 1991-2001 using data from the multiple indicator surveys and focused surveys and suggest some adjustments to the full immunization levels obtained from multiple indicator surveys.

Prior to 1990s, few immunization Coverage Evaluation Surveys (CES) were conducted to validate the reported coverage and for planning activities to improve the coverage levels, but as these were limited to only few states, the nation-wide evaluated coverage figures were not available. However, after 1992, many large scale household surveys were conducted in India and from these surveys we have immunization coverage data for six reference points for the decade of 1991-2001.

Various evaluation surveys globally have experimented the ways to obtain information on immunization coverage among children in various countries. In the beginning, to obtain reliable and valid estimates, the information was gathered from immunization cards only. However, this proved to provide lower estimates of immunization coverage and therefore the questionnaires were modified to include information based on mothers re-call as well. Fisher and Vaessen (1987) have highlighted this, "relying on cards as an indication of immunization coverage will help establish the prevalence of card holders but certainly not the real prevalence of children immunized". Further, it is not very clear that reliance on estimates from card coupled with mother's re-call may result either in an underestimate or an overestimate. Therefore, it is important to present the immunization prevalence separately for children whom the information was obtained from immunization cards and from mother's re-call.

Even after presenting the information in segregated formats, the real prevalence of immunization was not available because of lapses in mother's re-call. Therefore, an attempt has been made here to adjust the immunization coverage obtained from mother's re-call using information available from card. This became possible when the multiple indicator surveys start providing immunization coverage rates separately by card and re-call.

DATA AND METHODOLOGY

The NHFS 1 & 2, MICS and various CES data sets[2] were used to analyze the trend in immunization coverage rates. The adjustments in the percent of children fully immunized obtained from NFHS 1 & 2 and MICS were carried out using a simple ratio method approach, subject to the following assumptions:

1. The immunization coverage obtained from Card is accurate. This means that the immunization coverage for children who has a vaccination card does not need any adjustment and can be considered as gold standard.

2. Though mothers/care-givers have difficulties in re-collecting all vaccinations the child might have received over time, the under reporting of any dose of DPT vaccine is negligible.

3. The dropout rate of DPT1 to DPT3 for children whose information obtained from Re-call is equal to the total (all children, i.e., both card and re-call) dropout rates. This assumption is based on our best guess and one can make necessary changes if required.

4. The ratio of 'difference between DPT3 and full immunization' to DPT3 for children with immunization Card and without card (Re-call) is same. Here the adjusted DPT3 value obtained using the assumption 3 is used for the without card children, for whom the information is obtained using re-call method.

Based on the above assumptions, the data was analyzed in the following way: First, drop out rates from DPT1 to DPT3 were calculated separately for children for whom the information obtained from Card and Re-call (without card).

Secondly, using assumption 3, the adjusted DPT3 estimates were obtained for children with no immunization cards.

In the third step, as per the assumption 4 the ratio of 'difference in the DPT3 coverage and fully immunized (FI)' to DPT3 for Card is equal to the similar ratio for Re-call. That is,

$$\frac{DPT3_{card} - FI_{card}}{DPT3_{card}} = \frac{DPT3_{Re\text{-}call}^{Adjusted} - FI_{Re\text{-}call}^{Adjusted}}{DPT3_{Re\text{-}call}^{Adjusted}}$$

where FI_{Card} is the percent of children fully immunized among those who have immunization card and $FI_{Re\text{-}call}^{Adjusted}$ is the adjusted full immunization rates (%) for children with no immunization card from whom the information obtained through Re-call method.

The percent of all children fully immunized is obtained by computing the weighted average of the FI_{Card} and $FI_{Re\text{-}call}^{Adjusted}$. The mathematical expression of this is given below:

$$FI_{Adjusted} = \frac{FI_{card} \times N_{card} + FI_{Re\text{-}call}^{Adjusted} \times N_{Re\text{-}call}}{N_{card} + N_{Re\text{-}call}}$$

Here N_{Card} and $N_{Re\text{-}call}$ are number of children for whom the information on immunization was obtained from immunization Card and from mother's/caregiver's Re-call.

Further, for analyzing the trend in the immunization coverage, we assume that focused surveys like CES do not underestimate the child immunization coverage and therefore no adjustments were made to CES data. The CES estimates were used for the years 1997, 1998, 2000 and 2001. As we do not have any source for data on immunization coverage for the years 1991 & 1993-1996, estimates were obtained using trend line (See graph).

RESULTS AND DISCUSSION

The NHFS-1 shows that 35.4% of children age 12-23 months were fully immunized in 1992. The CES during 1997 show an upward trend in the level of immunization (51.8%) and has declined in 1998 (48.5%). However, the NFHS-2 showed that only 42.0% children age 12-23 months were fully immunized in 1998 and even lower by MICS (37.9%) in 1999. The CES conducted during the years 2001 and 2002 also have shown that the children fully immunised are 49.8% and 56.6% respectively. The downward trend observed from NFHS - 2 and MICS provided us an opportunity to look into the data more critically and come out with some refined estimates for the NFHS 1 & 2 and MICS estimates that have shown lower coverage levels compared to CES.

It is evident from Table 1 that the coverage levels vary significantly between the two groups of children who have an immunization card and those who have no card. NFHS-1 shows that about 60.6 percent children are fully immunised among those who have an immunization card compared with only 24.3 per cent among those who have no card. The gap is similar for NFHS-2 and is even higher for MICS. This is true for all the vaccines as well. They corroborate with the results from studies that show that the immunization coverage levels among children with no immunization cards will be lower compared to that among children who have an immunization card. Children hail from higher socio-economic strata of the community is more likely to have an immunization card compared to their counter parts (Fisher and Martin, 1987 and Boerma et al., 1990). However, attempts to cover-up the gap between actual coverage and reported coverage among children with no immunization card are rare and have not gained attention of the researchers as well as programme planners.

Table 1. Percent of children age 12-23 months vaccinated any time before the survey by type of vaccine, according to source of information, from NFHS-1& 2 and MICS 2000

Source of information	BCG	DPT1	DPT3	OPV1	OPV3	Measles	Fully immu- nised[1]	Number of children
NFHS-1, 1992-93								
Immunization Card	90.5	98.9	84.3	98.5	84.6	66.8	60.6	3630
Mother's Re-call	49.7	51.9	37.3	53.1	39.6	31.3	24.3	8223
Total	**62.2**	**66.3**	**51.7**	**67.0**	**53.4**	**42.2**	**35.4**	**11853**
NFHS-2, 1998-99								
Immunization Card	95.2	98.6	85.5	98.1	85.4	73.2	69.1	3393
Mother's Re-call	59.6	57.6	39.7	76.2	51.3	39.3	28.3	6684
Total	**71.6**	**71.4**	**55.1**	**83.6**	**62.8**	**50.7**	**42.0**	**10076**
MICS 2000								
Immunization card	95.5	99.0	84.0	99.1	85.3	79.3	73.0	4719
Mother's Re-call	54.9	48.4	29.3	56.5	46.7	37.0	21.8	7368
Total	**67.7**	**64.3**	**46.5**	**69.9**	**58.9**	**50.3**	**37.9**	**12087**

[1] Children fully immunized are those who have received BCG, 3 doses of DPT, 3 doses of OPV and Measles vaccines.
NFHS: National Family Health Survey; MICS: Multiple Indicator Survey.

Table 2 presents the actual and adjusted values of children fully immunised using the procedure guide lined in the data and methodology section. The adjusted values are 10-15% higher than the direct estimates obtained from the multiple indicator surveys studied in this paper. The adjusted fully immunization coverage for the year 1992 from the NFHS-1 is 38.9%, for the year 1998 from NFHS-2 is 47.3% and for the year 1999 from MICS is 47.1%. The CES estimate for full immunization coverage is 49.8% for the year 2000 and 56.6% for year 2001. The above trend in the immunization coverage suggests that, during the late 1990s the immunization program suffered a set back but picked up momentum from 2000 onwards. (See Graph).

Table 2. Observed and adjusted percent of children age 12-23 months fully immunized from NFHS, MICS and CES

Year	Source	% of children fully immunized		
		Observed	*Adjusted*	*Trend*
1991	Estimated	32.1	36.3	36.3
1992	NFHS-1	35.4	38.9	38.9
1993	Estimated	38.9	41.5	41.5
1994	Estimated	42.0	44.1	44.1
1995	Estimated	45.2	46.6	46.6
1996	Estimated	48.5	49.2	49.2
1997	CES	51.8	-	51.8
1998	CES	48.5	-	48.5
1998	NFHS-2	42.0	47.3	47.3
1999	MICS	37.9	47.1	47.1
2000	CES	49.8	-	49.8
2001	CES	56.6	-	56.6

NFHS: National Family Health Survey; MICS – Multiple Indicator Survey.
CES: Coverage Evaluation Survey.

The limitation of this method of adjustment is its dependence on assumptions listed in the methodology section. Further this can be improved or a more refined estimate could be obtained by generating a set of adjusted fully immunised from various combinations of ratios and averaging that.

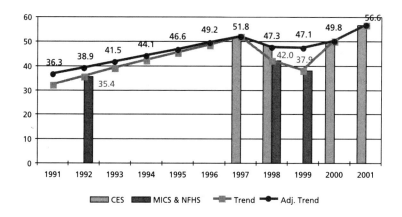

CONCLUSION

Analyzing the trend of child immunization coverage in India was always a challenge. This became more difficult when there were multiple sources and variation across sources very high. An attempt has been made to bridge this gap by adjusting the level of children fully immunised from multiple indicator surveys using a simple ratio method approach.

The results reveal that, there is a gap in the reported coverage of immunization and the actual coverage for those children with no vaccination cards. Therefore, the adjusted fully immunization coverage among children obtained using ratio method might be very close to the actual coverage. This method can be adopted to obtain more refined coverage rates provided the information is collected separately for children who have an immunization card and with out a card.

However, the real and long lasting solution of trusting the level of immunization coverage lies in providing immunization cards to all children. Further, there is a need to find the difference between the actual coverage and re-call coverage among those who have cards to validate this adjustment procedure. The limitation of this analysis is that of the assumption that, focused surveys captures immunization coverage correctly and does not require any adjustments. But, at the same time, due to emphasis on specific issues in the focused surveys it is likely that the estimates will be on the higher side, and may need some downward adjustment. This inflation in the estimates could be both due to sampling as well as non-sampling errors, but more so due to non-sampling error.

NOTES

[1] NFHS is also considered as a Multiple Indicator Survey, because that provides estimates for a set of indicators.

[2] CES rates for 1997 and 1998 were weighted estimates to be consistent with the 2000 & 2001 rates.

REFERENCES

Boerma J. Ties, Elisabeth A. Sommerfelt, Shea O. Rustein and Guillermo Rojas (1990). *Immunization: Levels, Trends and Differentials*, Institute for Resource Development/Macro Systems Inc., DHS Comparative Studies No.1.

Department of Women & Child Development and UNICEF (2001). "Multiple Indicator Survey (MICS 2000), India Summary Report", December.

Department of Women & Child Development and UNICEF (2001). "Multiple Indicator Survey (MICS 2000) – India Report", New Delhi, India (mimeo).

Fisher, A. and Vaessen Martin (1987). *Measuring Immunization Prevalence*, Maryland: Institute for Resource Development Inc.

Gupta, J.P. and Murali, I. (1989). *National Review of Immunization Programme in India*, New Delhi: National Institute of Health and Family Welfare.

International Institute for Population Sciences (1995). *National Family Health Survey (NFHS), 1992-93*, India: Mumbai-IIPS.

International Institute for Population Sciences (IIPS) and ORC Macro (2000). *National Family Health Survey (NFHS-2), 1998-99*, India: Mumbai-IIPS.

Lemeshow, Stanley and David Robinson (1985). "Surveys to measure programme coverage and impact: A review of the methodology used by the expanded programme on immunization". *World Health Statistics*, Vol. 38, No.1.

WHO/UNICEF (2003). *Review of National Immunization Coverage 1980-2002 – India*, June 2003 (Draft).

Chapter 5

Triangulating Research Methodologies and Practices to Promote Childhood Poverty Policy Change

*Nicola Jones**

INTRODUCTION

Over the last decade, poverty research and assessment has attracted considerable international attention and resources, as exemplified by international initiatives such as the UN Millennium Development Goals or the Poverty Reduction Strategy Paper framework. During the same period, a series of UN international conferences and conventions have highlighted and significantly expanded the concept of human rights beyond the civic and political spheres to encompass economic, social and cultural rights (e.g. Craske and Molyneux, 2002). These dual developments have provided the discursive and political space for researchers and activists to draw attention to the particular marginalization and deprivation of women and children living in poverty. Yet notwithstanding a growing body of research, there is still much to be done in terms of disseminating research results and strengthening relationships between NGOS, research networks and policy practitioners to ensure substantial policy change. *Where does the responsibility for dissemination, policy engagement and advocacy lie? What partnership strategies are likely to be most effective? How can these best be adapted to diverse political, social and cultural contexts?*

This paper draws on emerging work on policy processes as a lens to explore the challenges associated with linking poverty assessment tools, research dissemination and efforts to achieve concrete policy outcomes. Moving beyond more linear models of policy making, the policy process literature reconceptualizes policy formulation and implementation as dynamic processes involving multiple actor networks with varying interests and degrees of agency, informed by competing policy narratives

* Young Lives International Coordinator, Save the Children UK. The opinions expressed in this paper are those of the author only and do not necessarily reflect those of Young Lives partners nor Save the Children-UK.

(both local and global). It suggests that opportunities for influencing policy are more varied but perhaps also narrower and more incremental than conventionally perceived.

Empirically, I draw on experiences from *Young Lives*, an innovative international longitudinal study on the causes and consequences of childhood poverty, to explore wider challenges facing INGOs, policy practitioners and aid/donor organizations working on human rights and social policy issues. Framed within a sustainable livelihoods approach to child wellbeing, at the core of *Young Lives* (YL) research is a panel study tracking 8000 children and their families in four countries with distinct economic, political and socio-cultural trajectories (Ethiopia, India, Peru and Vietnam) over a 15-year period. I contend that the lessons garnered from conducting the first phase of the YL quantitative survey (2001-4) within a wider multi-partner policy analysis-advocacy-dissemination project can contribute to debates on the efficacy of other international poverty assessment initiatives, including UNICEF's work with MICSs.

The paper begins by discussing the complementarity of MICS and YL data in monitoring progress towards the Millennium Development Goals in an increasingly evidence-based international policy environment. The analysis then considers the limitations of quantitative approaches in affecting holistic social policy outcomes and presents findings from policy processes literature as a means to conceptualize these weaknesses. These wider theoretical points are in turn used to highlight the ways in which YL has been designed to grapple with the complexities and dynamism of the policy process in different national contexts, in terms of both the *project process* and its *research foci*. The paper concludes by reflecting on the role of values in policy research, the difficulties of balancing efforts to change social-policy with stakeholder-led research demands, and the need to develop more sophisticated analytical tools to capture macro-micro policy linkages.

QUANTITATIVE METHODOLOGIES FOR EVIDENCE-BASED POLICY-MAKING ON CHILDHOOD POVERTY

In the world of development policy, where policy making has historically been viewed as a matter of the rational application of technical expertise, the failure of efforts to reduce poverty has largely been interpreted as a problem of assumption-based rather than evidence-based policy making. Premised on the belief that better research tools would lead to superior policies and outcomes, the 1990s/2000s saw the creation of multiple poverty assessment initiatives, as well as an array of international development and poverty reduction targets (McGee and Brock, 2001:4). In order to monitor and potentially hold national and international policy makers accountable to their official commitments to poverty amelioration, researchers and activists alike recognized the importance of quantifiable indicators and related data collection.

It is within this broader context that both MICS and YL surveys were established. As Komarecki (2003) argues, MICS was established to provide crucial missing data to monitor progress in relation to the Convention on the Rights of the Child. Similarly, YL was established under the auspices of the UK DFID's Millennium Development Fund in the context of debates about how to monitor the MDGs to ensure substantive progress by 2015. Partially influenced by the Blair administration's use of longitudinal data in the "war on child poverty", the YL project aims to draw attention to the complex, often indirect but far-reaching impact of macro-economic policies on the physical, cognitive and pyscho-social wellbeing of children born in 2000 until their adolescence in 2015.

Whereas many poverty assessment tools have taken the form of large-scale quantitative household surveys focusing narrowly on income or consumption-based variables and obscuring issues of (inequitable) intra-household distribution, both MICS and YL adapted more multi-dimensional definitions of poverty and poverty assessment. Established in 1995, MICS was path-breaking because of its move away from a focus on aggregate household indicators that typify household surveys, towards a concern for individuals and intra-household distribution of power/ resources and the impact thereof on women and children (i.e. traditionally more vulnerable family members). YL, with a focus on caregivers and children, shares a similar perspective, but is rooted in a modified sustainable livelihoods framework,[1] incorporating a wider range of assets –financial, physical, natural, human (time, knowledge, skills) and social– that families and communities need to pursue a sustainable livelihoods strategy. In addition to more routine questions on health, nutrition and education, the YL questionnaire incorporates modules on family livelihoods, child cognitive development, mental health, as well as cognitive and structural social capital.

Because of different sampling and research methodologies as well as content foci, the potential contributions of MICS and YL to national and international-level policy debates will diverge, as seen in the case of Vietnam where both assessment tools have been carried out. In Vietnam, MICS (especially MICS 2 which has had greater buy in (An, 2004 personal communication) has provided a cost-effective nationally representative sample of data on largely nutritional and health indicators, but also some education and child rights variables for children under 5 years. This has enabled UNICEF and local partners to highlight, for example, the still high prevalence of chronic malnutrition in Vietnam, the importance of investment in early childhood education, differential immunisation rates across regions and wealth groups, and the reasons for the registration or non-registration of children's births. Its questionnaire on women aged 15-49 has allowed for a focus on the close linkages between maternal and child wellbeing, especially the importance of breastfeeding, as well as raised awareness about contraceptive usage and women's knowledge of HIV transmission and prevention. Because these cluster surveys are conducted at 5-year intervals, MICS has the potential to give policy-makers access to relatively up-to-date data and to ensure that issues of child and maternal welfare are kept on the public agenda. The solid evidence base developed by MICS should allow concerned advocates to more effectively critique Vietnam's rapid economic development strategy in addressing the needs of society's more vulnerable, frequently excluded social groups.

Young Lives' longitudinal, purposeful sentinel site surveillance methodology affords some distinct but complementary advantages. First, born in the tradition of the British Birth Cohort Studies[2] and Seven Up (a life-course study of British citizens followed up at 7 year intervals), and modelled partly on the South African Birth to Twenty analysis of children begun in 1990, Young Lives' longitudinal methodology should provide firmer ground for causal inference than cross-sectional snapshots. In particular, with data sweeps of index children at ages 1, 4, 8, 11, 14 years, the survey is designed to reveal transitions, processes and histories which one-off studies are ill designed to capture (Wilson and

Huttly, 2003).[3] For example, YL will be able to examine whether "tendencies toward advantage or disadvantage cumulate over time, generating increasing long-term inequalities" (Joshi, 2001), whether direct interventions enable disadvantaged children to catch up fully or only partially with their peers and explore the characteristics of children living through transitory as compared to chronic poverty. Such information will enable researchers and policy practitioners to better understand the relative costs and timing implications of preventative policies as compared to policies that seek to reverse earlier disadvantage.

Second, although YL's non-representative sampling technique limits the kinds of national level conclusions that can be drawn, its purposeful over-sampling of the poor and the selection of community sites that represent a range of different infra-structural, agro-ecological, livelihood, socio-cultural, ethnic, administrative etc. characteristics, facilitates in-depth analyses of the causes, manifestations and consequences of poverty in a variety of settings. In other words, it provides a useful middle ground between national level but limited descriptive statistical statements, and single qualitative case studies that tend to carry little credibility with target audiences and are difficult to integrate into the policy formulation process (ibid.; McGee and Brock, 2003).

This site-level focus also encourages a greater involvement and engagement with regional and local governments in the survey implementation, analysis and dissemination processes, which tends to be overlooked by the "big picture" orientation of national surveys. For example, in the Vietnamese case, the Young Lives team is now organizing workshops with provincial and communal government leaders to disseminate and discuss results from the first round of data analysis, particularly reasons for inter- and intra-provincial differences in child wellbeing.

THE CHALLENGE OF NON-LINEAR, DYNAMIC POLICY PROCESSES

The respective strengths of the MICS and YL as data sources on children and their caregivers notwithstanding, quantitative surveys are likely to be of limited value in shaping social policy if not contextualized within the complexities of the policy process itself. Lucinda Platt (2003) in her survey of the interaction between research on child poverty and related social policies in the UK between 1800 and 1950, aptly notes:

> The impacts of research may occur neither at the time of the research, nor in ways that are predictable. The influence of research is not necessarily in the direction in which researchers intend and is mediated by the options available to policy makers at a particular time. [There is a] ...need for research to be both radical and relate to its time and place... Its influence will vary with the political complexion of the country and ideological and religious factors. It is both to make an impact but also to accord, at least in part, with existing mores (2).

The penchant for quantifiable poverty assessment approaches is understandable in that they help to address important information lacuna concerning the patterning, distribution and identity of those living in poverty. However, because their expected utility is premised on a linear model of policy-making involving the rational execution of technically-informed evidence, we should not be surprised that in isolation such methodologies are unlikely to have a significant impact on real world policy processes and outcomes. As McGee and Block emphasize "The view that government officials should be convinced of the instrumentality of poverty knowledge illustrates an obscuring of the political and social dynamics which other commentators suggest are at play in the policy process" (2001:8).

In trying to account for the complexities of policy formulation and implementation, a newly emerging body of policy processes literature underscores the importance of reconceptualizing policy making as a non-linear, dynamic process. Theorists such as Keeley and Scoones (2003) argue for a "structuration approach" which combines the insights of three different schools of thought as to what drives policy change: political interests derived from actors' structured interests, actor agency stemming from an on-going process of inter-actor negotiation and bargaining, and discursive practices (reflecting a Foucauldian understanding of the inter-relationship between power, knowledge and policy) (27-8). Attempting a middle ground between policy as a linear process and policy as chaotic and accidental, this approach recognizes structural constraints and the difficulties inherent in negotiating the complex and messy dynamics of the policy process, but nevertheless leaves room for agency and change:

Policy approaches are likely to be influenced by dominant policy discourses and narratives, by powerful combinations of political interests and by effective actor-networks...but this should not lead to the conclusion that policy processes inevitably end in impasses. Each discourse, actor-network or policy network involves institutional practices and interactions that are made up of the activities of individuals. At these multiple interfaces there may be "policy spaces" or "room for manoeuvre" to promote alternative approaches to policy (29).

Of importance here is the recognition of policy influencing as an iterative process –rather than assuming a simple linear progression from technical evidence, to policy design to accurate implementation, the policy processes school instead sees the potential of multiple but comparatively narrow opportunities to affect change. It argues that policy is shaped significantly by interpretation and practice, and by policy actors from multiple sectors (line ministries and departments) and levels of government decision-making (i.e. central, regional, local) that are involved in implementation.

If we understand the policy environment as an arena with multiple, shifting but relatively narrow access points, two basic types of interaction are open to those pursuing policy engagement and dissemination strategies. The first can be characterized as "argumentative interaction" –a more critical or combative approach involving strategies to "build alternative actor networks [and ...] dislodge dominant positions and their associated networks" (Keeley and Scoones: 2003:30). However, while there is clearly a place for challenging extant paradigms that underlie inappropriate policy decisions, proponents of "participatory" or "deliberative democracy" (e.g. Fraser, 1989 Dryzek, 1994) contend that political change is often more effective and enduring if proponents attempt to foster more participatory forms of governance and decision-making. This second "communicative interaction" approach seeks to build participatory, consultative partnerships involving research networks, community groups and NGOs, and national and local government stakeholders, in which a diversity of values, perspectives and goals are negotiated and reflected (Keeley and Scoones, 2003:31). The extent to which these policy engagement strategies are available to proponents of change will depend in part on the specific political and social climate of a given country, and especially the degree of administrative and political decentralization.

YOUNG LIVES PRACTICE

Drawing on these wider theoretical points, I now turn to a discussion of how YL has sought to grapple with the complexities and dynamism of the policy process in different national contexts, both in terms of the *project process* and its *research foci.* This section is concerned with the following questions:

- What kinds of partnership arrangements best facilitate research-based advocacy and policy engagement?

- Whose responsibility is it to disseminate research results?

- In what ways and with what aims should dissemination be approached?

- How can we best design policy-relevant research questions and analyses?

Partnership and Policy Change

Whereas other longitudinal studies on poverty and development have been conceived primarily as a data resource and its impact on policy influencing in many cases developed later and even accidentally (Joshi, 2001), YL was established as a multi-partner project with an explicit emphasis on social/policy change. Significantly, it involves partnerships between Northern and Southern research institutes, an INGO and in some cases local NGOS and government partners. The academic consortium has lead responsibility for the data collection and analysis, while Save the Children UK is charged with leading the policy analysis, engagement, advocacy and dissemination aspects of the project.[4]

In keeping with Scoones and Keeley's (2003) communicative interaction approach to policy influencing, one of the central aims of YL has been to promote government and community buy-in from the outset.

Accumulated learning by researchers and activists alike has shown that a sense of government and community "ownership" of a research project is likely to facilitate the acceptance and recognition of the research findings (e.g. Kabakchieva, 2000; Pham, 2003). Accordingly, country-level advisory panels comprised of experts from academia, civil society, INGOs, international donors and government ministries have been established. These stakeholders are consulted regularly regarding survey design and content, and the discussion of research findings prior to publication. To foster widespread interest in and engagement with the project, a public launch of Phase 1 was organized in each country to discuss the project's aims and solicit input from participants prior to data collection. As Vietnamese Young Lives national co-ordinator Pham Thi Lan notes:

> Holding public consultative meetings before research findings are available is very new in Vietnam and people were puzzled at first. But over the past three years we have seen the fruits of this consultative approach as policy makers and government officials now identify with the project, and having had some input, view it as legitimate (personal correspondence, 2004).

Similarly, meetings with regional and local government officials and community leaders are now being held to disseminate results from the first round of data analysis, and to solicit suggestions for information needs and appropriate policy-relevant research foci going forward. While the logistical and organizational burden of regular stakeholder interaction is high compared to traditional modes of research where interaction is typically limited to the compiling of reports and making datasets available, over the long duree it is likely to be more effective given the iterative nature of the policy process. That is, policy change does not derive from a single decision implemented in a linear fashion but is an inherently political process and consists of a "web of inter-related decisions" which evolve over the course of policy implementation (Keeley and Scoones, 2003:4). In this regard, the interface between national governments and the international donor and creditor community is important..., more important still for successful poverty reduction policy are the interfaces [and the construction and use of poverty knowledge in all these spaces] between national governments, civil society and local policy actors (McGee and Brock, 2001:35).

Dissemination and advocacy

While limited policy change can be partially ascribed to a lack of commitment by national government leaders and a dearth of economic and human resources to implement much-needed reforms (e.g. Komarecki, 2003), responsibility also lies with researchers and NGOs who must effectively disseminate research results to policy makers capable of acting upon new evidence. This process entails three key challenges: a) capacity building, b) understanding the policy process and advocacy environment, and c) the development of multi-pronged, flexible and context-sensitive methodologies and discursive tactics.

First, because many developing countries have only recently made the transition from authoritarian to democratic politics or are still in various stages of that process, it is not surprising that the dissemination/ advocacy capacity of local researchers and NGOs is still under-developed. In order to address this, YL has prioritized capacity building in understanding and implementing dissemination and advocacy strategies. This has involved joint working relationships between Save the Children UK headquarters staff and country-level National Coordinators as well as facilitating short-term intensive training workshops on media work, policy brief development, development education, and methodologies for working with children. The first three-year phase of the project has utilized an eclectic range of public communication methods that include:

Young Lives Dissemination Methodologies

- Working papers and related policy briefs
- Print, radio and television media work - both local and international
- Discussion forums with experts as well as children
- Face-to-face interactions with policy practitioners
- Photography projects which "serve as a mirror for communities and children to reflect on their lives" (Eliana Villar, personal correspondence, 2004)
- Video case studies of children and their care-givers
- Essay competitions for children about poverty experiences
- Newsletters to stakeholders

- Participatory poverty assessment projects with children about their aspirations, likes and dislikes
- Interactive websites (both international and in local languages)
- Journalism fellowships and media workshops to encourage more in-depth coverage of child poverty issues
- Workshops using regionally-disaggregated data with local government officials

In order to work successfully in distinct political contexts, these methods have been informed by conceptual think-pieces on the policy process, advocacy and discursive environments of our four research countries (see <www.younglives.org.uk>). Key points identified include the importance of mapping appropriate dissemination and advocacy targets, spaces and civil society/ state partners; understanding the "access" and "veto points" at both the national and decentralized government levels; and unpacking existing discourses on children and poverty in order to identify tensions between local and international discursive strategies.

Based on these conceptual maps, efforts have been made to develop policy engagement and dissemination strategies in a context-sensitive manner. Young Lives teams in Ethiopia and Vietnam for instance have recognized that policy change requires alliances with government officials and parliamentarians from the beginning. To take a specific example, in order to address the lack of attention to child wellbeing issues in the Vietnamese PRSP, Save the Children Alliance, including Young Lives, collaborated with the governmental Committee for Population, Families and Children to identify priority areas. This alliance resulted in the successful incorporation of child-specific goals in the final version of the document. However, attempts by international organizations to address the neglect of HIV/AIDS in the same document was largely unsuccessful due in part to a lack of efforts to foster government allies (Pham, 2003). By contrast, in Peru –a country characterized by high political instability and low levels of policy planning, monitoring and civil servant accountability– there are fewer opportunities for effective partnerships with government bodies. Instead, YL has sought to maximize the potential of a comparatively open media by using, for example, video documentaries and public photo exhibitions to raise awareness of childhood poverty among the public and government officials (Villar, 2003).

LESSONS AND CHALLENGES FOR SOCIAL POLICY CONTESTATION

This concluding section reflects on three key challenges involved in influencing child-related social policy contestation processes through evidence-based policy research:

- balancing project human resources,

- possible tensions between stakeholder demands and change-oriented goals,

- the importance of seeking more appropriate research methods to capture macro-micro policy linkages.

Balancing partner skills and professional goals

In striving to develop policy-relevant research, a key challenge lies in balancing the respective strengths and interests represented in a multi-partner, multi-disciplinary policy research project. In the case of YL, our research partners were selected based on their ability to handle the rigors of large-scale field-based data collection, data management and quantitative analyses, but less attention was given to balancing quantitative with qualitative research and policy analysis skills. However, such inputs are essential to understand the underlying causal mechanisms or pathways of variables that have been found to have statistically significant associations as well as to provide nuanced policy evidence. For example, while YL research in Andhra Pradesh suggests that maternal social capital (defined as membership in women's self-groups) has a positive influence on some child well-being indicators, without complementary qualitative work we are unable to offer a robust explanation as to how maternal civic involvement is translating into improved child well-being, and therefore what if any policy interventions would be appropriate. Similarly, because YL national coordinators were selected largely based on their dissemination/advocacy, policy analysis and stakeholder networking skills, they are less experienced in critically engaging with quantitative analyses. None of these problems is insurmountable, but it does suggest the need for considerable capacity building, as well as a willingness for partners to move beyond disciplinary comfort zones and grapple with new research foci and methodologies.

Consideration also has to be given to divergent audience demands –i.e. academia, policy practitioners and popular media. This impacts not only the language and style of outputs (academic journals, policy briefs, news articles), but also the framing of research questions. In particular, policy-relevant research not only depends on having the "correct tools" (e.g. an appropriate dataset), but also setting up questions and a research design that will yield new findings that contribute to both national and international policy debates. It is therefore important that project partners engage in a critical dialogue about what policy research priorities are, how the data developed can help close knowledge gaps, and reflect on the policy implications of the research findings. In addition to discussing current policy weaknesses, cost-effective, politically feasible policy alternatives (possibly drawing on best practices from other country contexts) should also be discussed.

Balancing social change goals with stakeholder demands

Unlike mainstream development practitioners who continue to frame poverty alleviation and development as a domain of technical expertise, policy processes theorists make a convincing case that policy engagement is not neutral but value-laden. How does a multi-partner project reach conclusions about the value content of its policy recommendations? While policy implications need to be drawn from research findings, the interpretation of these results will necessarily entail value judgements. Should a North-South partnership project attempt to reach a consensus on the desired direction of policy change or leave such decisions largely up to national teams with a more intimate understanding of local socio-cultural and political specificities?

A related challenge concerns the need to strike a balance between social/policy change goals and responding to demand-led analyses. Large-scale data collection enterprise such as MICS or Young Lives are designed to address particular issues of social deprivation or inequalities, yet in order to ensure the relevance of the research to policy practitioners and civil society actors analyses must also respond to stakeholder information needs. Given resource constraints, how can a project best balance the possibly conflicting demands of international and national audiences? For example, while one objective of Young Lives is to inform international donors and policy-makers about the child-related impacts of macro-economic policies, such analyses may be of lower priority to especially provincial-level policy practitioners concerned with the efficacy of specific child-targeted policy interventions, such as new day-care programs or nutritional supplementation packages.

Collaborative multi-partner projects must also be cognizant that local stakeholder groups may shy away from research topics that call for greater cross-sectoral or politically sensitive policy initiatives, because of particular individual career or institutional interests. It is therefore vital that project directors remain faithful to a change-oriented vision, while remaining sensitive to stakeholder concerns.

Balancing macro/micro levels of analysis

A final challenge concerns the general dearth of appropriate methodologies that link macro, meso and micro-levels of analysis in order to produce policy-relevant findings. As Ravi Kanbur (1999) argues, the research community still lacks a "grammar and a language to bridge the micro-macro gap". While YL has developed policy matrices for each country that trace major macro-economic and sectoral policy changes over the last 5-10 years, marrying this information with our household and community-level surveys in a persuasive manner has proven more difficult. The breadth of our survey enables us to capture the multi-dimensionality of childhood poverty, but provides weaker purchase on the impacts of specific policy interventions, particularly if their impact is expected to be more diffuse. Progress here will require more in-depth analyses of carefully designed questions that investigate the impact of macro-economic policies (such as the effect of trade liberalization on a specific state-owned enterprise like KonaCoffee in Vietnam or Ethiopia's Agriculture-led Industrialization Development strategy) on children in our sentinel sites. Indeed, it is in this area that triangulating the insights of nationally representative data sets such as MICS, with more detailed, purposively selected meso-level data from YL household and community questionnaires, as well as in-depth qualitative micro-level information, has much to offer in developing a context-sensitive understanding of the dynamics of childhood poverty. By discussing the ways in which YL results are in line with or differ from MICS national-level findings, YL should be able to counter critiques that its findings are unrepresentative and hence of limited policy-relevance at the national level. By the same token, researchers interested in how MICS findings play out in more depth within and across provinces or regions will be able to turn to YL meso-level community and micro-level household surveys. Interesting contrasts could also be made between the cross-sectional time-series MICS data that will illustrate broad population-level changes, and YL panel data, which will highlight the impact of accumulated policy and socio-economic shifts on the same cohort of children over time. The causal mechanisms underpinning these quantitative findings could in turn be unpacked by qualitative case studies selected based on patterns identified in the database.

NOTES

[1] While the sustainable livelihoods framework focuses on productive strategies, reproduction can be introduced by noting the importance of human capital –in terms of time, skills and knowledge– in successfully reproducing healthy, well-nourished and developed children.

[2] The first Birth Cohort Study was initiated in the 1940s/50s to provide insights into the interaction of health, employment, and educational trajectories (Joshi, 2001; Platt, 2003).

[3] Given considerable start-up costs, stakeholders must be persuaded of the value of a longitudinal dataset as a long-term resource, whereby policy relevance pay-offs are likely to compound over time. This depends on the extent to which survey questions represent a balance between issues of contemporary relevance and those that are sufficiently far-sighted to anticipate questions that will be of significance in the future (Joshi, 2001).

[4] In recognition of the diversity of YL countries, no single partnership model was imposed, rather variations on this triple alliance (academics, INGOs, and government partners) were developed to suit the local environment (see <www.younglives.org.uk>).

REFERENCES

Craske, Nikki and Maxine Molyneux (2002). *Gender and the Politics of Rights and Democracy in Latin America.* Hampshire: Palgrave Macmillan.

Dryzek, John (1994). *Discursive Democracy: Politics, Policy and Political Science.* Cambridge: Cambridge University Press.

Frazer, Nancy (1989). *Unruly Practices: Power, Discourse and Gender in Contemporary Social Theory.* Minnesota: University of Minnesota Press.

Joshi, Heather (2001). "Longitudinal data as an aid to the policy maker: some British Examples". Paper for the Annual Conference of the Economists, Australia: Perth.

Keeley, James and Ian Scoones (2003). "Understanding Environmental Policy Processes: A Review". IDS Working Paper 89, University of Sussex.

Komarecki, M. (2003). *Promoting Human Rights and Social Policies for Children and Women: The role of multiple cluster indicator survey (MICS).* (Partly reproduced as chapter 1 of this volume).

McGee, Rosemary and Karen Brock (2001). "From Poverty Assessment to Policy Change: Processes, Actors and Data". Working Paper 133. Sussex: Institute of Development Studies.

Pham, Thi Lan (2003). "Managing Research and Advocacy in Vietnam". Paper Presented at "Childhood Poverty: Longitudinal Studies for Policy Making", Young Lives Conference, 8-9 September, 2003.

Platt, Lucinda (2003). "Putting Childhood Poverty on the Agenda: The Relationship Between Research and Policy in Britain 1800-1950". Young Lives Working Paper No. 7, UK.

Shanks, Edwin and Carrie Turk (2003). "Refining policy with the poor: local consultations on the draft comprehensive poverty reduction and growth strategy in Vietnam". Policy Research Working Paper, World Bank.

Tefera, Bekele (2003). "Advocacy in the Ethiopian Context and Implications for Young Lives". Paper presented at "Childhood Poverty: Longitudinal Studies for Policy Making", Young Lives Conference, 8-9 September, 2003.

Villa, Eliana (2003). "The Experience of Policy Making for Childhood in Peru". Paper presented at "Childhood Poverty: Longitudinal Studies for Policy Making", Young Lives Conference, 8-9 September, 2003.

Wilson, Ian and Sharon Huttly. 2004. "Young Lives: A Case Study of Sample Design for Longitudinal Research". Young Lives Working Paper No. 10: UK.

Personal communication

Dr An V. N. Director General, Committee for Population Family and Children, Vietnam.

Bekele Tefera, YL National Coordinator Ethiopia.

Piush Antory, YL National Coordinator India.

Pham Thi Lan, YL National Coordinator Vietnam.

Eliana Villar, YL National Coordinator Peru.

Chapter 6

Evaluating Child Poverty in Niger: a Participatory Learning Process

*Marco Segone**

CONCEPTUAL FRAMEWORK OF POVERTY BASED ON THE HUMAN RIGHTS APPROACH

Poverty remains among the most important human rights challenge facing the world community. A human rights-based approach means that the situation of poor people is viewed not only in terms of welfare outcomes but also in terms of the obligation to prevent and respond to human rights violations. For example, any action that excludes children from school or discriminates against girls constitutes such a violation. The human rights approach aims to empower families and communities to secure assistance and advocates the fair and just distribution of capabilities and opportunities.

Vandemoortele (2001) suggests that Poverty has many faces; and because poverty means very different things to people, there is no universally accepted definition or indicator. A family can be considered as poor because of inadequate income or due to unmet basic needs or both. Should a family with an income above the poverty line but without a school for its children to attend considered as poor? The answer depends on the interpretation of poverty. According to a money-metric interpretation, this family would not rank among the poor, while a basic-needs interpretation would consider this family as poor.

Nowadays, the International development community recognizes that poverty is not only about material deprivation (Income poverty) but also

* The author wishes to thank Alberto Minujin, Enrique Delamonica, Edilberto Loaiza and Kate Spring, Policy and Planning Department at UNICEF Headquarters in New York, and Santosh Mehrotra and John Micklewright at UNICEF Innocenti Research Center in Florence, for their valuable comments and feedback. This paper does not necessarily reflect the policy or viewpoint of UNICEF.

about low opportunities in health and education, among others (Basic needs poverty or Human poverty). The World Bank, in its World Development Report 2000/2001 on "Attacking poverty", broadened the notion of poverty to include vulnerability and exposure to risk and, based on its Participatory Poverty Assessment, voicelessness and powerlessness (two new dimensions that, together with weak Social capital, could tentatively be named as Social poverty).

Income poverty

Poverty was most commonly defined as having insufficient income to buy a minimum basket of goods and services. Drawing solely on quantitative measures, this interpretation is known as "Income poverty". The most commonly used indicator associated with income poverty is the Income poverty index, which gives the proportion of people or households whose income falls below a particular poverty line. The demarcation of the poverty line depends on the composition of the basic basket of goods and services.

The international community commonly defines the poverty line as $1 per day per person –expressed in purchasing power parity for 1985 to adjust for differences in prices between countries. Based on this definition, the World Bank estimates that 1.2 billion people in developing countries lived in poverty in 1998. An additional 1.5 billion people lived in marginally better conditions on less than $2 per day. Sub-Saharan Africa is the region where income poverty is most widespread, while the majority of the income-poor live in Southern Asia.

Human Poverty

Because of its multidimensional nature, a definition of poverty should go beyond a strictly material condition, recognizing poverty's broader characteristics such as high mortality rates, frequent illness, low access to basic social services, and low educational levels, among others. Indeed, there are dimensions of poverty that cannot be monetized but that are felt by millions of people in their daily lives.

The term Human poverty was coined by the United Nations Development

Programme in 1997 to distinguish broad human deprivation from the narrower Income poverty. If income is not the sum total of well-being, lack of income cannot be the sum total of poverty. Human poverty does not focus on what people do or do not have, but on what they can or cannot do. It is about deprivation in the most essential capabilities of life, including leading a long and healthy life, being knowledgeable and having adequate economic provision.

Social Poverty

Poor people are often treated badly by the institutions of state and society and excluded from voice and power positions in those institutions (World Bank, 2001). Voicelessness and powerlessness, social and political exclusion, or discrimination based on gender, age or on any other ground have been identified as important dimensions of poverty by poor people.

Edwards (2000) argues that Social capital is the crucial missing ingredient in poverty reduction strategies. Recent research shows that membership in voluntary associations has more impact on household incomes than educational attainment. Also the World Bank report on Attacking poverty (2001) states that in addition to removing social barriers, effective efforts to reducing poverty require complementary initiatives to build up and extend the social institutions of the poor. Social institutions refer to the kinship systems, local organizations, and networks of the poor and can be usefully discussed as different forms or dimensions of Social capital.

Multidimensionality of Poverty

A multidimensional approach is thus indispensable in devising an effective and sustainable solution to poverty. Poverty reduction is more than merely transcending a particular income threshold. It will also require a sustained increase in the capabilities of all people, including poor people, to live long, healthy and productive lives, to participate in the development process as full partners, and to enjoy the fulfillment of their human rights.

CHILD POVERTY

According to estimations (Minujin, 2000), children represent at least half of the world's total population and, at the same time, poor children are over-represented among children. In other words, the proportion of poor children among all children is substantially higher than the share of all the poor in the total population.

Bradbury, Jenkins and Micklewright (2000) argue that the focus on child poverty as opposed to any other group in the population needs little justification. Children represent a country's future, an obvious reason for societal concern with child well-being. There are the innate feelings of protection towards the young and assumptions of their blamelessness for the situation in which they find themselves. Children are unable to take full responsibility for their circumstances, and are dependent on others to look after and raise them. Their vulnerability provides a powerful moral imperative in favor of collective action in general to help them, and a welfare state in particular. To implement this requires prior knowledge of the nature of child poverty and its consequences, plus knowledge of what the causes are.

Moreover, impoverished children become transmitters of poverty–as parents–to the next generation. In this vicious circle, malnourished children grow up to become malnourished mothers who give birth to underweight babies; parents lacking access to crucial information are unable to optimally feed and care for their children; and illiterate parents cannot support children in their learning process. As such, children run the risk of becoming the next generation of poor. To transform this vicious circle into a virtuous one, poverty reduction must start with children.

In the words of Jim Grant, former Executive Director of UNICEF, "children can be the Trojan Horse to attacking the citadel of poverty". Recognizing the need to break the vicious cycle of poverty transmission, the World Summit for Social Development called on policy-makers to prioritize the needs of children in devising sustainable poverty reduction solutions–aimed not only at the household level, but also at community and national levels.

MONITORING CHILD POVERTY: WHAT GETS MEASURED, GETS DONE

Santos Pais (1999) argues that in the light of the principle of universality, all children, from birth to childhood and adolescence, boys and girls, of whatever color, race, language or religion and wherever they may live, need to be considered. Special attention should be paid to the most vulnerable groups in society. Understanding their situation calls for a special effort, but it is an imperative guided by the values of equity, solidarity and social justice. We clearly need to understand who they are, the conditions in which they live, the most urgent problems affecting them and the root causes for their vulnerability. Only by ensuring visibility of their situation, Santos Pais continues, will it be possible to formulate effective and relevant policies and envisage adequate strategies to address their vulnerability. Failing to do so, we will simply increase their marginalisation and fail to honor the commitment made to the universal rights of children.

Table 1. Framework for assessing progress on Human Rights

Period	Average perspective	Deprivation perspective	Inequality perspective
One period	What is the national average? How has the national average changed?	Who are the most deprived? By: • Income quintile • Gender • Region • Rural or urban • Ethnic group • Education level	What is the disparity? Between : • Bottom and top income quintiles • Females and males • Worst-off and best-off regions • Rural and urban • Worst-off and best-off ethnic group • No education and higher education
Over time		How have the most deprived social groups progressed?	How have disparities between social groups changed- have they widened or narrowed?

Statistical indicators are a powerful tool to ensure visibility of Child poverty. When data are carefully collected, analyzed and interpreted, when the findings are released and turned into messages, they become an important means for promoting human rights of children and fighting Child poverty. Using statistics to go deeper into poverty issues can help reveal the disparities and inequalities behind average figures and help focus attention on what needs to be done to address the situation. UNDP (2000a) suggests the following framework to analyze disparities and inequalities.

As previously stated, poverty is multidimensional and thus monitoring child poverty should cover the three dimensions of poverty: Income, Human and Social poverty. For each of them, different tools are used.

Monitoring Income poverty and Socio-economic status

Traditionally, Income poverty has been monitored through Household income and consumption surveys. Due to the high cost of these surveys, not all countries have up-dated income data. This is why some non-income surveys attempt to tackle the challenge of assessing the economic status of households when income or consumption data are not available, usually by including questions on type of house construction, whether the household has a radio or bicycle and so on. However, practical analysis and use of these data has been sparse and generally localized to a particular survey or country.

Recent work by the World Bank, Macro International (via the Demographic and Health Surveys [DHS]) and UNICEF (via the Multiple Indicator Clusters Survey [MICS]), has shown what can be done for the many countries in which DHS and MICS have been implemented. The DHS and MICS surveys lack questions on household income or consumption expenditures, but an asset or "wealth" index (Davidson, 2000) has been constructed from: whether any member owns a radio, television, refrigerator, bicycle, motorcycle or car; whether electricity is used, the source of drinking water, the type of sanitation, how many rooms and the type of materials used in dwelling construction.

Monitoring Human Poverty

Since its first publication in 1990, the UNDP Human Development Report has developed and constructed several composite indices to measure different aspects of Human development. The Human development index (HDI) has been constructed every year since 1990 to measure average achievements in basic Human development in one simple composite index and to produce a ranking of countries. The concept of Human development is much deeper and richer than what can be captured in any composite index or even by a detailed set of statistical indicators. Yet, UNDP argues, a simple tool is needed to monitor progress in Human development. Thus the HDI reflects achievements in the most basic human capabilities, that is, leading a long life, being knowledgeable and enjoying a decent standard of living. Three variables have been chosen to represent those dimensions: life expectancy, educational attainment and income.

The UNDP Human Development Report 1997 introduced the concepts of Human poverty and formulated a composite measure of it, the Human poverty index (HPI). The HPI for developing countries (which differs from the one for developed countries) is composed of the following variables: percentage of people not expected to survive to age 40; adult illiteracy rate; percentage of people without access to safe water; percentage of people without access to health services; and percentage of underweight children under five.

Regarding Human poverty of children, at the World Summit for Children (WSC) in 1990, the international community pledged to meet an ambitious set of goals to improve the quality of life of the world's children. Targets were set for reductions in infant, child and maternal mortality rates, improvements in child nutrition, better access to basic education, improvements in early childhood care and primary health care, safer water and environmental sanitation, and the protection of children from abuses and exploitation.

The governments that signed the WSC Declaration and the Plan of Action for Children committed themselves to monitoring progress toward these goals and objectives. The Plan of Action called for each country to "establish appropriate mechanisms for the regular and timely collection, analysis and publication of data required to monitor social indicators related to the well-being of children." Many governments have taken substantial steps to do this in their own National Programmes of Action. Measurement of these indicators is an essential part of the process, both for providing information for action and for assessing change. Generally, social indicators are collected by national Health and Education systems, and/or by surveys, such as the DHS and MICS.

In the case of Niger, the Ministry of Public Health and the Ministry of Education have a National information system. Two DHS surveys have been carried out in 1992 and 1998, and two MICS surveys in 1996 and 2000.

Monitoring Social Poverty

Voicelessness and powerlessness are new aspects that emerged from different Participatory Poverty Assessments carried out by International organizations, notably UNDP and the World Bank. The World Bank, as a background research to the World Development Report 2000/2001, carried out "The Voices of the Poor Study" based on realities of more than 60,000 poor women and men in 60 countries. The study shows that poor are active agents in their lives, but are often powerless to influence social and economic factors that determine their well-being. In the Voices of the Poor study poor people discussed, in small groups, the range of the institutions importançe to their daily life and then identified the criteria that were important in rating institutions. Characteristics included trust, participation, accountability, ability to build unity, responsiveness, respect, fairness, caring, listening and loving.

However, measuring voicelessness and powerlessness in an accurate, robust and consistent way so that comparisons can be made across countries and over time will require considerable efforts on both the methodological and data-gathering fronts. The same can be said about measuring Social capital. No standard indicators are internationally accepted and collected to measure bonding, bridging and linking Social capital.

CHILD POVERTY ANALYSIS IN NIGER

Adopting the above approach of multidimensionality of poverty and the UNDP framework for assessing progress on Human Rights, Child poverty in Niger has been analyzed taking into consideration major disparities and inequalities for Income, Human and Social poverty.

The major finding of this analysis is that Niger is a country of wide extreme poverty. Regarding Income poverty and socio-economic status, 63% of Nigeriens are poor, only 43% have access to drinkable water, 18% to sanitation and 6.5% to electricity. Only 41% own a radio, 19% a cart, 5.9% a bicycle and 1.9% a car.

Regarding Human Poverty, Niger ranks 173 out 174 countries in the Human Development Index (HDI) with a value of 0.270. Niger has the third worst under 5 mortality rate in the world (280), after Sierra Leone (316) and Angola (295). 40% of Nigerien children are chronically malnourished, only 16% of deliveries are attended by skilled health personnel, only 30% of children attend primary school and only 20% of adults are literate. Only 45% of children are registered at birth, and 70% currently work.

Nevertheless, averages do not tell the full story of how far countries have gone in fulfilling the development aspirations of their people. Groups for which socioeconomic progress has been faster seldom represent the disadvantaged people. Thus, while averages give a good sense of overall progress, they can be misleading (UNDP/UNICEF, 2002). The poor are often by-passed by "average" progress. As disparities are widening for a range of indicators, the informational value of national averages gradually decreases. A good assessment, therefore, should go beyond averages and aggregates to shed light on the situation of the most disadvantaged groups in a society.

For this reason, the relevant data available in Niger was disaggregated by region, rural/urban, gender, wealth, and level of education.

Table 2. *Spatial analysis of Income poverty, Socio-economic status and Human poverty in Niger*

Region	Human Poverty	Socio-economic status	Income poverty
Agadez	0.22	0.28	0.44
Diffa	0.33	0.57	0.49
Dosso	0.33	0.57	0.76
Maradi	1.00	0.85	0.65
Tillaberi	0.22	0.71	0.80
Tahoua	0.88	0.85	0.51
Zinder	0.88	0.71	0.59
Niamey	0.00	0.14	0.42

Source: Enquête national sur le budget et la consommation des ménages. 1993, and MICS 2000.

Based on the analysis carried out in the next pages, Human poverty, Income poverty and Socio-economic status have been compared in table 2. The Region of Maradi seems to be the poorest region in Niger in terms of Human poverty, Income poverty and Socio-economic status. The next poorest regions seem to be Tahoua, Zinder, Tillaberi and Dosso. Niamey and the Region of Agadez seem to be the richest ones.

Nevertheless, Niger is a country with significant inequalities. The Male/female ratio regarding Literacy is 2.860 at national level, but in the region of Zinder is 5.169 and in the poorest quintile is 4.714. Regarding Primary school attendance, the Male/female ratio is 1.400 at national level, but in the Region of Dosso is 1.786 and in the second poorest quintile is 5.735.

Significant inequalities exist also within Wealth quintiles. The Poor/rich ratio is 0.145 for Delivery attendance, 0.256 for Literacy, 0.328 for Primary school attendance, 0.369 for Antenatal care and 0.396 for Polio immunization.

Significant inequalities exist also regarding the level of education of the mother or women. The Low/high mother's education ratio is 2.184 for Under 5 Mortality, 1.726 for Stunting, 0.159 for Delivery attendance and 0.383 for Polio immunization.

Nevertheless, Gender, Wealth and Mother's education inequalities have been slightly narrowing in 1998/2000.

Income poverty of children in Niger

Over the last decade, Niger is facing a serious economic crisis. In average, the GNP has increased by 1.9% yearly, while the population has increased by 3.3%. This means a decreased of GNP per capita from $ 210 in 1995 to $ 190 in 2001 (République du Niger, 2001a).

Graphic 1. Evolution of the GNP per capita

Source: Live data base, World Bank.

According to the latest Income survey carried out (République du Niger, 1993), 63% of Nigeriens (5.2 millions inhabitants) are poor, and 34% (2.8 millions inhabitants) are extremely poor. Important disparities exist between urban and rural areas. In urban areas 52% is poor and 26% extremely poor, as opposed to respectively 66% and 36% in rural areas.

Table 3. Spatial analysis of the Poverty Index in Niger

Region	Rank	% Population	Poverty Index	Contribution to the national Poverty Index
Tillaberi	1	18.71	0.80	23.72
Dosso	2	14.52	0.76	17.32
Maradi	3	19.62	0.65	20.00
NIGER	-	-	**0.63**	-
Zinder	4	19.43	0.59	17.92
Tahoua	5	17.22	0.51	13.76
Diffa	6	2.33	0.49	1.79
Agadez	7	2.22	0.44	1.53
Niamey	8	5.94	0.42	3.95

Source: Enquête national sur le budget et la consommation des ménages. 1993.

123

Table 4: Spatial analysis of the Socio-economic status (access to or ownership of assets) in Niger

Region	Indicators worst than national Average	Water		Sanitation		Electricity		Radio		Cart		Bicycle		Car	
		R	V	R	V	R	V	R	V	R	V	R	V	R	V
Maradi	0.85	4	37.7	4	13.3	3	2.4	2	33.8	7	26.6	4	5.7	3	1.1
Tahoua	0.85	5	44.2	2	10.2	2	2.1	4	43.9	4	13.3	3	2.8	5	1.3
Tillaberi	0.71	2	35.2	3	10.3	4	3.4	5	45.2	5	14.7	6	8.4	6	1.4
Zinder	0.71	6	49.3	1	6.4	1	1.8	1	26.4	6	21.7	1	1.3	2	0.4
Dosso	0.57	1	34.3	5	18.0	5	3.5	6	46.5	8	26.8	7	9.8	3	1.1
Diffa	0.57	3	35.4	7	35.2	6	8.6	7	58.3	3	6.0	2	1.7	1	0.0
Agadez	0.28	7	51.8	6	33.5	7	17.0	3	40.1	2	3.7	5	6.6	7	5.2
Niamey	0.14	8	73.3	8	83.7	8	76.3	8	76.3	1	3.6	8	12.8	8	11.7
NIGER	-	-	**43.2**	-	**18.1**	-	**6.5**	-	**41.1**	-	**19.1**	-	**5.9**	-	**1.9**

Source: MICS 2000.

The analysis of the Socio-economic status confirms that the poverty level of the Nigerien population is alarming. Only 1.9% owns a car, 5.9% a bicycle and 19.1 a cart. Only 6.5% has access to electricity, 18.1% to sanitation and 43.2% to drinkable water.

The Spatial analysis shows the Rank (R) and the Value (V) of each selected indicator by region, with Rank 1 meaning the worst and rank 8 the best. Regions are listed according to the number of indicators whose value is worst than the national average. The region of Maradi and Tahoua have 6 indicators out of 7 (0.85) with a value worse than the national average, Tillaberi and Zinder have 5 out of 7 (0.71), and Dosso and Diffa have 4 out of 7 (0.57). The region of Niamey ranked best with 1 indicator out of 7 (0.14), followed by Agadez with 2 out of 7 (0.28). In any event, as this calculation is not weighted, it should be interpreted with caution.

Human Poverty of children in Niger

The Human Development Index (HDI) in Niger increased in the last two decades from 0.230 in 1975 to 0.270 in 1999 (UNDP, 2001). However, Niger still ranks the 173rd country out of 174 with the worst Human Development Index in the world.

Graphic 2. Evolution of the Human Development Index

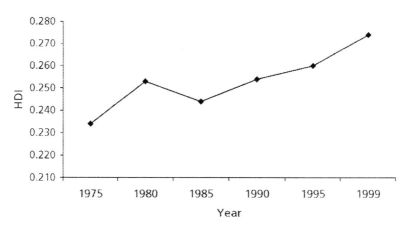

Source: Human Development Report, 2001.

To analyze the Human poverty of children in Niger, nine major indicators have been selected:

• Under-five mortality rate (U5M): Probability of dying between birth and exactly five years of age, per 1000 live births

• Stunting prevalence: Proportion of under-fives who fall below minus 2 and below minus 3 standard deviations from median height for age of WHO reference population

• Polio immunization: Proportion of children immunized against poliomyelitis

• Antenatal care: Proportion of women aged 15-49 who were attended at least once during pregnancy by skilled health personnel

• Delivery attendance: Proportion of births attended by skilled health personnel

• Net primary school attendance: Proportion of children of primary school age attending primary school

• Literacy rate: Proportion of population aged 15 years and older who are able, with understanding, to both read and write a short simple statement on their everyday life

• Birth registration: Proportion of children 0-59 months of age whose births are reported registered

• Child labour: Proportion of children 5-14 years of age who are currently working

These indicators have been selected because they have a significant relevance on Child and Mother Health, Nutrition, Education and other Child rights. For each indicator the following detailed analysis has been carried out:

• Longitudinal

• Gender

• Spatial

• Wealth

• Mother's education level

Table 5. Longitudinal analysis of Human poverty of children in Niger

Indicator	1991/1992	1996/2000	Trend
U5M	335.1	273.8	Improving
Stunting	32.3	39.8	Worsening
Polio Immunization	20.1	40.6	Improving
Antenatal care	30.1	40.4	Improving
Delivery attendance	14.9	15.7	No change
Primary school	18.2	30.3	Improving
Literacy rate	12	19.9	Improving
Birth registration	NA	45.4	NA
Child Labour	NA	70.1	NA

Source: DHS 1992, MICS 1996, DHS 1998 and MICS 2000.

Longitudinal analysis of Human poverty of children in Niger

The situation has generally improved in Health and Education, and deteriorated in Nutrition. The positive trend in Health and Education confirms the positive trend of the Human Development Index. Because of unavailability of data regarding Birth registration and Child labour before 2000, it is not possible to make any longitudinal analysis for these two indicators.

However, it is important to underline that the positive changes in Health and Education during the decade 1990/2000 have not reached the expected objectives. According to the Niger End Decade Report (République du Niger, 2001), Niger did not meet any of the World Summit for Children objectives. Moreover, Niger is one of the countries with the worst indicators in Health, Nutrition and Education not only within West Africa, but all over the world.

Gender analysis of Human poverty of children in Niger

Table 6. Gender analysis of Human poverty of children in Niger

Indicator	Male/Female ratio		Trend
	1993/1998	*1995/2000*	
U5M	1.141	1.032	Improving
Stunting	1.075	1.022	Improving
Polio Immunization	1.051	1.012	Improving
Primary school	1.750	1.400	Improving
Literacy rate	3.800	2.860	Improving

Source: DHS 1998 and MICS 2000.

Gender inequalities are not important regarding Health (U5M, Stunting and Polio immunization), but are extremely significant regarding Education, with a Male/Female ratio of 1.400 for the Primary School attendance and 2.860 for Literacy.

However, it is important to underline that Gender inequalities have narrowed in 1998 and 2000 both in Health and Education.

As the situation is worst in Education, a more detailed analysis was carried out in this sector, to highlight the disparities and better understand the situation.

Table 7. Spatial analysis of Gender Inequalities

Indicator	Worst/best region Ratio	Male/Female Ratio by Region							
		Agadez	Diffa	Dosso	Maradi	Tillabéri	Tahoua	Zinder	Niamey
Primary School	1.802	1.020	1.083	1.786	1.481	1.378	1.590	1.543	0.991
Literacy Rate	3.671	1.819	2.483	3.168	3.373	3.243	2.777	5.169	1.408

Source: MICS 2000.

As shown in table 7, significant disparities exist among regions. Regarding Primary school attendance, the Male/female ratio ranges from 0.991 in Niamey and 1.020 in the Region of Agadez to 1.786 in the Region of Dosso and 1.590 in Tahoua. The Worst/best region ratio regarding Gender inequalities is 1.802. Important disparities exist also regarding Urban and Rural areas. In Urban areas the Male/female ratio is 1.033 and in Rural areas is 1.632.

Regarding Literacy rate, the Male/female ratio ranges from 1.408 in Niamey and 1.819 in the Region of Agadez to 5.169 in the Region of Zinder and 3.373 in Maradi. The Worst/best region ratio regarding Gender inequalities is 3.671. Important disparities exist also regarding Urban and Rural areas. In Urban areas the Male/female ratio is 1.607 and in Rural areas is 4.937.

Table 8. Wealth Analysis of Gender inequalities

Indicator	Poor/rich ratio	Male/female ratio by Quintiles				
		Poorest	Second	Middle	Fourth	Richest
Primary School	1.451	1.739	1.648	1.686	1.368	1.198
Literacy Rate	3.133	4.714	5.735	5.244	5.081	1.830

Source: MICS 2000.

As shown in table 8, significant disparities exist among Wealth quintiles. Regarding Primary school attendance, the Male/female ratio ranges from 1.198 in the richest quintile to 1.739 in the poorest one. The Poor/rich ratio regarding Gender inequalities is 1.451.

Regarding Literacy rate, the Male/female ratio ranges from 1.830 in the richest quintile to 5.735 in the second poorest one. The Poor/rich ratio regarding Gender inequalities is 3.133.

Spatial Analysis of Human poverty of children in Niger

Table 9: Spatial analysis of Human poverty of children in Niger

Region	Indicators worst than Average	U5M		Stunt.		Polio		Antenatal		Delivery		School Attend		Literacy		Birth Reg.		Child Labour	
		R	V	R	V	R	V	R	V	R	V	R	V	R	V	R	V	R	V
Maradi	1.00	3	306	2	47.3	3	29.3	2	29.2	3	13.9	3	30.3	4	17.7	3	40.5	1	83.3
Zinder	0.88	1	366	1	47.8	1	17.8	1	22.7	1	3.7	2	23.9	5	19.1	1	28.8	5	66.7
Tahoua	0.88	5	263	4	40.1	2	22.1	3	33.4	2	8.9	1	11.4	1	11.5	5	45.3	4	74.8
Diffa	0.33	2	356	3	42.1	4	43.2	6	59.1	7	43.0	6	36.2	7	32.3	6	47.6	3	76.3
Dosso	0.33	4	294	5	37.3	7	75.7	7	69.3	5	16.3	4	31.9	2	15.6	7	60.8	2	80.8
Tillaberi	0.22	6	213	7	28.4	6	45.4	5	44.6	4	15.9	5	34.4	3	6.3	2	36.4	7	53.7
Agadez	0.22	7	172	6	32.0	5	43.4	4	38.5	6	21.3	7	40.1	6	28.9	4	40.9	6	58.6
Niamey	0.00	8	132	8	18.1	8	82.8	8	89.2	8	77.7	8	69.7	8	59.1	8	90.5	8	46.7
NIGER	-	-	280	-	39.8	-	40.6	-	41.2	-	15.7	-	30.3	-	19.9	-	45.4	-	70.1

Source: MICS 2000.

The Spatial analysis shows the Rank (R) and the Value (V) of each indicator by region, with Rank 1 meaning the worst, and rank 8 the best. Regions are listed according to the number of indicators whose value is worse than the national average.

The region of Maradi has 9 indicators out of 9 (1.00) with a value worse than the national average, Zinder and Tahoua have 8 out of 9 (0.88), Diffa and Dosso 3 out of 9 (0.33). Niamey is the best with 0 indicators out of 9 (0.00), followed by the Region of Agadez and Tillaberi with 2 out of 9 (0.22). However, as this calculation in not weighted, it should be interpreted with caution.

Regarding Under 5 Mortality, there are four regions with a value higher than the national average (280), notably the regions of Zinder (366), Diffa (356), Maradi (306) and Dosso (294), and four regions with a value lower than the national average, notably the regions of Tahoua (263), Tillaberi (213), Agadez (172) and Niamey (132).

Regarding Stunting and Polio Immunization, the table shows that three of the four regions with the higher Under 5 Mortality also have a higher Stunting (Zinder, Maradi and Diffa) and a lower Polio immunization (Zinder, Maradi and Diffa), suggesting a potential correlation.

Table 10. Rural/Urban analysis of Human poverty of children in Niger

Rural/Urban	U5M	Stunt	Polio	Antenatal	Delivery	School Attend.	Literacy	Birth Reg.	Child labour
School	1.802	1.020	1.083	1.786	1.481	1.378	1.590	1.543	0.991
Rural	293	41.8	33.8	35.5	9.7	24.8	13.7	39.6	73.4
Urban	168	26.4	79.3	83.6	64.7	61.3	50.5	84.6	53.1
R/U ratio	1.744	1.583	0.426	0.424	0.149	0.404	0.271	0.468	1.382

Source: MICS 2000.

Regarding the Rural/Urban analysis, table 10 shows significant disparities for all the indicators.

Wealth analysis of Human poverty of children in Niger

Table 11. Wealth analysis of Human poverty of children in Niger

Indicator	Poor/Rich ratio		Trend
	1998	2000	
U5M	1.534	1.350	Improving
Stunting	1.297	1.279	No change
Polio Immunization	NA	0.396	NA
Antenatal care	0.292	0.369	Improving
Delivery attendance	0.067	0.145	Improving
Primary school	0.272	0.328	Improving
Literacy rate	0.255	0.256	No change
Birth registration	NA	0.415	NA
Child labour	NA	1.288	NA

Source: DHS 1998 and MICS 2000.

The situation has generally improved in Health and primary Education, and did not change in Nutrition and adult Literacy. Due to unavailability of data regarding Birth registration and Child labour before 2000, it is not possible to make any longitudinal analysis for these two indicators.

Nevertheless, it is important to underline that inequalities related to Wealth remains alarming high for all the indicators analyzed.

Human poverty of children in Niger based on Mother's education analysis

Table 12. Inequalities based on the Mother's education analysis

Indicator	Low/High education ratio		Trend
	1998	2000	
U5M	2.415	2.184	Improving
Stunting	1.792	1.726	Improving
Polio Immunization	0.318	0.383	Improving
Antenatal care	0.417	0.409	Worsening
Delivery attendance	0.201	0.159	Worsening
Birth registration	NA	0.456	NA

Source: MICS 2000.

Regarding the inequalities between children whose mother has no education and children whose mother has an high education, the situation has improved for Under 5 Mortality, Polio immunization and Stunting, and slightly deteriorated in Antenatal care and Delivery attendance. Because of unavailability of data regarding Birth registration before 2000, it is not possible to make any longitudinal analysis for this indicator.

Nevertheless, it is important to underline that inequalities for children whose mother has no education and children whose mother has an high education remains alarming high for all the indicators analyzed.

Social Poverty of children in Niger

The first time a Poverty Participatory Assessment in Niger had been carried out by the Ministry of Planning in cooperation with UNDP and the World Bank was in 2001 in the district of Mayahi and Bankilare (Republique du Niger, 2001b). The Permanent Secretariat of the Poverty Reduction Strategy Paper is planning to carry out a similar study at national level.

According to the above mentioned study, those surveyed defined poverty as the opposite of wealth. Wealth is defined as autonomy regarding material resources, access to opportunities and a social and psychological equilibrium. Regarding the definition of poverty:

40% mentioned the dependence on somebody

37% mentioned social exclusion (poor is somebody alone, without support, who is not consulted, who is not involved in anything)

36% mentioned lack of something (lack of food, animals, money)

26% mentioned the restriction of freedom and rights (poor is someone who has no right to speak, somebody who never wins in social conflicts)

21% mentioned an incapacity (incapacity to decide, to set up an independent initiative)

According to this study, those surveyed perceive poverty as an incapacity and privation of means of subsistence or access to basic social services. Social factors such as divorce, unemployment, the size of the family and some socio-cultural attitudes, worsen the level of vulnerability of young, elders and women.

CONCLUSION

This analysis oo Child poverty in Niger tested the conceptual framework of Child poverty based on a Human rights approach. The results have been encouraging, even if the methodology still needs to be further developed.

The paper furnishes data and information to operationalise the conceptual framework of Child poverty in Niger. It clearly highlights which regions are the poorest (the region of Maradi, Tahoua and Zinder), in which sector funds should be allocated to narrow the most important gender inequalities (for example, literacy in the region of Zinder or primary school in the region of Dosso) and which strategies should be implemented to attack poverty in Niger (for example, to attack malnutrition, efforts should be made to change behavior and not necessarily to increase income, as demonstrated by the wealth analysis of stunting).

It is hoped that the analysis carried out in this paper will facilitate further development of the conceptual framework of Child poverty based on a human rights approach, and its application and operationalisation in other countries. The information produced by this kind of exercise proved to be very valuable in reaching decisions on how to attack poverty in developing countries.

REFERENCES

Bradbury, B., Jenkins, P. and Micklewright, J. (2000). *Child poverty dynamics in seven nations*. Innocenti working paper, No. 78. UNICEF Innocenti Research Center, Firenze.

Davidson, R., Gwatkin, Rustein S., Kiersten, J., Rohini P. and Wagstaff A. (2000). *Socio-Economic differences in Health, Nutrition and Population in Niger*.

HNP/Poverty Thematic Group, The World Bank, Washington

Edwards, M. (2000). "More social capital, less global poverty?" In: *Fighting poverty. Development Outreach*, Summer 2000. World Bank Institute, Washington

Malloch Brown, M. (2000). In: *Overcoming human poverty. Poverty report 2000.* UNDP, New York

Minujin A. (2000). "Making child poverty visible". Paper presented at the International Conference on Statistics, Development and Human Rights. Montreaux

Republique du Niger (1992). *Enquete de demographie e sante (EDSI)*. Niamey.

République du Niger (1993). *Enquête national sur le budget et la consommation des ménages*. Niamey.

République du Niger et UNICEF (1996). *Enquete a indicateur multiple (MICS)*. Niamey.

Republique du Niger (1998). *Enquete de demographie e sante (EDSII)*. Niamey.

République du Niger et UNICEF (2000). *Enquete a indicateur multiple de la fin de la decennie (MICS2)*. Niamey.

République du Niger (2001). *Rapport national sur le suivi du Sommet Mondial pour les Enfants*. Niamey.

République du Niger (2001a). *Version préliminaire du Diagnostic de la pauvreté*. Secrétariat permanent du DSRP. Niamey.

République du Niger (2001b). *Version préliminaire de l'Evaluation par le bénéficiaires appliqué à la pauvreté réalisée au niveau des deux antennes du PCLCP Mayahi et Bankilare*. Niamey.

Santos Pais, M. (1999). *A human rights conceptual framework for UNICEF*. Innocenti essay No. 9, International Child Development Center, Firenze.

Thomas, A. (2000). "Poverty and the end of development". In : *Poverty and development into the 21st century*. The Open University and Oxford University Press, Oxford.

UNDP (1997). *Human Development Report 1997*. New York

UNDP (2000). "The Commitment in poverty reduction". In : *Overcoming Human poverty*. New York, 2000.

UNDP (2000a). "Using indicators for human rights accountabilit"y. In: *Human rights and human development. Human Development Report 2000*. New York

UNDP (2000b). "Assessing progress in Human rights and Human development". In: *Human rights and human development. Human Development Report 2000*. New York

UNDP (2000c). "What do the Human development indices reveal?" In: *Human Development Report 2000*. New York.

UNDP (2001). *Human Development Report. New York UNDP and UNICEF (2002). The Millennium development goals in Africa: promises & progress*. New York.

UNICEF (2000). *Poverty reduction begins with children*. New York.

Vandemoortele, J. (2001). *Absorbing social shocks, protecting children and reducing poverty*. UNICEF, New York.

Woolcock, M. (2000). "Friends in high places? An overview of social capital". In: *It is not what you know. It is who you know! Economic analysis of Social capital*. Insights Development Research, n. 34, September 2000. Institute of Development Studies, University of Sussex, Brighton.

World Bank (2001). *Attacking poverty. World development report 2000/2001*. Washington.

Chapter 7

How to Make Children Come First: The Process of Visualizing Children in Peru

Enrique Mendizábal and Enrique Vásquez

INTRODUCTION

In 2000, at the Research Centre of the Universidad del Pacífico in Lima, and with the support of Save the Children Sweden, we began an in-depth study of social public expenditure targeted on children (1990[1]-2003[2])[3] in Peru. It showed that this vulnerable group was almost forgotten by the government. Furthermore, the political agenda of the Fujimori Administration had resulted in undermining the initial gains in the field of child welfare and created a system in which children not only seem to come last, but also were invisible.

We determined that the next step should aim to visualize and include children into the policy process to make the evidence relevant and crucial to policy making. Otherwise, the road towards achieving the Millennium Development Goals will be long and difficult, if not impossible to travel. In this paper, our objective is to describe how we developed a methodology to visualize children that can be used in the design, implementation and evaluation of targeted policies in favour of this group. We present the key findings of the Universidad del Pacífico/Save The Children Sweden's research on children in Peru since 1990 and the process carried out in two central government institutions, two local governments in the capital city of Peru, and two local governments outside Lima, to turn over this situation and visualize children in their budgets and government plans. We describe the way in which indicators developed from multiple sources were incorporated to tailor-made monitoring and evaluation systems and highlight the promising potential these systems have for the design of direct children-specific poverty reduction policies and interventions.

The paper highlights the challenges and limitations encountered, such as the need to introduce basic operational capacities in the local governments and the struggle to put aside partisan and individual political interests. The analysis also shows that although tools such as Multiple Indicator Cluster Surveys (MICS) or LSMS are useful, there is a need for context-specific data to design and calculate indicators and policy tools according to the needs of children, the internal organizational structure and constraints of the policy making institution and its external environment.

We also found that by transferring the initiative in the production of information and evidence to policy makers and implementers, we achieved a change in behaviour among them. This resulted in a more pro-children policy-making process and in policy makers being more receptive to and demanding of evidence and data as a key element of their decision making.

THE PROBLEM: CHILDREN ARE NON-VISIBLE IN PERU'S PUBLIC BUDGET

In this section the paper presents the key findings of the two phases of the Universidad del Pacífico/Save The Children Sweden four-year research. These findings represent the problems that Peru encounters in its obligation to eliminate child poverty and allocate public resources for an effective reduction of social exclusion and inequality among children.

Building an approach

Our study of the problematic of children can be divided in four non-linear stages. Our first attempt to identify children in the public budget took us through a thorough review of the printed versions of the budget between 1990 and 2000. In the process we identified the functions, programs, projects and activities that could be related to children according to the five categories of basic social services (health and sanitation, nutrition, education, justice and well-being). This was complemented by a study of the institutional memories of the key public institutions.

As this effort proved to be unsuccessful, we extended the scope of our study with the intention of assessing the situation of children during the decade; the objective being to illustrate the effects of *blind*-social policies on children. To do this we used the information gathered and processed by household surveys, particularly the ENNIV[4] (a LSMS funded privately), the ENAHO[5] (a LSMS run by the public sector) and the ENDES[6] (a DHS run by the public sector). The use of multiple surveys allowed us to complement the information provided by each and to construct a reliable diagnosis of the situation of children in Peru, by age, gender, household poverty level and geographical location, among other indicators. Thus, we noticed how the situation of Peruvian children is still difficult.

The third stage involved the study of children living in vulnerable situations. This was done through a series of focus groups and in-depth conversations with children living in the streets, children who work and teenage mothers. The information provided by the children themselves offered a benchmark with which to interpret the results obtained from the survey analysis. Together, they proved to be an optimum tool.

Finally, we carried out additional studies such as an analysis of the international cooperation focused on children in Peru and an exercise to determine the magnitude of the public deficit on children spending.

Key findings

Throughout all categories we identified four main problems that were supported by uncontested and rich evidence. In the first place, our study showed that no more than 25% of the public budget was targeted at children when it should have been at least 45% according to our study of the public deficit on children spending.[7] It revealed that this meagre proportion was pro-cyclical to GDP and total public budget trends. Consequently, targeted social public spending reached its peak by the middle of the 1990s and collapsed after the Asian Crisis and the effects of the El Nino Phenomenon.

Secondly, targeted social expenditure did not reach the extreme poor nor the most socially and, particularly, geographically excluded. As a consequence, the situation of children in the rural Sierra and Jungle had not improved by the end of the decade and they remained entirely unprotected. Leakage was particularly high among nutrition and food programs.

Thirdly, children's invisibility in the public budget is part of an opaque public policy culture that does not allow nor encourage monitoring and evaluation of policies and results. Hence social expenditure was suffering (and still does) from high levels of leakage and the unnecessary overlapping of programs.

Finally, the State had not confronted the drama of children living in high-risk conditions. As a result, children living in the streets, using drugs, working in unhealthy and inhuman conditions and pregnant teenagers in a highly violent and excluding society depend entirely on charity and eventual short-lived public initiatives to survive.

Individually, each area of study provided important insights regarding the welfare of children in Peru since 1990. In the absence of MICS, LSMS and DHS surveys were our primary source of information to diagnose the situation of children. However, these surveys had to be complemented with qualitative information obtained through participatory research methods. This evidence is described below.

Health and sanitation

The achievements in health levels and access to health services in the 1990s are only relatively positive. For instance, while infant mortality rates dropped from 57.2 per 1000 children born alive in 1990 to 34 in 2000,[8] the gap between rural and urban remained high at about 26 children per every 1000 born alive in the rural areas with respect to urban. This inequality is more obvious when total personal health expenditure is analysed according to income deciles. In 2000, after a decade of market reforms, the richest 10% spent 30% of the total health expenditure while the bottom 40% did not even reach 20%. In recent years the government of Mr. Alejandro Toledo has tried to change this inequality by setting up a special Health Insurance for the poorest. However, the mismanagement of this governmental health program resulted in a leakage of over 50% and generated a US$40 million financial deficit for the health sector by 2003. In conclusion, the same social management problems and flawed health policies persist.

Child Mortality Rate: 1990-2000
(per 10,000 children under 5)

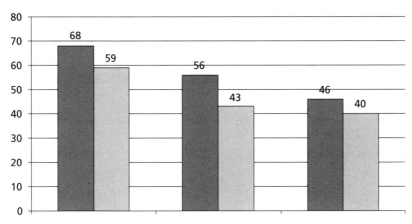

Source: Health National Survey (ENDES) 1992-2000.

Nutrition

The performance of the public sector in this area can be best described by the embarrassing impact of the more than US$1.2 billion spent in 'nutrition and food' programs in Peru, between 1996 and 2000. The result was a meagre 1-percentage point decrease in the level of chronic malnourishment among children under 5 years old. In addition to this, it is important to note that by the year 2000, public food and nutrition initiatives showed a level of juxtaposition of 36%.[9]

Besides juxtaposition, the main reasons for the failure to address malnutrition in the 1990s in Peru rest on the high levels of leakage and the poor quality of the rations offered to beneficiaries.[10]

Despite these management failures, a massive budget was awarded to this sector (US$300 million per year since 1996). This can be explained by the role these programs and projects played in the political machinery of the Fujimori Regime (1990-2000). In this way, expenditure in food and nutrition programs remained high after 1997 and considerably grew towards 2000 to coincide with general elections, even though the rest of the public social sector budget was constrained. Therefore, evidence of mismanagement and the problematic of children could have had little impact on food security policy making during the 1990s. These policies, however inefficient, proved to be good politics for Mr. Fujimori's government; and the incoming Toledo Government unfortunately readily adopted this vision.

Child Chronic Malnutrition; 1990-2000
(In percentages)

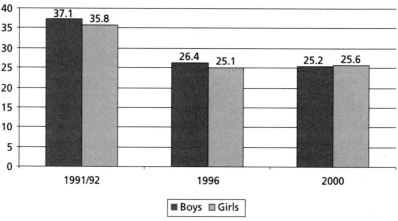

Source: Health National Survey (ENDES) 1992-2000.

Education

Regarding the education sector, of most significance is that during the 1990s a large proportion of resources was channelled to infrastructure. The institutions in charge of educational infrastructure increased their budget from about U$32,000 in 1990 to US$112 million in 1994[11]. Nonetheless, the urban-rural divide remained extremely high by the end of the decade: while Lima's children were an average 0.99 years behind their grade according to their age, the rural Selva demonstrated a 2.06 years gap. Similarly, the situation of rural girls lacked the political interest that the subject deserved and their situation was considerably worse than that of boys. In all these cases it is clear that the most excluded where those further away from the reach of the Central Government and its institutions.

Illiteracy Rate in Rural Areas by Gender: 1997-2000
(In percentages)

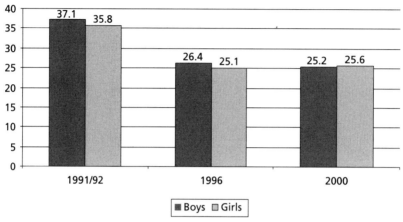

Source: National Household Survey 1997-2001.

Furthermore, the emphasis on physical access to a school building missed a significant element of education: its quality. The investment in schooling facilities did not breed quality, nor did it achieve the desired quantity[12]. Hence the recent significant rise in public investment shown in the budgets for this sector must be considered wisely. The choice of INFES during the second part of our project responds to this concern.

Justice and well-being

Very little has been achieved with respect to children that face the law; whether as victims or aggressors. Similarly, child labour in Peru is still a problem that is addressed timidly and that needs to be tackled across other sectors. Cases of children in the Armed Forces are not rare and domestic violence remains highly unreported (70%), particularly in the rural areas[13]. Information on expenditure on child related justice services was virtually non-existent and it was only possible to identify complementary support services from local governments and civil society organizations.

Child well being during the 1990s was synonymous with sport. As with schools and feeding programs, the Fujimori regime built high profile sporting facilities mostly in newly upgraded squatter settlements in urban areas. Hence the budget assigned to well being increased significantly during the decade; however, it left little to show for except derelict football and volleyball courts.

Children in vulnerable situations

When it came to direct conversations with children living in the most vulnerable situations in Peru, we encountered the true face of their invisibility. Street children are not, as many Peruvians including policy makers and politicians think, those waiting on street corners begging or selling candies to motorists. They sleep under bridges, are often subject to an abusive police force, and can live within a vicious cycle of drugs and violence. Our attention was drawn to them, even though they constitute a proportionally small group in the country, because they highlight the true structural characteristics of extreme child poverty: they do not belong. Street children have severed all connections with their family, school and friends. Successful interventions have recognized this and reach them by slowly rebuilding their ties with these social institutions. Their invisibility from public policy, however, is total.

The analysis of the situation of children provided evidence to the extent and magnitude of the problem. The following section focuses on a methodology developed to solve it. Our key concern was raising the visibility of children in the policy process.

THE SOLUTION: A METHODOLOGY TO VISUALIZE CHILDREN IN PUBLIC BUDGETS

Using Evidence to Influence Policy

Following the completion of the study of children and public spending on children in Peru during the 1990s we engaged in a process of dissemination of the evidence. Ours contributed to the pool of studies and surveys on children in Peru and the wealth of evidence that highlighted the problem of child poverty and the deficiencies of public management.

Unfortunately, reform was absent. The culture of research that has developed throughout civil society and, in particular, academic institutions in Peru, is lacking in the public and private sectors. This can be in part attributed to an educational system, which has failed to develop the capacities to gather, classify and use information. Or also due to a culture of "*caudillismo*",[14] present throughout Latin America, which awards considerable social value and pride to un-aided leadership. In this way, it is not often that evidence is demanded for policy making.

Based on our study, it became clear to us those public institutions, in general, lack the proper systems for the generation and processing of information. This is vital because without it, the State is unable to fulfil its Child Rights commitments. For that reason we decided to develop and implement a methodology to visualize children in the public budgets.

The Methodology offers an invaluable tool not only to improve the quality of the investment on the welfare of children but also to sensitise public opinion; which has been absent from the public debate on this subject. Additionally, it presents an opportunity to institutionalise a culture of transparency and accountability of public policy.

The methodology of the Methodology

The rationale behind the Methodology is that if children are invisible or absent in the policy making process, then it is impossible to guarantee appropriate policies in their favour. Additionally, evidence was having very little impact on policy makers and politicians. Therefore, there was a need to bring both the policy process and the development of evidence together and make the latter an intrinsic part of the former. Only this, we believe would bring about a significant behavioural change among policy makers: they would become aware of the problem, its implications and their power to find plausible solutions.

The first part of the Methodology consisted of selecting 6 different institutions. These were:

1. National Fund for Compensation and Social Development (FONCODES); Lima.[15]

2. National Education and Health Infrastructure (INFES); Lima.[16]

3. Municipality of Lima; Lima.[17]

4. Municipality of San Borja; Lima.[18]

5. Municipality of La Banda de Shilcayo; San Martin.[19]

6. Municipality of Tarapoto; San Martin.[20]

For its development and implementation, our team worked in four areas. In the first instance, we analysed the budget process at each institution with particular emphasis on the areas related to child welfare. In this we were guided by national LSMS and DHS style surveys as well as other primary and secondary data and documentations available within each institution.

In second place we developed a legal framework in which the Methodology would be introduced into each institution. This was accompanied, in the third place, by the development of context specific instruments to facilitate and strengthen the new Methodology. These instruments included monitoring and evaluation systems, information cards system, information storage and processing software, etc. It is important to note that although some of the indicators used are the same, the tools and instruments to obtain them in each case were different. This responded to the availability of financial, human and physical resources. For instance, in Lima, a software package to manage the budget information was used, while in San Martin, a cards system to gather and manage data was designed.

The fourth component of the Methodology involved the provision of technical assistance for the development and maintenance of the new budget processes. Assistance was provided in a demand-driven basis with emphasis on the less qualified staff and institutions.

These components, which were carried out within the institutions and with their full participation, resulted in a Monitoring System to Visualize Children in the Public Budget. The system is composed of 5 modules to ensure the integral evaluation of the institution's efforts.

Alerts Module: This module is based on information gathered through both subjective and objective means. The role of MICS, LSMS and DHS is central to the elaboration of a detailed diagnosis of the problem at the national and regional scale. In the case of smaller municipalities, however, data collected from schools, medical centres and neighbourhood associations is crucial for a correct and prompt alert on the situation of child welfare.

Activities Module: This module provides a description of the social programs focused on children. It includes basic information such as its name, the target population, its scope of action, its operative annual budget, etc. This information serves as a guideline and sets the foundations for a more transparent system.

Results module: The objective of this module is to calculate, assess and present the institutions' performance. To determine the social gains derived from the execution of each project, we designed indicators to assess the levels of Efficiency, Effectiveness, Equity and Transparency.

Processes Module: The objective of this module is to determine the optimal way to execute a program. Indicators were designed in Specialization, Synergy, Outsourcing, Graduation and Citizen Participation. It is important to note that concepts such as graduation and synergy are absent from the policy process in Peru. Graduation challenges the process and demands a close monitoring of individual beneficiaries.

Inputs Module: The objective of this module is to determine the institution's resource requirements for an efficient execution of the program. To achieve this, we designed indicators to measure the Procedures followed in the production and provision of public services, the quality of information systems, the quality of human resources and social management skills present and the institution's relation with users, suppliers and financers.

Lessons

The main lessons for monitoring the formulation and implementation of focalized social policy on children in Peru can be summarized as follows:

First, the central government institutions and local government need to set up basic information systems which allow them to 'see' the children as beneficiaries. This should begin with the setting up of an 'identification tool' of the boys and girls who must be supported by public social intervention. Although household surveys (and the MICS) might be useful for aggregated analysis, local authorities must find a way of developing tools for individual analysis. Because of this, it is critical to invest on the institutional building of the public institutions in two directions. On the one hand, upgrading their information technology; and on the other, training the staff in the use of the information in a manner that increases child wellbeing and fulfils children's human rights.

Information systems should be user-friendly to the extent that they act not only as a tool of evaluation for policymakers but also for children and those who are represent them. Neighbourhood associations must play a partner rather than a clientelism role in social policymaking.

Most local governments lack systems and human resources that would allow them to deliver social programs in an efficient and effective way in the context of increased budgets and responsibilities.

At the same time, the implementation of the Methodology showed the strengths and weaknesses of the public institutions involved in the study. Aspects like poor visualization and the lack of a monitoring and evaluation system dramatically hinder the impact of the programs and the efforts to differentiate policies according to gender. Visualization was difficult because of the lack of capacity and willingness to develop indicators which may show the situation in the program. This makes it impossible to monitor or evaluate programs at the child level and, as a consequence, the impact on children is ignored.

Fortunately, some strength existed. The institutions, particularly local governments, showed an interest for change. Hence their participation in the development of the Methodology was very positive and amounted to far more than merely providing information. They engaged in the process allowing us to meet their own requirements and concerns. For instance, in the Municipality of Lima, the implementation of the Methodology was based upon a complete fulfilment of the requirements established by the functionaries; often political. This was crucial to ensure the success and cooperation of the key decision makers.

An important issue to highlight is that since this initiative, policy makers within the chosen institutions are paying attention to the importance of developing programs which differentiate by geographical domain and, particularly, by gender. Nonetheless, the research group is well aware that the Methodology must be continuously supported to ensure its sustainability.

Finally, an important lesson from this project is that the process was more important than the result. As a consequence of the process, the local stakeholders involved have become aware of their problems and their power to solve them. They have developed indicators and gathered information that is relevant to their unique context in a way that is compatible with national official standards.

POLICY IMPLICATIONS

The diagnosis of the problem and the visualising methodology suggest, above all, that the social policy process needs to be opened and made to work in favour of the beneficiaries. Disclosing information via the internet, as the Peruvian government has emphasized since the year 2000,[21] or publishing the budget, is not enough.

The problem goes beyond the public budget itself. If children are not clearly identified within the public budget, policies oriented towards them will be vague or inaccurate. This blind policymaking is endemic in Peru. To challenge it we need to introduce monitoring and evaluation systems and make them an integral part to the policy process.

Size does not matter. Large and small institutions show the same problems when it comes to visualizing children in their budgets and policy process. The level of opacity was high in FONCODES where many were involved in child welfare programs and in the municipalities in San Martin where only one person was responsible for a few initiatives. The difference rests on the magnitude of the effect stemming from these blind-policies. Hence the same objectives and principles should apply to all public institutions.

However, information systems need to be designed to serve the beneficiaries by providing them and the policy makers with useful, up to date and reliable qualitative and quantitative evidence. This means designing carefully chosen instruments and tools according to the limitations and potentials of the institution and its resources. In a similar fashion, public initiatives must be tailored to the specific contexts in which they will be implemented. The vast diversity of geographical, cultural, economic, social and political settings in Peru should be taken into account.

The indicators developed, when taken together, can provide an important insight about the whole policy process, the implementation and the impact of the programs or projects. They combine desktop, qualitative and primary and secondary quantitative information sources. They were designed to be flexible to each institution's requirements, needs and constraints and to work with a variety of data management instruments. The government should invest in making these sources of information and their conclusions more readily available for civil society and local governments.

Efforts to improve the production of relevant information must be part of an inter-sectoral process involving both national and local level public institutions, as well as the private sector. Information from private schools and clinics should be readily available for policy makers and civil society.

Similarly, the use of specialised and comparable surveys such as MICS needs to be promoted in Peru. Currently, only LSMS and DHS surveys are available to researchers, civil society and policy makers. Although they provide useful information for policymaking they do not address the needs of children, and children in vulnerable situations specifically. Rather they only offer general statistics of child welfare that have only a relative impact.

Demand for evidence is not strong in Peruvian policy making. This stems from an education system, which has failed to develop the capacity to gather, classify and use information. A crucial policy implication is that the development of a culture of information has to be a priority in the educational agenda.

Finally, empowerment of local policy makers and civil society must involve breaking the monopoly of information. In our methodology we developed the basic skills to allow local stakeholders to gather, process and use information relevant to them. As a result they will no longer depend on external agents for information or for solutions to their problems. Therefore, the production of information to inform as well as to guide the policy process must be part of the official policy making guidelines of the public sector.

NOTES

[1] Vásquez, E and E. Mendizabal (2002). *Children First? Study of Focalized Social Expenditure in Children in Peru: 1990-2000*, Lima: Universidad del Pacífico/Save The Children Sweden.

[2] Vásquez , E. (2004). *Children First? How much the Peruvian State invested on children: 2001-2003*, Lima: Save The Children Sweden.

[3] The Period between 1990 and 2000 captures the full length of the Government of Alberto Fujimori. The Period from 2001 to 2003 captures the first years of the Government of Alejandro Toledo. Between late 2000 and July 2001, an interim government led by the President of Congress held office.

[4] Encuesta Nacional de Niveles de Vida. This survey was run by Instituto Cuanto, which is a private consultancy firm.

[5] Encuesta Nacional de Hogares. This survey is run by the National Institute of Statistics.

[6] Encuesta Nacional Demográfica y de Salud Familiar. This survey is run by the National Institute of Statistics.

[7] This study considered the difference in spending between children living in poverty and extreme poverty to those well above the poverty line.

[8] Health Ministry of Peru (2002), See <http://www.minsa.gob.pe/LOGROS/>.

[9] Vásquez, E. and E. Mendizabal (eds.) (2002), op. cit.

[10] Vásquez, E., "Nutritional programs", pp. 268-272, in: Beltrán, A. R. Cortez, J. Chacaltana y E. Vásquez (eds.) (2000), *Development for a social strategy for Peru*.

[11] Vásquez, E. and E. Mendizabal (eds.) (2002), op. cit.

[12] UNESCO-OECD (2002), *Basic aptitudes for the world of tomorrow*.

[13] Mendizabal, Enrique and Giovann Alarcon (2002), "Study of domestic violence in Huancayo (Promudeh/IDB)", mimeo., Lima.

[14] The Encyclopaedia Britannica defines Caudillos as Latin American military dictators: "In the wake of the Latin American independence movement in the early 19th century, politically unstable conditions and the long experience of armed conflict led to the emergence in many of the new countries of strongmen who were often charismatic and whose hold on power depended on control over armed followers, patronage, and vigilance. Because their power was based on violence and personal relations, the legitimacy of the caudillos' rule was always in doubt, and few could withstand the

challenges of new leaders who emerged among their own followers and wealthy patrons", <http://concise.britannica.com/ebc/ article?eu=385370>.

[15] FONCODES is an antipoverty social fund of the central government that manages US$500mn of public budget and loans from multilateral organizations like World Bank and Inter-American Development Bank.

[16] INFES is the Institute for Educational and Health Infrastructure which aims to build public schools and medical centres mainly on poverty districts in Peru. INFES' budget is less than US$100mn and part of it comes from international loans.

[17] Lima is the capital city of Peru. Its population is over 7 million.

[18] This is a middle-class district which population is under 200,000 people. However its local government is well managed and organised which enabled to do the research.

[19] Tarapoto is a flourishing city of San Martin Region which is located in the jungle of Peru.

[20] La Banda de Shilcayo is a rural district close to Tarapoto City.

[21] See <www.mef.gob.pe> in order to navigate the SIAF (Sistema Integrado de Administración Financiera). The data available facilitates to see the public spending, however it is not possible to examine if the resources reached the children or the poor people, for instance.

REFERENCES

Beltrán, A. R. Cortez, J. Chacaltana y E. Vásquez (eds.) (2000), *Development for a social strategy for Peru*, Lima: Universidad del Pacífico.

Encyclopaedia Britannica, <http://concise.britannica.com/ebc/article?eu=385370>.

Health Ministry of Peru, (2002), <http://www.minsa.gob.pe/LOGROS/>.

Instituto Cuanto (1994, 1997, 2000), *Living Standard Nacional Survey (ENNIV)*, Lima: Instituto Cuanto.

Instituto Nacional de Estadistica e Información (1997-2002), *National Household Survey (ENAHO)*, Lima: INEI.

Instituto Nacional de Estadistica e Informatica (1992-2002), *Demographic and Family Health Survey, (ENDES)*, Lima: INEI.

Ministry of Economy and Finance, *Sistema de Intergrado de Informacion financiera (SIAF)*, <www.mef.gob.pe>.

UNESCO-OECD (2003), *Basic aptitudes for the world of tomorrow*.

Vásquez, E. (2002), *Boys and girls visualization methodology in public budgets in Peru: Local Municipality of San Borja (Lima)*, Lima: Universidad del Pacífico/Save the Children Sweden.

— (2002), *Boys and girls visualization methodology in public budgets in Peru: Municipality of Lima*, Lima: Universidad del Pacífico/Save the Children Sweden.

— (2002), *Boys and girls visualization methodology in public budgets in Peru: Social Development and Compensation National Fund (FONCODES)*, Lima: Universidad del Pacífico/Save the Children Sweden.

— (2003), *Boys and girls visualization methodology in public budgets in Peru: Educative and Health Infrastructure National Institute (INFES)*, Lima: Universidad del Pacífico/Save the Children Sweden.

— (2003), *Boys and girls visualization methodology in public budgets in Peru: Local Municipality of La Banda del Shilcayo (Tarapoto, San Martin)*, Lima: Universidad del Pacífico/Save the Children Sweden.

— (2003), *Boys and girls visualization methodology in public budgets in Peru: Municipality of San Martin*, Lima: Universidad del Pacífico/Save the Children Sweden.

— (2004), *Children First? Study of Focalized Social Expenditure in Children in Peru: 2001-2003 Volume II*, Lima: Universidad del Pacífico/Save the Children Sweden.

Vásquez, E. and E. Mendizabal (eds.) (2002), *Children First? Study of Focalized Social Expenditure in Children in Peru: 1990-2000*, Lima: Universidad del Pacífico/Save the Children Sweden.

Vásquez, E. and D. Winkelried (2003) *Looking for the well-being of poor people: How far we are?* Lima: Universidad del Pacífico.

Vásquez, E. and J. Porras (2003). *The social programs and the manoeuvre margin of the local governments within the framework of the decentralization process.* Lima: Universidad del Pacífico.

Chapter 8

Maternal and Child Health Status in Diber Prefecture, Albania

Malik Jaffer, Karen Z. Waltensperger, Erika Lutz, Fabian Cenko, Ermira Brasha, Gazmend Koduzi, James Ricca

BACKGROUND

The Republic of Albania, located in South East Europe. Slightly smaller than the US State of Maryland, the country has a population of approximately 3.1 million. Albania's geography and history have shaped it into a modern nation with isolated populations, poor infrastructure, and low socio-economic status as reflected by its gross national income (GNI) per capita of $1,380. Albania ranks 95/151 ("medium human development") on the Human Development Index. Life expectancy is 73.4 years; and the adult literacy rate is 85.3% (UNDP, 2003, Human Development Report, p. 242).

The *health status of children* in Albania has declined steadily since the fall of communism in the early 1990s and throughout the turbulent decade of transition that followed, particularly in the underserved northern region. Diber Prefecture is an impoverished, underserved, rural mountainous area in northeastern Albania spanning 2,356 square kilometers with over 26% of the population living in poverty *(income less than $2 per day)* and 44% living in extreme poverty *(income less than $1 per day)* (INSTAT, 1998, Results of Household Living Survey). Over 72% of the active population is engaged in the small-scale private agriculture (UNICEF, 2000, Assessment of Social and Economic Conditions of Districts in Albania). Diber Prefecture is composed of the three districts of Mat, Bulqize, and Diber with 3 main urban centers, 32 communes and 279 rural villages.

Diber and Bulqize Districts are reported to have the highest rates of infant mortality in the country, but accurate district-level data is unavailable. Albania 2000 MICS reports national infant mortality rate (IMR) at 28/1,000, and the under five mortality rates (U5MR) at 33/1,000

(UNICEF, 2000, Albania MICS Report, p 7). Albania's IMR is nearly double that of the Eastern European average (14/1,000). According to the Ministry of Health (MOH)/ Institute of Public Health (IPH), the main causes of infant mortality in Albania are respiratory infections, congenital abnormalities, diarrhea, and infectious diseases (UNICEF, 2000, Albania MICS Report, p. 19). Lower respiratory infections (especially pneumonia) and diarrhea are the leading causes of under five morbidity and mortality nationwide and in Diber Prefecture. Malnutrition is an important underlying cause of infant mortality and morbidity. Additionally, the Albania 2000 UNICEF Multiple Indicator Cluster Survey (MICS) reported a nationwide stunting rate of 17% (severely stunted) (UNICEF, 2000, Albania MICS Report, p. 23). Albania's health service delivery system is centralized, with no current prefectural-level health authority. The District Public Health Directorates are responsible for health service delivery at the district level.

In 2002, the American Red Cross (ARC) and Albania Red Cross (AlbRC) used the results of the MICS in mobilizing resources for the population in one of the most underserved regions of Albania; children and women in the impoverished, underserved northeast region, specifically in Diber Prefecture. The ARC and AlbRC used the MICS results, along with the UNICEF Global Database, to portray a compelling picture of the Albania child health needs in a proposal submitted to the United States Agency for International Development (USAID) Global Bureau Child Survival and Health Grant Program. This proposal resulted in the first ever USAID Child Survival grant awarded for Albania in 2003.

The five year USAID grant for Albania, dubbed "The Albania Child Survival Project" (ACSP) broadly aims to improve the use of child health and family planning services and key family practices by targeting 19,950 children under five years old, 55,417 women of reproductive age (15-49 years), and 68,153 men (15-59 years) in Diber Prefecture. To gain a better understanding of the specific health issues and possible interventions in Diber Prefecture, a baseline Knowledge, Practice, and Coverage (KPC) household survey was undertaken in October 2003. The data obtained was compared with the information in the MICS. The methodology and the results of the KPC survey and its comparison to the MICS are presented in this paper.

METHODOLOGY

The target population for the KPC survey were mothers with living children aged 0-23 months (born between November 1, 2001 and October 31, 2003), living in Diber Prefecture. In addition, to assess nutritional status, anthropometric data was collected for all children 0-59 months in the household.

Sampling Design

The design used for the KPC survey was a two-stage 30-cluster sampling method. Each district was considered as a study unit, and the two-stage sampling technique involved a) cluster sampling in each district and b) simple random sampling for children 0-23 months within each cluster. Random sampling was obtained in both stages.

The indicators requiring the largest sample size were those related to stunting. For these, a sample size of 600 was estimated to be satisfactory. This sample size ensured statistical significance for all the other indicators when evaluated in time. The resulting sample size was n=569 with two mothers with children refusing to answer questions.

Questionnaire

The Knowledge, Practice and Coverage questionnaire was adapted from KPC 2000+ (Espuet D., MACRO Child Survival Technical Support Project), with additional complementary feeding questions drawn from *Generating Indicators of Appropriate Feeding of Children 6-23 Months from the KPC 2000+* (Arimond M. and Ruel, M. T., 2003, International Food Research Policy Research Institute). Local partners and stakeholders were consulted in survey development; and survey questions were compared to MICS to make them as comparable as possible.

Data Collection

In the first half of October 2003, the project team developed a 3-day curriculum to train six supervisors, who in turn trained 29 female interviewers during a 5-day period that included a day of field testing. Supervisors and interviewers comprised members of the project technical team, representatives of the MOH, IPH, Tirana University Hospital, USAID/JSI reproductive health project and volunteers.

Data Analysis

Data was analyzed following recommendations from the KPC 2000+ Field Guide (Espeut D., MACRO Child Survival Technical Support Project) and <http://www.childsurvival.com/kpc2000/kpc2000.cfm#FieldGuide>). Anthropometric data was analyzed using EPI INFO v 6.04. EPINUT *Anthropometry* was used to calculate height-for-age. Indicators were calculated for prefecture and district, and the prefecture level data was weighted to account for differing district sizes.

RESULTS

The results are separated into four key categories: Nutrition and Micronutrients, Control of Diarrheal Diseases (CDD), Acute Respiratory Infection (ARI), and Family Planning (FP). A summary of comparable MICS results and KPC results are in Table 1.

Nutrition and Micronutrients

Anthropometry: Results of the KPC survey indicate that 18.6% of *children under five* in Diber Prefecture are stunted. This prefecture level result is comparable to the countrywide stunting rate of 17% reported in the MICS. Rates for both underweight and wasting are higher in Diber Prefecture than in Albania as a whole. The proportion of children underweight in the prefecture is 14.3% (compared to 4% countrywide); and the proportion of children wasted is 14.3%, compared to 4% countrywide.

Immediate breastfeeding: At a behavioral level, the KPC survey reveals sub-optimal breastfeeding practices in the prefecture. Although 90% of births in the prefecture take place in health facilities, and 98% are attended by trained health workers; only 31% of neonates benefit from initiation of breastfeeding within the first hour after delivery.

Exclusive breastfeeding: KPC results for the prefecture reflect exclusive breastfeeding rates as follows: 64.1% for children 0-1 month; 45.3% for children 0-3 months; *34.3% for children 0-5 months.* On a positive note, the 45.3% exclusive breastfeeding rate found for children 0-3 months in the prefecture is significantly higher than the countrywide rate of 9% reported for this age group by UNICEF (UNICEF, 2000, Albania MICS Report, p. 23).

Continued breastfeeding: While 82% of children 6-11 months benefit from continued breastfeeding; 59.7% are still breastfed at 12-17 months compared to the 65% reported by UNICEF for children 12-15 months (UNICEF, 2000, Albania MICS Report, p. 23); and only 28.2% of children 18-23 months are still breastfed compared to 6% (children 20-23 months) reported in the MICS report.

Complementary feeding: The KPC findings shows the proportion of children aged 6-9 months who receive breast milk plus solid or semi-solid foods is 81.9% in contrast to 24% reported by UNICEF (UNICEF, 2000, Albania MICS Report, p. 23). The proportion of children 6-8 months and 9-23 months that are fed at least the minimum recommended number of times daily is 89.6%. More than ninety percent (91.1%) of children 6-23 months are given food from animal sources on a daily basis. Eighty-seven percent (87%) are fed dairy products; 35.7% are fed eggs; and 29.7% are fed meat, poultry, or fish. KPC findings for complementary feeding seem to suggest more positive household behaviors than for breastfeeding. However, because of the disparity between MICS finding and the project's KPC results for complementary feeding, further investigation into infant and young child feeding practices will be undertaken through qualitative and quantitative studies as the project progresses.

Nutritional management during illness: The KPC survey found that half (50.3%) of all children 0-23 months had been sick in the past two weeks. This is higher than the 15% of children reported to have had diarrhea or some other illness in the previous two weeks prior to the MICS (UNICEF, 2000, Albania MICS Report, p. 27). Of the children who were reported sick in the KPC, only a third (33%) had been offered the same amount or more fluid or food during the illness compared with 62% during the MICS (UNICEF, 2000, Albania MICS Report, p. 28). The KPC did however show that 93.9% of children had been offered increased food and fluid during recovery from the illness.

Use of iodized salt: Only half of all households (50.6%) surveyed in the KPC used iodized salt for cooking and family consumption. This is comparable to the rate of 47.8% for rural areas reported in the MICS results (UNICEF, 2000, Albania MICS Report, p. 24).

Low birth weight: The MICS report estimates that approximately 3% of newborns in Albania weigh less than 2500 grams at birth, but this is thought to be under-estimated. According to the MICS findings, prevalence of LBW does not vary much between urban and rural areas or by mother's education (UNICEF, 2000, Albania MICS Report, p. 25).

Antenatal nutritional management: While 86.6% of mothers in Diber Prefecture had had at least one antenatal visit during most recent pregnancy, less than 10% received iron or iron/folate supplementation. Of those that were supplemented, the average duration of iron supplementation was only 35 days. Of those mothers in the prefecture who received antenatal care, only 21% reported having been counseled on the importance of diet, workload, and rest during pregnancy. Routine post-partum vitamin A supplementation is not currently supported by MOH policies, norms, and protocols; and only 3.6% of mothers report having been supplemented with vitamin A following most recent delivery. The results of the KPC are congruent with the MICS results which indicates that about 3% of mothers who gave birth in the year prior to the survey were supplemented with vitamin A within eight weeks of the birth (UNICEF, 2000, Albania MICS Report, p. 25).

Control of Diarrheal Diseases (CDD)

Handwashing behaviors: While 86.6% of the surveyed mothers in Diber Prefecture reported hand washing with soap before food preparation, only 73.2% reported hand washing with soap prior to feeding children; and only 67.5% reported hand washing with soap following child's defecation. Only 31% of mothers reported hand washing at all appropriate times.

Breastfeeding practice: A significant proportion of infants are exposed to contaminants because of sub-optimal breastfeeding practices: only a third (34.3%) of children 0-5 months are exclusively breastfed; and a third (32%) of children 0-11 months are fed fluids by bottle.

Use of Oral Rehydration Therapy (ORT): Although three quarters (76.7%) of Diber Prefecture mothers surveyed at baseline were able to correctly prepare oral rehydration solution (ORS) from commercially-available sachets, only 16.3% of children 0-23 months with diarrhea in the last two weeks received oral rehydration therapy (e.g., ORS or recommended home fluids). This result compares unfavorably with the MICS finding of a national average of 94% of children with diarrhea who received one or more of the recommended home treatments (e.g., ORS or recommended home fluids).

Antibiotic use: Families of more than half (54%) of children with diarrhea in the last two weeks sought outside treatment. Three quarters (65.8%) of those children taken to health facilities were taken within 48 hours of diarrhea onset. Greater than a third of children with diarrhea (35.6%) received antibiotics from the health facility, pharmacy, or other source; a rate suggesting that simple diarrhea may be treated inappropriately with antibiotics. In Albania, most prescribed medications, including ORS and antibiotics, may be obtained without cost for children 0-11 months and are subsidized for children under five with a health card from the Health Insurance Institute.

At the community level, antibiotics are not available through village nurse midwives, even those trained in clinical IMCI. The results of a health facilities survey conducted by the ACSP indicate that less than two-thirds (61.4%) of village nurse midwives have ORS sachets available, and none of the commune health centers or rural ambulancas (generally defined as a village health post) visited had dedicated ORT corners. The health facilities assessments asked village nurse midwives for topics of home visits: more than half (52.9% indicated "handwashing" as a topic; and 17.6% indicated "management of diarrhea".

Immunization status: As measles is associated with diarrhea, it is useful to review the current status of measles in Albania. After 1992, measles cases were increasing annually and eventually reached approximately 10,000 per year at the end of the decade. During 2000-2002, the Albania MOH/IPH conducted two nationwide campaigns that led to the current "elimination phase" for measles. In 2003, only 28 suspected cases of measles were reported countrywide, and no cases were laboratory confirmed. Moreover, Albania has been able to achieve relatively high-performance routine vaccination against measles, with 98% national coverage for the first dose (at 12-14 months) and 90% for the second dose (at 5 years). KPC results for Diber Prefecture show 70.4% coverage, confirmed by vaccination card or mother's recall.

Water and sanitation: KPC results for water and sanitation in Diber Prefecture reflect conditions that prevail in much of Albania. Fewer than half of the families (42.4%) in Diber Prefecture have water piped into the house. About a fifth of families (19.7%) get water from a standpipe in the yard; and another fifth (18.9%) take water from a public standpipe or tap. A little more than half of households in the prefecture (54.4%) have indoor flush toilet systems; 14.5% have outdoor flush systems; and a third (31.1%) use pit latrines.

Acute Respiratory Infection

Recognition of danger signs and care seeking: At the household level, there is poor recognition of the most important danger sign for pneumonia in children under five which is cough with "fast and difficult breathing". Although 89.6% of mothers surveyed were able to cite at least two danger signs for illness in children, and 41.9% were able to cite four; however, only 8.3% were able to cite "fast or difficult breathing" as one of the danger signs. This differs from MICS results which indicate that 55% of mothers would take their children to a health facility right away if the children had difficulty breathing (UNICEF, 2000, Albania MICS Report, p. 28). For neonates, 22% of mothers cited "fast or difficult breathing" as a danger sign; and more than half (51%) cited "poor feeding". It is common practice to bundle children heavily against the cold and strap them into wooden cradles piled with warm covers. Often, this makes it difficult for mothers to observe a child's breathing.

"High fever" was the danger sign most commonly cited for children under five by 88.4% of mothers. UNICEF reports that 85% of mothers indicated that if their child developed a fever, they would take the child to health facility "right away" (UNICEF, 2000, Albania MICS Report, p. 28). "Vomits everything" was cited by 53.3% of mothers; "not eating or drinking" by 45.8% of mothers; "looks unwell" by 22.6% of mothers; "lethargic or difficult to wake" by 4.6% of mothers.

Prefectural level baseline results show that nearly three quarters (62.8%) of children 0-23 months who experienced cough and fast/difficult breathing in the two weeks prior to the survey were taken to a health facility and received antibiotics. However, only half (49.4%) of children with cough AND fast/difficult breathing were taken to a health facility for treatment *within 48 hours of illness onset.* Of those children with cough and fast/difficult breathing treated at a health facility, a majority (82%) received antibiotics. Of those not treated at a health facility, 6.5% received antibiotics from other sources.

Family Planning

Total fertility rate (TFR): *The recent (2002) National Reproductive Health Survey estimates Albania's TFR at 2.6 (Herold J., et al., 2003, Reproductive Health Survey Albania 2002: Preliminary Report, p. 11). The report further states that the rate is:*

> ...a bit higher than the rate published by WHO for 2001 (2.4) and the rate of 2.3 published by the UN Population Division (WHO, 2003; UN, 2003). There is no difference in the TFR by urban or rural residence...The TFR is the highest in Europe and higher than the TFR in 10 of the 13 countries in Eastern Europe and the former Soviet Union that have conducted similar Reproductive Health Surveys...

Adequate birth interval: KPC findings indicate that 74.4% of the children 0-23 months whose mothers were surveyed, were born at least 24 months after the previous surviving child; and 36% were born at least 36 months after the previous surviving child.

Contraceptive awareness: Contraceptive awareness is generally high in Albania. The national Reproductive Health Survey preliminary results indicate that nearly all women (96%) are aware of at least one family planning method, with 90% aware of at least one *modern* method, and 84% *aware* of a traditional method. Of the modern methods, the condom was most commonly known (81% of women), followed by the oral pill (68%), and tubal ligation (65%). Awareness of any method of contraception was also reported by the Reproductive Health Survey to be almost universal among men (98%). However, knowledge of specific methods was more limited, with only the condom (89%) and withdrawal (85%) being known by more than half of men (Herold J., et al., 2003, Reproductive Health Survey Albania 2002: Preliminary Report, p. 15).

A preliminary result is reported in the recent Reproductive Health Survey: "...the reported current practice of contraception is relatively high, at 75% for married women and 77% for married men" (Herold J., et al., 2003, Reproductive Health Survey Albania 2002: Preliminary Report, p. 16).

Contraceptive coverage (mothers of children 0-23 months): In Diber Prefecture, the proportion of mothers of children 0-23 months not currently pregnant and not desiring another child in the next two years, or not sure, who are using a modern method of contraception is 12.1%. This is similar to the data obtained from the MICS report. The report indicates that 15% of women married or in union use a modern contraceptive method (UNICEF, 2000, Albania MICS Report, p. 30). However, the KPC data shows that the contraceptive coverage rate varies significantly by district. In Mat District, where USAID promoted family planning through its bi-lateral contractor John Snow International, the coverage rate is 20.8%. In Bulqize District, it is 8.8%; and in Diber District, 7.4%. These findings are comparable to preliminary results reported by the National Reproductive Health Survey of 11% for urban women and 5% for rural women (Herold J., et al., 2003, Reproductive Health Survey Albania 2002: Preliminary Report, p. 17).

Use of non-modern methods of contraception: Most couples in union depend on non-modern methods of contraception. At the prefectural level, nearly half (49.7%) of mothers of children 0-23 months reported using withdrawal as a method. The results of the KPC are similar to the MICS results. The report indicates 42% of married or women in union use a traditional contraceptive method. The report further indicates that 33% of women using contraceptives use the withdrawal method of contraception (UNICEF, 2000, Albania MICS Report, p. 30). However, these rates are almost entirely due to the use of the traditional methods of withdrawal (67% and 72% for married women and men, respectively)

(Herold J., et al., 2003, Reproductive Health Survey Albania, 2002: Preliminary Report, p. 16).

Use of Lactational Amenorrhea Method (LAM): Although the rate of exclusive breastfeeding for children 0-5 months is 34.3%, only 2.7% of mothers of children 0-5 months (not pregnant and not wanting another child in the next two years or not sure) report using lactational amenorrhea method as a method of family planning. This corresponds to MICS results that between 3%-8% of women use LAM and periodic abstinence. (UNICEF, 2000, Albania MICS Report, p. 30)

DISCUSSION

Select findings from the KPC baseline survey in Diber Prefecture and the MICS are split into three categories: similar findings, better KPC findings, and better MICS findings. The difference in results regardless of source may be accountable to regional differences possibly attributable to cultural, social or educational disparities within the country. Additionally, it should be noted that the KPC survey data is drawn from one of the most economically disadvantaged and underserved prefectures in the country, whilst the MICS results represent a national sample of rural and urban areas.

The discrepancy in number of children with illness between the KPC and the MICS may be a result of seasonal differences for the two surveys. The MICS was conducted in summer, the high season for diarrhea; the KPC was conducted in late autumn, generally a low season for diarrhea, and just prior to the high season for acute respiratory infection.

Results from both the MICS and the KPC highlight areas where health care providers' practices and public health services can be improved. It is recommended and expected that a systematic process be established between stakeholders during the life of the project to continuously review progress and share best practices. It is anticipated that District Public Health Directors will share lessons learned with their MOH peers. The process of identification of need, design of intervention strategy and monitoring progress, builds capacity with Albanian partners and can influence decision making at various policy levels.

The four main foci of the KPC were Nutrition and Micronutrients, Control of Diarrhea Disease, Acute Respiratory Infection, and Family Planning.

Nutrition and Micronutrients

Anthropometric findings from the KPC survey conducted in Diber Prefecture reveal that nutritional deficiencies constitute a significant child health problem in the project catchment area and justify the selection of Nutrition and Micronutrients as one of the child survival project technical interventions.

Although a larger percentage of women deliver their children at health facilities and are attended by health practitioners, the rate of immediate breastfeeding within the first hour after birth is low. This finding suggests problems with health worker performance, as well as weak demand on the part of mothers to breastfeed immediately. Mothers remain in the maternity on an average of 72 hours following delivery. However, "rooming in" is not commonly practiced (except in certain facilities in Bulqize where Ministry of Health (MOH) and UNICEF have implemented "baby friendly" hospitals; and newborns are frequently kept in incubators. Further research of the attitudes and beliefs relating to breastfeeding practices, on the part of both mothers and mothers-in-law, is recommended and will be investigated in depth in the qualitative inquiry planned for August 2004.

Rates of continued breastfeeding differ between the KPC survey and MICS. This may be attributed to the different target groups surveyed. For example KPC surveyed for continued breastfeeding for children 18-23 months while UNCIEF surveyed for children 20-23 months. The rates for exclusive breastfeeding for children 0-3 months and complementary feeding of children 6-9 months is better in Diber Prefecture compared to the national data drawn from the MICS.

Control of Diarrheal Disease

WHO estimates that up to 90% of diarrheal episodes are attributable to three main environmental causes: 1) poor sanitation; 2) poor hygiene; 3) contaminated water and foods. Improper sanitation and poor hygiene in the form of low levels of appropriate handwashing may attribute towards high levels of diarrheal diseases. The KPC results of water and sanitation conditions in Diber Prefecture along with the behavioral findings cited in the results justify the selection of CDD as one of the child survival project technical interventions.

Acute Respiratory Infection

As a result of low recognition of "fast/difficult breathing", mothers, grandmothers, and household decision-makers need to be sensitized to the gravity of this danger sign. This is especially important in the young infant (during the first two months of life), who need prompt and appropriate care seeking within 48 hours of onset of illness.

Acute respiratory infection is one of the most common reasons for child health visits to health facilities both nationwide and in Diber Prefecture. Acute lower respiratory infection has been documented as the leading cause of infant mortality in the country (MOH/INSTAT, 2000, Causes of Death for the Year 1998, p. 30) and is named as a leading cause of U5 mortality nationwide (UNICEF, 2000, Albania MICS Report, p. 27) and in the project area as reported by the District Public Health Directors, justifying the selection of ARI as one of the child survival project technical interventions. Education on identifying danger signs and seeking appropriate care need to be an integral component of the intervention.

Family Planning

It is important to appreciate differences between reproductive health status in a Southeast European country like Albania versus other developing countries. To quote the recent national Reproductive Health Survey Preliminary Report (Herold J., et al., 2003, Reproductive Health Survey Albania 2002: Preliminary Report, p. 5):

> A key programmatic difference between policy objectives in Albania compared with those in some developing countries is that the emphasis is not on promoting a decline in fertility and

population growth, but on bringing about improvements in women's health through increased availability and improved use of modern contraceptive methods and reduced reliance on abortion.

A population based family planning survey is scheduled for fall 2004 to identify gaps and gain a fuller understanding of fertility behavior and the needs of Diber Prefecture. The results will influence the implementation of the ACSP family planning intervention. The low rate of use of modern contraceptive methods justifies the selection of family planning as one of the child survival project technical interventions.

CONCLUSION

The MICS Report was used as a foundation for the formulation of health interventions for a USAID-funded child survival project being carried out in Diber Prefecture, by the American Red Cross and Albania Red Cross. The KPC baseline survey confirmed the problems and assisted in narrowing the focus on key areas of knowledge and behavior of the community. These technical intervention areas for the project are: Nutrition, Control of Diarrheal Disease, Acute Respiratory Infection and Family Planning. The KPC in conjunction with the recommended studies has identified these areas to further guide the ACSP implementation strategies.

Table 1. Select Results from KPC and Albania MICS

	KPC	MICS
Stunting	18.6%	17%
Exclusive breastfeeding for children 0-3 months	45.3%	9%
Continued breastfeeding* (12-15/17 months)	59.7%	65%
Continued breastfeeding** (18-20/23 months)	28.2%	6%
Complementary feeding for children 6-9 months	81.9%	24%
Children with illness in last two weeks	50.3%	15%
Children with illness who receive additional fluids or food	33%	62%
Use of iodized salt for cooking or family consumption	50.6%	47.8%
Women who received vitamin A supplementation following birth	3.6%	3%
Children 0-23 months with diarrhea in the last two weeks who received oral rehydration therapy (ORT)	16.3%	94%
Recognition of "high fever" as a danger sign	88.4%	85%
Use of a modern contraceptive	12.1%	15%
Use of withdrawal as a contraceptive method	49.7%	33%
Use of lactational amenorrhea method of contraception	2.7%	3%-8%

*KPC sample includes children 12-17 months and MICS sample includes children 12-15 months
**KPC sample includes children 18-23 months and MICS sample includes children 20-23 months

BIBLIOGRAPHY

Arimond M. and Ruel, M. T. International Food Research Policy Research Institute, 2003.

Espeut D. MACRO Child Survival Technical Support Project.

Herold J., et al. Reproductive Health Survey Albania 2002: Preliminary Report 2003.

<http://www.childsurvival.com/kpc2000/kpc2000.cfm#FieldGuide>, April 2004.

INSTAT. Results of Household Living Survey, 1998.

MOH/INSTAT. Causes of Death for the Year 1998, 2000.

UNDP. Human Development Report, 2003.

UNICEF. Albania MICS Report, 2000.

UNICEF. Assessment of Social and Economic Conditions of Districts in Albania, 2000.

Chapter 9

Exclusive Breastfeeding as an Intervention to Reduce Morbidity and Improve Child Survival in Developing Countries

Seema Mihrshahi, Wendy Oddy and Jennifer K. Peat

INTRODUCTION

Children are the most vulnerable and dependent members of our society. All children have the right to the best start in life, which includes the right to the highest attainable standard of health and access to facilities for the treatment of illness (1). Yet the estimated number of child deaths worldwide in the year 2000 was 10.8 million. The majority of these deaths are in developing countries with the regions of Sub-Saharan Africa and South Asia carrying the greatest burden (2). Adequate monitoring of child mortality rates is essential for assessing the progress of children's human rights as well as overall national development. In the year 2000 as part of the Millennium Development Goals for health, nations pledged to ensure a two thirds reduction in child mortality by 2015 (3). This was based on the World Summit for Children goal in 1990, which had called for a worldwide reduction in child mortality to below 70 deaths per 1,000 livebirths by the year 2000 (4).

The most common diseases associated with child deaths worldwide are diarrhoea, pneumonia and malaria (2). Child deaths due to these diseases are a result of several determinants including nutritional status, environmental and maternal factors and lack of access to preventive and curative treatment (5, 6). Socioeconomic factors such as household income and access to clean water and sanitation also influence child mortality through the above determinants. Simple strategies and interventions to affect one or more of these determinants have the potential to make a significant and sustainable impact on child survival.

The importance of breastfeeding as a strategy for child survival has been established. Breastmilk provides protection against pathogens by providing antibacterial and antiviral substances including IgA, lactoferrin, oligosaccharides and cells that stimulate the infant's immune system (7). In developing countries, exclusively breastfed babies are less likely to be exposed to contaminated foods and this contributes to reductions in the incidence and severity of infectious diseases. Infants aged 0-5 months who are not breastfed have a seven-fold increased risk of death from diarrhoea and five-fold increased risk of death from pneumonia, compared with infants who are exclusively breastfed (8). Infants aged 6-11 months who are not breastfed also have an increased risk of death from these diseases. Improving breastfeeding rates can also have a positive effect on birth spacing, which also contributes to child survival (9). Recent estimates predict that exclusive breastfeeding in the first 6 months of life and continued breastfeeding for the first year could prevent 1.3 million child deaths worldwide, making promotion of breastfeeding a key strategy of child survival programs (10).

Other benefits of breastfeeding include improved child growth and development, and the reduced occurrence of chronic diseases, particularly obesity, diabetes and cancer (11). Maternal health effects identified include protection against severe post-partum haemorrhages, breast and ovarian cancers and a significant number of social and economic benefits (12). Breastfeeding also offers a benefit that cannot be measured, an opportunity for emotional bonding between mother and child, laying the foundation of a caring relationship (13).

The current recommendation of the World Health Organization (WHO) is that infants should be fed breastmilk exclusively to 6 months of age (14). Goal number 16 of the World Summit for Children states that nations should empower all women to breastfeed their children for four to 6 months and continue breastfeeding with complementary food well into the second year (4). Recent estimates predict that current breastfeeding patterns are far from recommended levels.

There are many factors that effect initiation and duration of breastfeeding. In developing countries women's heavy burden of responsibilities, the number of children in the family and frequency of pregnancies may affect the exclusivity and duration of breastfeeding. Other risk factors identified for lack of breastfeeding include low educational status and social class, lack of health advice and family support and availability and marketing of breastmilk substitutes (15). Cultural and religious beliefs also play a part in the early cessation of breastfeeding (16, 17). One of the most controversial and challenging issues for breastfeeding promotion in developing countries is the problem of high rates of HIV and possible mother to child transmission (18).

Interventions to promote breastfeeding have included health education, media campaigns, health sector programs such as the Baby-Friendly Hospital Initiative that provides counseling, rooming in, training of health professionals, and community-based initiatives such as peer counseling for pregnant and lactating mothers after discharge from hospital (19). Multifaceted programs that combine the above interventions have also been trialed throughout the developing world (20-25).

Given the importance of breastfeeding as a strategy for child survival this paper aims to use the Multiple Indicator Cluster Survey 2 data to:

1. Compare rates of breastfeeding and complementary feeding (exclusive breastfeeding 0-3 months, continued breastfeeding 12-15 months and 20-23 months, complementary feeding 6-9 months) between regions in the developing world.

2. Investigate the relationship between rates of exclusive breastfeeding and child morbidity, in particular on diarrhoea and acute respiratory infection prevalence.

3. Discuss whether breastfeeding promotion interventions in certain countries have made an impact on breastfeeding rates thereby improving the health, nutrition and progress of children.

METHODS

MICS Survey data

The Multiple Indicator Cluster Surveys 2 (MICS) are nationally representative surveys of households, women and children conducted in 2000. They include information about duration and exclusivity of breastfeeding and complementary feeding practices, childhood illnesses, education and vaccination coverage. Data were accessed from the website <www.childinfo.org> and analyzed in SPSS version 11.5.1.

Breastfeeding rates

Aggregated data on exclusive breastfeeding of children 0-3 months, continued breastfeeding of children 12-15 months and 20-23 months and complementary feeding of children 6-9 months were accessed from country reports. In order to compare breastfeeding rates between regions, countries were grouped into regions as follows: Sub-Saharan Africa, Asia, Latin America/Caribbean, Central and Eastern Europe, North Africa/Middle East. Results were expressed as mean breastfeeding rates with 95% confidence intervals.

Breastfeeding definitions

Breastfeeding status was based on women's report of children's consumption of breastmilk in the 24 hrs prior to the interview.

The exclusive breastfeeding rate was defined as percentage of children 0-3 months of age who received only breastmilk and vitamin, mineral supplements or medicine.

The timely complementary feeding rate was defined as percentage of children aged 6-9 months who received breastmilk and solid or semi solid food.

Outcomes

Distortions in the MICS data on death among children precluded obtaining estimates of mortality rates for most countries. Mortality rates were obtained from the publication State of the World's Children 2004 which listed accurate mortality rates from 2002 (26). Regional mean mortality rates and 95% CI were reported.

Morbidity definitions

Diarrhoea was determined as perceived by mother or caretaker or as three or more loose or watery stools per day, or blood in stool

Q. Has (name) had diarrhoea in the last two weeks?

Acute respiratory infection was defined as a positive response to all of the questions:

Q. Has (name) had an illness with cough in the last two weeks?

Q. When (name) had an illness with cough did she breathe faster than usual with short quick breaths or have difficulty breathing?

Q. Were the symptoms due to a problem in the chest?

Statistical analysis

For countries with available data on exclusive breastfeeding and illness, children 0-3 months who were exclusively breastfed were compared with those not exclusively breastfed. The rates of diarrhoea and acute respiratory illness in the last 2 weeks were compared using chi-squared tests. Relative risks and 95% CI were reported and univariate odds ratios and multivariate odds ratios adjusted for maternal education level and household wealth index were also calculated (data not shown).

RESULTS

Summary data on breastfeeding were available from 50 countries were available of which 23 countries were in Sub-Saharan Africa, 10 in Asia, 7 in Latin America/ Caribbean, 6 in Central and Eastern Europe and 4 in the North Africa/Middle East.

Child mortality rates

Child mortality estimates in 2002 showed large differences between regions. A total of 34 countries or more than two thirds of the total have a child mortality rate of 70 or greater. Mean child mortality rates were highest in Sub-Saharan Africa (171 per 1000 livebirths) and Asia (95 per 1000 livebirths) and lowest in Latin America/ Caribbean (36 per 1000 livebirths). Figure 1 shows the mean child mortality rates for these regions with error bars showing the 95% confidence intervals.

Figure 1. Mean child mortality rates in regions

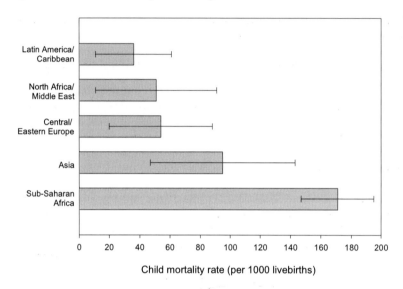

Child mortality rate (per 1000 livebirths)

Breastfeeding patterns

Mean exclusive breastfeeding rates in children aged 0-3 months of age ranged from 19% in North Africa and the Middle East, 20% in Latin America/Caribbean, 27% in Central and Eastern Europe, 28% in Sub-Saharan Africa and 40% in Asia. Mean exclusive breastfeeding rates are shown in Figure 2 with error bars showing the 95% confidence intervals. Mean rates of continued (any) breastfeeding are shown in Figure 3. Continued breastfeeding rates to age 12-15 months were high in Sub-Saharan Africa (83%) and Asia (81%) and much lower in Latin America and the Caribbean (42%), Central and Eastern Europe (50%) and North Africa/Middle East (49%). The breastfeeding rate to 20-23 months followed a similar trend with rates in Africa (45%) and Asia (47%) much higher than Latin America and the Caribbean (19%), Central and Eastern Europe (19%) and North Africa and Middle East (22%).

Figure 2. Mean exclusive breastfeeding rates in regions

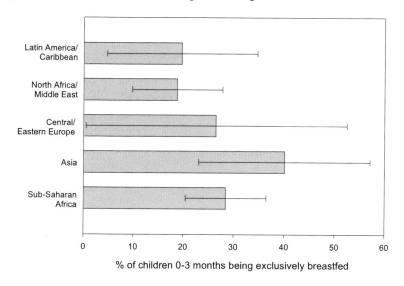

% of children 0-3 months being exclusively breastfed

Figure 3. Mean rates ofcontinued breastfeeding to 12-15 months and 20-23 months

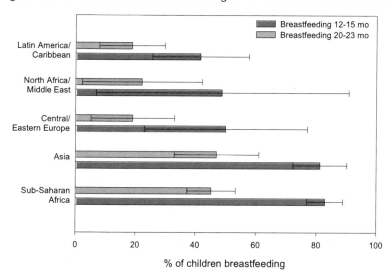

% of children breastfeeding

Rates of timely complementary feeding

Complementary feeding rates in children age 6-9 months ranged from 34% in Central and Eastern Europe, 40% in Latin America and the Caribbean, 49% in Asia, 50% in North Africa and Middle East to 56% in Sub-Saharan Africa and are shown in Figure 4.

Figure 4. Mean rates of timely complementary feeding in regions

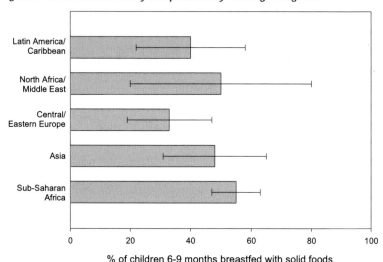

% of children 6-9 months breastfed with solid foods

Relation between exclusive breastfeeding and diarrhoea and acute respiratory infection prevalence

Individual MICS 2 datasets were available for 31 countries of which 21 had information on exclusive breastfeeding. Table 1 shows that diarrhoea prevalence in the last 2 weeks was significantly associated with lack of exclusive breastfeeding in 5 countries, all in Africa. Figure 5 plots the relative risks with error bars showing the 95% confidence intervals. A relative risk of less than 1 with error bars that do not overlap 1 shows a protective effect. When data were combined the pooled relative risk was 0.54. Even when the data was adjusted for maternal education level and wealth index (data not shown) there was an overall protective effect.

Table 2 shows of the 21 countries; only in the Central African Republic was lack of exclusive breastfeeding associated with acute respiratory infection (RR=0.33 95% CI 0.15-0.70, p=0.002).

Figure 5. Relative risk for diarrhoea in exclusively breastfed vs non-exclusively breastfed infants from 0-3 months

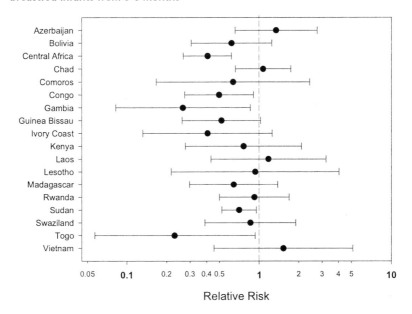

Table 1. *Relative risks for diarrhoea in the last 2 weeks in infants exclusively breastfed at 0-3 months compared with infants who were not exclusively breastfed*

Country	N (N)	EBF	Diarrhoea prevalence in last 2 weeks		% Diff	Relative Risk (95% CI)	P value
			Non-EBF group	EBF group			
Albania	78	7	11.3%	0%	11.30%		
Azerbaijan	106	16	27.8%	37.5%	-9.7%	1.35 (0.66-2.76)	0.431
Bolivia	232	127	15.2%	9.4%	5.8%	0.62 (0.31-1.25)	0.178
Central African R.	1212	243	22.2%	9.1%	13.1%	0.41(0.27-0.62)	0.0001
Chad	377	43	28.1%	30.2%	-2.1%	1.07 (0.66-1.75)	0.77
Comoros	250	18	17.5%	11.1%	6.4%	0.64 (0.17-2.42)	0.489
Congo	650	193	12.5%	6.2%	6.3%	0.50 (0.27-0.91)	0.018
Dominican Rep.	137	22	9.6%	0%	9.6%		
Gambia	247	79	14.3%	3.8%	10.5%	0.27 (0.08-0.86)	0.014
Guinea Bissau	457	125	14.2%	7.2%	7.0%	0.52 (0.26-1.03)	0.051
Guyana	124	21	5.8%	0%	5.8%		
Ivory Coast	709	66	11.0%	4.5%	6.5%	0.41(0.13-1.26)	0.100
Kenya	477	71	7.4%	5.6%	1.8%	0.76 (0.28-2.10)	0.596
Laos	390	96	4.4%	5.2%	-0.8%	1.18 (0.43-3.22)	0.78
Lesotho	226	36	5.9%	5.6%	0.3%	0.93 (0.22-4.03)	0.927
Madagascar	458	226	6.9%	4.4%	2.5%	0.64 (0.30-1.38)	0.253
Rwanda	227	137	16.7%	15.3%	1.4%	0.92 (0.50-1.69)	0.787
Sudan	1675	304	19.7%	13.8%	5.9%	0.70 (0.52-0.95)	0.017
Swaziland	207	56	14.6%	12.5%	2.1%	0.86 (0.39-1.90)	0.703
Togo	241	54	16.1%	3.7%	12.4%	0.23 (0.06-0.93)	0.018
Vietnam	135	41	6.40%	9.80%	-3.40%	1.53 (0.46-5.13)	0.491

Table 2. Relative risks for acute respiratory infection (ARI) in the last 2 weeks in infants exclusively breastfed at 0-3 months compared with infants who were not exclusively breastfed

Country	ARI prevalence in last 2 weeks		% Diff	Relative Risk (95% CI)	P value
	Non-EBF group	EBF group			
Albania	1.4%	0%	1.4%		
Azerbaijan	2.2%	0%	2.2%		
Bolivia	2.9%	7.9%	-5.0%	2.75 (0.78-9.71)	0.098
Central African Rep.	8.8%	2.9%	5.9%	0.33 (0.15-0.70)	0.002
Chad	8.1%	18.6%	-10.5%	2.30 (1.12-4.74)	0.025
Comoros	7.0%	5.6%	1.4%	0.79 (0.11-5.65)	0.817
Congo	6.6%	7.7%	-1.1%	1.18 (0.04-2.19)	0.596
Dominican Republic	14.8%	4.5%	10.3%	0.31 (0.04-2.43)	0.193
Gambia	4.2%	1.3%	2.9%	0.30 (0.04-2.43)	0.230
Guinea Bissau	4.4%	7.2%	-2.8%	1.63 (0.73-3.62)	0.231
Guyana	4.9%	4.8%	0.1%	0.98 (0.12-8.00)	0.986
Ivory Coast	2.4%	0%	2.4%		
Kenya	5.4%	4.2%	1.2%	0.78 (0.24-2.54)	0.677
Laos	0.3%	2.1%	-1.8%	6.13 (0.56-66.67)	0.090
Lesotho	0.5%	2.8%	-2.3%	5.13 (0.33-83.33)	0.195
Madagascar	3.0%	1.3%	1.7%	0.44 (0.12-1.68)	0.216
Rwanda	5.6%	6.6%	-1.0%	1.18 (0.41-3.41)	0.756
Sudan	3.2%	2.0%	1.2%	0.61 (0.26-1.42)	0.247
Swaziland	4.6%	5.4%	-0.8%	1.16 (0.31-4.31)	0.830
Togo	9.4%	3.7%	5.7%	0.39 (0.09-1.64)	0.176
Vietnam	6.4%	2.4%	4.0%	0.38 (0.05-3.08)	0.342

DISCUSSION

The goals set in the Millennium Declaration in relation to child mortality and breastfeeding are far from being achieved. Child mortality rates are unacceptably high in all developing countries and in 34 out of 50 countries included in the analysis, child mortality rates were higher than 70 per 1000 livebirths. With regard to breastfeeding, rates of exclusive breastfeeding are well below recommended levels in all regions. Although the rates of continued breastfeeding to one year are over 80% in Sub-Saharan Africa and Asia, less than half of infants are still breastfeeding at two years of age. The low rate of exclusive breastfeeding combined with high rates of any breastfeeding in the first year, suggest that although breastfeeding is widely practiced, children are being supplemented with foods that are inadequate for their nutritional needs in the critical first months of life. This leaves them susceptible to infectious diseases, which are the primary cause of child mortality.

In five of 21 countries, lack of exclusive breastfeeding was associated with higher prevalence of diarrhoea in the 2 weeks preceding the survey. We found that even after controlling for factors such as mother's education level, the risk of diarrhoea was increased in infants who were not exclusively breastfed. However the same association was not apparent in regard to acute respiratory infection. These results are similar to the findings of other studies (9, 27) and confirm that exclusive breastfeeding is important in regions where child deaths due to infectious diseases are high.

The MICS 2 data remain, for many countries, the only data collection tool for the assessment of the Millennium Development and World Summit for Children goals and the only reliable source of information for the monitoring of children's rights and wellbeing. Despite this, limitations in MICS 2 data are apparent. In regard to figures for exclusive breastfeeding, there are very small numbers of children aged 0-3 months in most of the surveys and larger numbers are needed in order to estimate accurate rates of exclusive breastfeeding. In addition, the use of 24 hr recall questionnaires tend to overestimate the percentage of infants who have been exclusively breastfed since birth because infants who are given other liquids irregularly may not have received them in the 24 hrs before the survey.

With regard to the morbidity data, the illness questionnaire required the mother to give a response based on her understanding of diarrhoea and other illnesses and may have required more than yes or no responses. This raised the possibility of interviewer and responder error, which could not be corrected for in these analyses. Other biases include reverse causality and confounding which occurs when factors relating to breastfeeding practices are also related to morbidity (28, 29). Common confounding variables include socioeconomic status, maternal age or education status and presence of clean water and sanitation facilities. We corrected for maternal education and used a household wealth index as a measure of socioeconomic status. However, we were not able to correct for other factors that were associated with morbidity, for example, maternal nutrition or low birth weight.

There are also inherent biases associated with ecological analyses and the use of aggregated data as was the case in our calculation of breastfeeding and mortality rates. The units of observation were summary statistics from the populations studied rather than measurements from individual subjects. This method of analysis is appropriate for monitoring crude rates and describing variations between populations, however we could not use these rates to identify effects of breastfeeding on mortality or to infer causation because it was not possible to control for confounding. Hence, we used the disaggregated data from the limited number of countries for which it was available to examine the association between exclusive breastfeeding and diarrhoea and acute respiratory illness. More evidence from such cluster surveys needs to be collected, so that the true effectiveness of breastfeeding in reducing child mortality and morbidity can be measured and such biases can be minimised.

Governments will not be successful in their attempts to improve economic development unless optimal child nutrition and health, through appropriate infant feeding practices, are ensured. Wide dissemination of the MICS 2 results could be used as an opportunity to encourage governments to reassess their priorities in regard to children's well-being and breastfeeding promotion. Many governments, for example, have adopted the Baby Friendly Hospital Initiative (BFHI), which has made a significant impact on breastfeeding practices globally. Breastfeeding promotion and support is also a key element of the Integrated Management of Childhood Illness strategy, which encompasses a range of specific interventions to prevent and manage the major causes of morbidity and mortality and integrate breastfeeding as an essential part of clinical care.

Simple breastfeeding promotion interventions that have been trialed in developing countries are showing encouraging results. Two case studies have been chosen to illustrate examples of strategies that have the potential to achieve a significant public health impact, that of Madagascar in Africa and the state of Haryana in India. Both these case studies are in regions of the world where child mortality is at its highest levels.

Madagascar

The child mortality rate for Madagascar is 136 per 1000 children livebirths (26). It has been estimated that a total of 54% of all deaths in children aged less than 5 years are due to malnutrition. A major cause of death and malnutrition is sub-optimal breastfeeding practices. In 1999, a community based child survival and reproductive health project was launched. The project goals were to improve breastfeeding, related complementary feeding, control micronutrient deficiencies and improve family planning practices (25). The strategy combined interpersonal communication, women's group activities and large-scale media involvement. The communication component included home visits and counseling at health clinics. Women's groups facilitated nutrition promotion, health talks and drama workshops. The media component featured radio and television advertisements, traditional singers and appointment of a pop star as the country's breastfeeding and nutrition ambassador.

An assessment of the program and control sites was conducted in October 2001. Comparisons were made with the 1999 baseline survey. The results demonstrated significant improvements in practices as measured by key indicators:

• Initiation of breastfeeding within the first hour increased from 34% at baseline to 69% in 2001

• Exclusive breastfeeding among women with infants less than 6 months of age increased from 46% at baseline to 79% in 2001.

• Timely complementary feeding among infants 6 months of age more than doubled in the program area (75%) compared with the control area (33%).

• Infants under 6 months of age who were not exclusively breastfed had a relative risk of diarrhoea of 3.75 compared with exclusively breastfed infants (p=0.02).

India

India has the highest number of child deaths in the world, estimated at 2.4 million (2).

In the state of Haryana, a large-scale cluster randomised controlled trial was conducted from 1998 to 2002. The purpose was to evaluate the effectiveness of community based interventions to improve exclusive breastfeeding during the first 6 months and complementary feeding thereafter and to assess the impact on diarrhoeal illness and growth (23). The study covered a population of 40,000 out of which a cohort of 552 infants in intervention communities and 473 infants in control communities were enrolled for evaluation.

The design of the intervention was highly participatory and involved community representatives, and health workers including traditional birth attendants, nurses and midwives, and local village based workers (Anganwadi workers) who belonged to the Integrated Child Development Service (23). Community representatives were selected to provide nutrition counseling to mothers throughout their infants first year. They helped to convert nutrition recommendations into local culturally acceptable messages at regular neighbourhood meetings by using songs and theatre. Communications materials that were developed included flipcharts, clinic posters and feeding recommendation cards for mothers.

Evaluation data indicated that

- Exclusive breastfeeding at 3 months of age was 79% in the intervention communities and 48% in the control communities (p<0.001)

- Inappropriate feeding of newborns dropped to 31% in the intervention communities compared with 75% in the control communities (p<0.001).

- The seven day prevalence of diarrhoea was significantly reduced by 8% at 3 months (p=0.028) and 3% at six months (p=0.037) in the intervention group infants when compared with the control group infants.

These two community-based strategies show that potentially sustainable interventions to promote optimal infant feeding are effective and could be replicated on larger scales to achieve an impact on child health and survival. Common elements of both interventions included partnerships between government health services, non-governmental agencies, traditional birth attendants, community leaders and community groups. Both interventions involved a substantial amount of preliminary research to clarify local values, beliefs and practices that affect breastfeeding behavior. Through this, culturally appropriate and effective messages were developed. Most importantly, both interventions involved the active engagement of women's groups and this served a dual purpose of empowering women with the knowledge and resources that could improve their child's nutrition and health while at the same time improving their status in the community.

CONCLUSION

This paper focuses on the potential of breastfeeding as a strategy to improve the health, nutrition and survival of children. Children have the right to optimal nutrition and health. The Convention on the Rights of the Child specifically calls for informing all segments of society about child health and nutrition including the advantages of breastfeeding. The World Summit for Children in 1990 called for the empowerment of all women to breastfeed their children exclusively for four to six months and to continue breastfeeding, with complementary foods well into the second year. We found that fewer than half of all infants are being exclusively breastfed for up to three months. Although levels of continued breastfeeding are relatively high at one year of age, less than half of infants are still breastfeeding at two years of age. Thus, the current breastfeeding patterns are well below recommended levels. The MICS 2 data show that in many countries exclusive breastfeeding in the first months of life is associated with a reduced prevalence of diarrhoea, a major cause of ill health and child mortality in developing countries. Simple community based interventions have been shown to be effective in increasing breastfeeding rates and improving child health. Well designed and locally acceptable communication strategies including the media, training of health care workers and community representatives to provide appropriate counseling to mothers and active involvement of women's groups provide the foundation on which to base breastfeeding promotion as a child survival strategy.

REFERENCES

1. Convention on the Rights of the Child. UN General Assembly resolution 44/25 of 20 November 1989. <www.unicef.org/crc/crc.htm>, accessed 3/1/2004.

2. Black, RE, Morris SS, Bryce J. Where and why are 10 million children dying every year? Lancet. 2003; 361(9376): 2226-34.

3. UN General Assembly, 56th Session. Road map towards the implementation of the United Nations Millennium Declaration: a report of the Secretary-General. New York: United Nations, 2001.

4. UNICEF. Progress since the world summit for children: a statistical review. UNICEF: New York 2001.

5. Hill K. Frameworks for studying the determinants of child survival. Bull World Health Organ. 2003; 81(2):138-9.

6. Mosley WH, Chen LC. An analytical framework for the study of child survival in developing countries. 1984. Bull World Health Organ. 2003; 81(2):140-5.

7. Victora CG, Kirkwood BR, Ashworth A, Black RE, Rogers S, Sazawal S, Campbell H, Gove S. Potential interventions for the prevention of childhood pneumonia in developing countries: improving nutrition. Am J Clin Nutr. 1999; 70(3):309-20.

8. Victora CG, Smith-PG, Vaughan JP, Nobre LC, Lombardi C, Teixeira AM, Fuchs SC, Moreira LB, Gigante LP, Barros FC. Infant feeding and deaths due to diarrhea. A case-control study. Am J Epidemiol. 1989; 129(5):1032-41.

9. Effect of breastfeeding on infant and child mortality due to infectious diseases in less

developed countries: a pooled analysis. WHO Collaborative Study Team on the Role of Breastfeeding on the Prevention of Infant Mortality. Lancet. 2000; 355(9202):451-5.

10. Jones G, Steketee RW, Black RE, Bhutta ZA, Morris SS; Bellagio Child Survival Study Group. How many child deaths can we prevent this year? Lancet. 2003; 362 (9377):65-71.

11. Leon-Cava N, Lutter C, Ross J, Martin L Quantifying the benefits of breastfeeding: A summary of the evidence. PAHO document.

12. Labbok MH. Health sequelae of breastfeeding for the mother. Clin Perinatol. 1999; 26(2):491-503.

13. UNICEF. Breastfeeding: Foundation for a healthy future. UNICEF: New York 1999.

14. Global Strategy for Infant and Young Child Feeding. Geneva, World Health Assembly, May 2002.

15. Sachdev HP, Mehrotra S. Predictors of exclusive breastfeeding in early infancy: operational implications. Indian Pediatr. 1995; 32(12):1287-96.

16. Guerrero ML, Morrow RC, Calva JJ, Ortega-Gallegos H, Weller SC, Ruiz-Palacios GM, Morrow AL. Rapid ethnographic assessment of breastfeeding practices in periurban Mexico City. Bull World Health Organ. 1999; 77(4): 323-30.

17. Kramer M. Commentary: Breastfeeding and child health, growth, and survival. Int J Epidemiol. 2003; 32(1):96-8.

18. Brahmbhatt H, Gray RH. Child mortality associated with reasons for non-breastfeeding and weaning: is breastfeeding best for HIV-positive mothers? AIDS. 2003; 17(6):879-85.

19. World Health Organisation. Community-based strategies for breastfeeding promotion and support in developing countries. World Health Organisation, Geneva 2003.

20. Morrow AL, Guerrero ML, Shults J, Calva JJ, Lutter C, Bravo J, Ruiz-Palacios G, Morrow RC, Butterfoss FD. Efficacy of home-based peer counselling to promote exclusive breastfeeding: a randomised controlled trial. Lancet. 1999; 353(9160):1226-31.

21. Barros FC, Halpern R, Victora CG, Teixeira AM, Beria JU. Promotion of breast-feeding in urban localities of southern Brazil: a randomized intervention study. Rev Saude Publica. 1994; 28(4):277-83.

22. Froozani MD, Permehzadeh K, Motlagh AR, Golestan B. Effect of breastfeeding education on the feeding pattern and health of infants in their first 4 months in the Islamic Republic of Iran. Bull World Health Organ. 1999; 77 (5):381-5.

23. Bhandari N, Bahl R, Mazumdar S, Martines J, Black RE, Bhan MK; Infant Feeding Study Group. Effect of community-based promotion of exclusive breastfeeding on diarrhoeal illness and growth: a cluster randomised controlled trial. Lancet. 2003; 361(9367):1418-23.

24. Kramer MS, Chalmers B, Hodnett ED, Sevkovskaya Z et al. PROBIT Study Group. Promotion of Breastfeeding Intervention Trial (PROBIT): a randomized trial in the Republic of Belarus. JAMA. 2001; 285(4):413-20.

25. Madagascar LINKAGES project: www.linkagesproject.org/country/madagascar.php Accessed 3/1/2004

26. UNICEF State of the World's Children 2004- Girls, Education and Development. UNICEF: New York 2003

27. Arifeen S, Black RE, Antelman G, Baqui A, Caulfield L, Becker S. Exclusive breastfeeding reduces acute respiratory infection and diarrhea deaths among infants in Dhaka slums. Pediatrics. 2001; 108(4):E67.

28. Jakobsen MS, Sodemann M, Molbak K, Alvarenga IJ, Nielsen J, Aaby P. Termination of breastfeeding after 12 months of age due to a new pregnancy and other causes is associated with increased mortality in Guinea-Bissau. Int J Epidemiol. 2003; 32(1):92-6.

29. Simondon KB, Costes R, Delaunay V, Diallo A, Simondon F. Children's height, health and appetite influence mothers' weaning decisions in rural Senegal. Int J Epidemiol. 2001; 30(3):476-81.

Chapter 10

Analysis of Chronic Malnutrition in Children by Wealth and Urban/Rural Residence[*]

Gina Kennedy

INTRODUCTION

At the Millennium summit in September 2000, world leaders arrived at consensus on a set of eight multi-sectoral development goals, which address, poverty, hunger, health, education, gender equality and the environment. Each of the eight goals has a specific target to be achieved by 2015. There are many synergies between the goals and progress toward one will likely lead to improvements in others. Improving nutrition particularly that of young children and women has been cited as a vital for nearly all of the MDGs (SCN, 2004). It is within this context that chronic malnutrition of children will be explored in greater detail using MICS survey data.

Nutritional status of children under the age of five years is considered a good barometer of the well-being of a community or nation (De Onis, Frongillo and Blossner, 2000). In particular, chronic malnutrition in children is a reflection of extended deprivation and poor environment for growth. Malnutrition is implicated in over half of all childhood deaths (WHO, 2003). Malnourished children are less likely to enroll in school and less likely to fully benefit from educational opportunities (SCN, 2004).

Africa and Asia have the highest rates of malnutrition, in terms of both absolute number of children affected and prevalence. Recent estimates indicate that 45.1 million (35.2%) preschool children in Africa and 109.4 million (30.1 %) preschool children in Asia suffer from chronic malnutrition (SCN, 2004). If the Millennium Development Goals are to be achieved, there will need to be a greater focus on these two regions.

[*] This research was undertaken with the support and direction of the Nutrition Planning, Assessment and Evaluation Service of the Food and Agriculture Organization of the United Nations as part of an overall program of ongoing activities to assess the impact of globalization on the nutritional status of urban populations.

Study of urban areas is relevant in the context of the Millennium Development Goals given the prediction that nearly half of the populations in Africa and Asia will live in urban areas by 2015, the year the Millennium Development Goals are to be achieved (United Nations Population Division, 2002). There is need for a greater understanding of the dynamics of child malnutrition and more broadly poverty across urban and rural contexts. It is widely considered that children in urban areas are better off than children in rural areas. When direct comparisons of child nutritional status are made, this does appear to hold true. When measures of socio-economic status are added to the analysis, however, the apparent advantage of urban children is obscured.

This paper will explore the prevalence of chronic malnutrition in children using MICS data from one case study country in Africa and another in Asia. The prevalence of chronic malnutrition across and within urban and rural populations of different wealth quintiles will be analyzed. Causal factors of malnutrition related to health and care practices will also be examined.

METHODOLOGY

The UNICEF Multiple Indicator Cluster Surveys were reviewed to find surveys from sub-Saharan Africa and Asia, which contained both child anthropometric measurements and measurement of wealth. Several data sets from sub-Saharan Africa containing anthropometric and wealth data were available. The survey from Kenya (2000) was chosen as the case study for Africa based on the comprehensiveness of the data and patterns of urbanization. The survey covered 8993 households and 7266 children under the age of five. Twenty percent of the sample was urban.

Of the available data sets from Asia, only two contained both anthropometric and wealth measurements. The data set from Viet Nam (2000) was chosen to illustrate the case for the region. The survey covered 7628 households and 3104 children under the age of five. Twenty four percent of the households lived in urban areas.

The data was analyzed using SPSS Statistical software package version 11.5. The data were stratified by urban/rural residence and wealth index quintile.

The first part of the analysis focuses on the prevalence of chronic malnutrition, which is calculated based on cut-off points for height relative to age and gender. The WHO recommended cut-off points of <-2.00 standard deviations of height-for age Z scores of the NCHS/WHO child growth curves were used to define children as chronically malnourished (WHO, 1995). After all flagged records were discarded; the prevalence of chronic malnutrition in each group was calculated. In order to have a denominator of at least 25 in each sub-set as recommended in the MICS manual (UNICEF, 2000) the two wealthiest and least wealthy quintiles were combined. Chi-square test for significance was performed in Epi Calc 2000 version 1.02.

Health and care indicators were also analyzed by wealth and residence. These indicators are based on respondent recall of the two weeks preceding the survey for health indicators and the previous day for use of bednet. For the health indicators, missing answers or "don't know" were discarded. Use of iodized salt was considered as another care/health behavior practice. Salt was considered iodized if it was above 15 ppm. Only households where salt was tested were considered in the denominator.

PATTERNS OF URBANIZATION

Prior to entering into a discussion on the prevalence of malnutrition in urban and rural areas, the pattern of urbanization in each country should be described to put the situation into perspective.

Urbanization in Kenya

The current population in Kenya is 31.2 million, with an urban population of 10.7 million (United Nations Population Division, 2002) and an urban growth rate of 4.93 percent (UN-HABITAT, 2001). The urban population is expected to reach 47.2 percent by 2015. Nairobi is by far the largest city with an estimated population of 2.5 million (World Gazetteer, 2004). The remainder of the urban population is dispersed in smaller cities of less than one million inhabitants. According to estimates by UN Habitat, 70 percent of the urban population lives in slums (UN-Habitat, 2003).

Urbanization in Viet Nam

Over 79 million people live in Viet Nam, 19 million of them in urban areas (United Nations Population Division, 2002). By 2015 the urban population is predicted to reach 31.6 percent. The urban growth rate is 2.86 percent, much slower than that in Kenya. Ho Chi Minh City and Hanoi are the largest cities, the former with nearly 3.5 million inhabitants and the latter with 1.4 million (World Gazetteer, 2004). Forty seven percent of the urban population lives in slum areas (UN-Habitat, 2003).

In a city development index used by UN-Habitat which considers development sub-indices such as infrastructure, waste, health and education, Hanoi received a relatively high score of 74.2. To put the number into context, of the cities considered, Stockholm achieved the highest reported score of 97.4 and Niamey the lowest 21.7 (UN-HABITAT, 2001).

RESULTS

Table 1. Prevalence of chronic malnutrition across urban/rural areas

Wealth Index (quintiles)	Prevalence of Chronic Malnutrition				pvalue (X^2)
	Urban		Rural		
	(n)	(%)	(n)	(%)	
Kenya					
Poorest (1 and 2)	42	45.2	2917	41.4	0.60
Richest (4 and 5)	1018	23.1	893	27.2	0.04*
Viet Nam					
Poorest (1 and 2)	60	36.6	1657	45.8	0.15
Richest (4 and 5)	402	20.6	399	28.8	0.007*

* Indicates significant at $p<0.05$.

The prevalence of chronic malnutrition is lower in urban compared to rural areas in all cases except for the poorest segments of the urban population in Kenya. In both Kenya and Viet Nam the prevalence of chronic malnutrition is not statistically different for children in the poorest urban compared to poorest rural households. For the richest strata, chronic malnutrition is significantly lower in urban compared to rural children. In the case of the examples above, there would appear to be some added benefit of living in an urban over a rural area, when a certain level of economic status is attained.

Prevalence of chronic malnutrition within urban and rural areas

Figure 1. Prevalence of chronic malnutrition within urban and rural areas by wealth

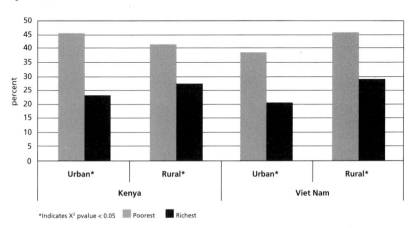

*Indicates X^2 pvalue < 0.05   ░ Poorest   ■ Richest

Figure one illustrates the magnitude of the difference in chronic malnutrition among the rich and poor in urban and rural areas. In all cases, the prevalence of malnutrition is significantly higher for the poorest when compared to the least poor in both urban and rural areas. Findings of others (Menon, Ruel and Morris, 2000; Zere and McIntyre, 2003) are consistent with this analysis. Inequalities between the rich and poor are often cited as being higher in urban areas (World Bank, 2003). Menon et al. find this to be the case for both underweight and chronic malnutrition in ten out of eleven countries in Asia, Africa and Latin America.

Inequalities in health and care practices

Food, health and care as first described in a conceptual framework by UNICEF (1997) are now widely accepted as underlying causes of malnutrition in young children (UNICEF, 1998). The figures below compare data on health (prevalence of fever and diarrhea) and chronic malnutrition in poor and rich urban and rural populations of Kenya and Viet Nam.

Figure 2a. Children's health and chronic malnutrition by wealth and residence in Kenya

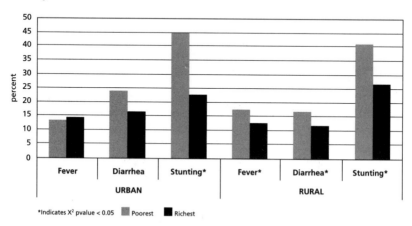

Figure 2b. Children's health and chronic malnutrition by wealth and residence in Viet Nam

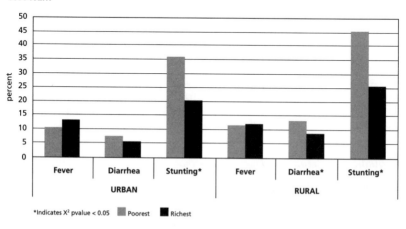

Figures 2a and b illustrate the gap between chronic malnutrition and poverty to be more striking than that of the other indicators considered. The relationship between chronic malnutrition and poverty is the only one which is statistically significant for urban and rural areas of both countries.

The prevalence of fever is significantly higher in Kenya, between the rural rich and rural poor. There are no significant differences in Viet Nam where the prevalence of fever in either wealth or residence bracket ranges from 11-14 percent.

Diarrhea prevalence is most consistently related to poverty in both urban and rural areas. The prevalence of diarrhea is higher in urban compared to rural children in Kenya, while the prevalence of diarrhea is remarkably low in urban Viet Nam, even for the poorest in the population. This could be a reflection of access to improved water and sanitation as partly reflected in the high city development index for Hanoi. However, this conclusion is contradicted by data from a national survey in Viet Nam in 1998 where sharp disparities in access to safe water and sanitation were found across lower and higher income deciles (World Bank, 2003).

The data in the MICS survey allow for some analysis of care practices beneficial to health and nutrition. For this analysis two indicators were chosen, the number of children who slept under a bed net and households consuming iodized salt. Figure 3 shows the number of households where children slept under a bednet or where iodized salt is used (only available for Viet Nam in children's data set). In Viet Nam over 90% of the households reported children slept under bednets. There was little differentiation in use by either residence or wealth. Discrepancy in use of bednets in Kenya is greatest along urban/rural lines, with the use of bednets by the urban poor exceeding that of the rural rich. This may be reflective of greater availability and/or cheaper price of bednets in urban areas, as well as greater access to information on the importance of using bednets.

In Viet Nam use of adequately iodized salt differed by wealth and residence. Urban residents were more likely than rural residents to have adequately iodized salt. The disparities between the rich and poor are also marked in both urban and rural areas. The differences between the rich and poor most likely result from the higher purchase price for iodized salt.

Figure 3. Use of bednets and ionized salt in Kenya and Viet Nam

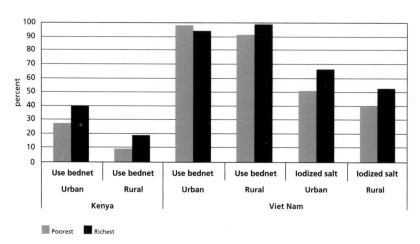

DISCUSSION

There is a strong relationship between poverty and chronic malnutrition in urban and rural areas. This relationship can be masked when simple urban rural comparisons are made. Children in the poorest households are more likely to be chronically malnourished whether living in an urban or rural area.

From the two data sets analyzed, there is evidence to suggest that once a certain level of wealth is achieved, living in an urban area may provide some advantage in terms of the nutritional outcome of children. This may be due to a greater diversity of food accessible by wealthier populations and/or access to higher quality health and education services. A previous study using data from three countries in Africa (Angola, Central African Republic and Senegal) and single instead of combined wealth index quintiles showed that there was no significant difference in the prevalence of chronic malnutrition between urban and rural areas, even among the wealthy. (Kennedy and Nantel, 2003). More research needs to be undertaken to better describe the socio-economic profile of urban chronic malnutrition, given the specific characteristics and patterns of urbanization in different countries.

Inequalities have been shown to be wide between the rich and poor in urban areas (Haddad, Ruel and Garrett, 1999). The urban context, may compound social, political or institutional barriers, which can impede an escape from poverty. Aspects such as legal or illegal city residence status, spatially segregated settlements and lack of political voice all point to the likely occurrence of greater inequalities (World Bank, 2003).

Health indicators analyzed showed a relatively consistent rich/poor bias in Kenya and to a lesser extent in Viet Nam, although the correlation with poverty is not as consistent as the pattern seen with chronic malnutrition. In Viet Nam the prevalence of fever did not differ much by wealth. The high usage rate of bednets among both the rich and poor in Viet Nam may negate any wealth effect for this indicator.

Using the data sets

One problem faced with analysis of urban and rural population by wealth quintile arises due to sample size. The MICS manual advises each sub-set analyzed include a minimum of 25 observations. When breaking down populations into smaller and smaller sub-sets it becomes difficult to analyze all variables of interest (maternal education, feeding practices). The only solution to these basic statistical constraints is to increase sample size. The benefit of increasing sample size should be weighed against budget and time constraints, to arrive at the best possible solution.

Large discrepancies in the proportion of urban and rural population classified as rich or poor occur with current measures used to create wealth indices. This further constrains analysis by sub-sets. One solution to this would be to apply a relative wealth measure as done in the inequality study by Menon and colleagues (Menon, Ruel and Morris, 2000).

Similarly, it may be necessary to refine the indicators used to assess poverty in urban environments. There is current debate regarding assessing poverty in urban and rural areas using a single measure. For example the dollar per day measurement has been strongly criticized as being an unfit measurement of poverty in urban areas due to reliance on cash income for needs such as shelter, food and transportation

(Satterthwaite, 2003). Although the wealth index quintiles used in MICS may decrease the possibility of error as they combine several variables, they may also be biased toward classifying households in rural areas as poor and urban areas as wealthier. For example, when considering access to safe water and sanitation, the services may be more available to urban residents, but only if they can afford the usage fees commonly associated with them. Poor urban residents may have water and sanitation facilities close by, but they may be unable to access the services due to limited cash income. In homogenous communities it can be difficult to accurately categorize the poor and better off, the task becomes more complex given the diversity in environment between urban and rural areas.

CONCLUSION

Improving the nutrition of children in Africa and Asia is fundamental to reaching the MDGs. Failure to do so would mean the first goal of eradicating hunger and poverty would not be achieved, and efforts toward improving child health, achieving universal primary education and promoting greater gender equality would be undermined. Furthermore such failure would jeopardize the next generation.

This paper has demonstrated that the prevalence of malnutrition is similar for low income populations in urban and rural areas. Generalized statements that urban children are better off than rural counterparts should be used cautiously. Given the predicted increase in urbanization over the next decade, more focus on urban areas is warranted. However, it should not be assumed that a shift in development resources from rural to urban areas is the answer. Increased investment in reducing both rural and urban malnutrition is needed to generate the level of impact embodied in the MDGs.

The current research contributes to the growing body of evidence that chronic malnutrition in children reflects poverty. The relationship between being poor and chronically malnourished appeared more consistent than that of other health indicators. Additional studies could expand the range of countries analyzed, examine other secondary indicators such as dietary diversity, care practices and gender disparities or test alternative measures of poverty.

REFERENCES

De Onis, M., Frongillo, E. & Blossner, M. (2000), "Is malnutrition declining? An analysis of changes in levels of child malnutrition since 1980", *Bulletin of the World Health Organization,* vol. 78, no. 10, pp.1222-1233.

Kennedy, G. & Nantel, G. (2003), "Analysis of disparities in nutritional status by wealth and residence: examples from Angola, Central African Republic and Senegal". Paper presented at the World Bank Urban Research Symposium 2003. Available: <http://www.worldbank.org/urban/symposium2003/docs/papers/kennedy.pdf>.

Haddad, L., Ruel, M. & Garret, J. (1999), "Are Urban Poverty and Undernutrition Growing? Some newly assembled evidence". Food Consumption and Nutrition Division Discussion Paper No. 63. Washington D.C.: International Food Policy Research Institute.

Menon, P., Ruel, M & Morris, S. (2000), "Socio-economic differentials in child stunting are consistently larger in urban than in rural areas", *Food and Nutrition Bulletin,* vol. 21, no. 3, pp. 282-289.

Satterthwaite, D. (2003), "The Millennium Development Goals and urban poverty reduction: great expectations and nonsense statistics", *Environment and Urbanization,* vol. 15, no. 2, pp. 181-190.

SCN (Standing Committee on Nutrition). (2004), 5th Report on the World Nutrition Situation. Nutrition for Improved Development Outcomes. Geneva: SCN Secretariat.

UN-Habitat. (2001), *The State of The World's Cities.* United Nations Centre for Human Settlements, Nairobi.

UN-Habitat. (2003). *Slums of the world. The face of urban poverty in a new millennium.* United Nations Human Settlement Program.

United Nations Population Division. (2002), *World Urbanization Prospects The 2001 Revision.* Population Division, Department of Economic and Social Affairs. United Nations Secretariat.

UNICEF. (1998), State of the World's children. Available: <http://www.unicef.org/sowc98/silent4.htm>, Accessed: 2004, April 2.

UNICEF. (2000), *Monitoring Progress Toward the Goals of the World Summit for Children.* End-Decade Multiple Indicator Survey Manual. Division of Policy and Planning, Programme Division. NY:United Nations Children's Fun.

WHO. (1995), *Physical status: The use and interpretation of anthropometry.* WHO Technical Report Series 854. Geneva.

WHO. (2003), "What do we mean by malnutrition" (2003, March 9), (WHO.int), Available: <http://www.who.int/nut/nutrition2.htm>, Accessed: 2003, April 5.

World Bank. (2003). "Urban Poverty in East Asia. A review of Indonesia, the Philippines and Vietnam". Urban Development Working Paper No. 11. East Asia Infrastructure Department. The World Bank.

World Gazetteer. (2004), "Current Population figures for cities, towns and places of all countries", Available <http://www.world-gazetteer.com>, Accessed: 2004, April 2.

Zere, E. & McIntyre, D. (2003), "Inequities in under-five child malnutrition in South Africa" *International Journal for Equity in Health* vol. 2, no. 7.

Chapter 11

Children Living Only with Their Mothers –Are They Disadvantaged?

*Enrique Delamonica, Asmaa Donahue and Alberto Minujin**

INTRODUCTION

A traditional bias assumes that most children live in a household comprised of a father who works and a mother who stays home to care for her children. In the real world, however, families come in many sizes and shapes ranging from a single parent and child to multi-generational, extended households. In fact, contrary to the nuclear family model, about 20% of the world's households are headed by women (Vecchio and Roy, 1998). Policy makers have often treated these households as somehow incomplete, assuming poorer outcomes for children as the result of gender discrimination and the "feminization of poverty." Such assumptions leave the causes of poverty unexamined and fail to recognize the various strategies those different types of households use (Chant, 1997, 2004). Are children who grow up living only with their mother necessarily worse off than children who live with both of their parents? What opportunities and challenges do children face when raised only by their mother?

In order to design appropriate policies to support the efforts of mothers in raising their children, we need to better understand the impact of living arrangements on child well-being and on their mothers and caregivers. This study is a preliminary attempt to use MICS2 data to analyze development outcomes for children who live in different household arrangements.

BACKGROUND

In discussing poverty and vulnerability, economists traditionally viewed households as homogenous, nuclear family units in which members had equal control over resources and equal power in decision making. In this

---

* We thank the colaboration of Erik Bell in the data analysis.

scenario, household decisions would be based on rational choice and comparative advantage would compel men to enter the work force and women to stay home. Gender-based research has since challenged these assumptions, showing that households are heterogeneous and mutable. They may be headed by men or women of any age; as the HIV/AIDS pandemic rages on in Sub-Saharan Africa, grandmothers and sometimes even adolescents are heading households on their own. Households may be small, nuclear units, or include extended family. Members may move in and out as some marry and begin lives elsewhere or as others need support, such as divorced female relatives or unemployed young men. Households may also reconstitute themselves when single parents begin new relationships with each other, combining their families to form new, larger households. Regardless of the type of household, relationships within it are not necessarily harmonious and differ between individuals: some may share resources and cooperate to achieve certain goals, some may struggle for control, others may act independently (Moser, 1993). Fatima Mernissi's description of struggles for control over the "cupboard key" between Moroccan women and their mothers-in-law gives but one example of intra-household power dynamics (Mernissi, 1987).

In challenging hackneyed notions about the structure and dynamics of families, gender theorists have also written about a broad spectrum of women's and girls' productive and nonremunerative roles at home and in the community. Caroline Moser (1993) identifies the triple role of women: 1) reproductive (childrearing and household management), 2) productive (income generating) and 3) community management (voluntary community work including care giving and distribution of resources). Because development policy traditionally prioritized wage-earning productive work, it tended to overlook the pivotal, nonremunerative roles that women play in managing households and communities. Within the home, women not only cook, clean and raise children but also manage finances, supervise the health and education of family members and generally keep the household's productive labor force functional. Outside the home, women supervise the distribution of community resources such as water and attend to social welfare through care giving and other volunteer activities. Women are expected to carry out community management roles in their loosely-defined "spare time" (Moser, 1993). Although these tasks are unpaid and often unacknowledged, they provide many of the assets and capabilities that allow households and communities not only to engage in productive activities but to manage risks. Indeed, it is because women's multiple roles are vital to the functioning of communities and households that women's participation in development is critical.

The various roles that women perform impose an extra burden on mothers who also support their families. Working mothers, for example, must juggle low paying jobs with unpaid domestic responsibilities, so that they typically work longer hours than men (Buvinic and Gupta, 1997). Gender discrimination imposes other constraints as well, such as a lack of access to resources and opportunities or lower wages. Yet women attempt to mitigate these risks by organizing their households to make the best possible use of available resources (Chant, 2004). Sometimes this involves bringing in other family members to share in productive labor or to take over reproductive tasks, freeing up the household head for remunerative work. Migrant worker's remittances and other contributions from the wider kin network are another resource (Chant, 2004; Van Driel, 1994). This may partly explain why, despite the disproportionate representation of women among the poor, female-headed households for the most part are not significantly poorer than those headed by men (Quisumbing, et al., 2001). Indeed, a growing number of women are choosing to raise their children independently rather than tie themselves to an unreliable or abusive partner (Chant, 1997, 2003; Van Driel, 1994).

The ability of poor women to draw upon kin networks and organize scant household resources is reflected in the finding that children may do just as well if not slightly better in a female-headed household, while suggesting that some types of female headed-households may protect against vulnerability, whereas others may reproduce it (Quisumbing, et al., 2001; IFAD; Rogers, 1996; Buvinic and Gupta, 1997). This is partly because women are able to act upon their preferences more when they are the main decision maker, and those preferences tend to favor the well-being of their children (Rogers, 1996; Buvinic and Gupta, 1997). Women's decision making and command of resources is as important to improving children's development outcomes as the availability of those resources.

These findings do not diminish the fact that women face challenges in supporting their children on their own. As noted earlier, women who work to support their household are still responsible for reproductive tasks at the end of the day. If there is no other adult in the household, their children may be under greater pressure to take on more reproductive work or find work outside the home (Buvinic and Gupta, 1997). Moreover, not all women choose to raise their children alone and may face discrimination based on stigmas about single motherhood or widowhood. Given these circumstances, one must ask whether mothers who raise their children on their own are sacrificing their own well-being for the sake of their children's. There is also the question of inequality within households, particularly in the case of single mothers who must move with their children into the home of their parents or relatives. As a result, a growing body of literature calls for a more complex analysis of female-headed households that takes into consideration the challenges and opportunities presented to mothers who raise their children on their own.

CONCEPTUAL FRAMEWORK

Given the limitations of the information provided by the MICS2 data, this study defines children's living arrangements based on the presence of a biological parent. They are described as children who are:

1. living with both parents (LBP);

2. living only with their mother (LM);

3. living only with their father (LF); or

4. living with neither parent (LNP).

The attempt to find a term that adequately describes the four living arrangements analyzed here has proved less than satisfying.[1] A traditional bias assumes that families in which children are raised by less than two parents are necessarily lacking. While for some families the loss of a parent is devastating, other families with nontraditional living arrangements are able to provide children with healthy and fulfilling lives. Furthermore, much of the language currently in use to describe mothers who raise their children without a partner is wanting. Since children and not households are the unit of analysis in this study, we simply refer to "children living only with their mother." This includes children who are raised by their biological mother but not their father, whether it is because the mother is divorced, separated, widowed, unmarried or remarried. Likewise, "children living only with their father" refers to children raised by their biological father but without the biological mother.

Although this study is concerned with the different kinds of families that children live in, the terms "household" and "living arrangements" are used instead. The term "family" is generally used in contemporary debates to define living units in which members are related by blood or marriage. The term 'household,' on the other hand, recognizes that not all members living in the same unit are related to each other (Chant 1997, 2003) and perhaps better represents the diverse living arrangements that children call home. It is usually in terms of 'female-headed households' that living arrangements for mothers and their children are discussed in development literature, with an emphasis on women's role in decision making. Although detailed information on household heads was not available in the MICS data, it is nevertheless useful to understand the different types of households that single mothers form with their children:

Female-headed households, by most definitions, are those in which the woman is the main decision maker and provider, and bears the majority of family responsibilities (Vecchio and Roy, 1998). Women, who are divorced, widowed, separated or who have never married become *de jure* household heads in their own right, having no adult male to take on this role. *De facto* heads are temporarily in charge during their partner's absence: the husband or partner seasonally migrates for work, is sick, or has abandoned his responsibilities (Van Driel, 1994). A woman might also become de facto head of the household simply because she is more capable than her husband (Vecchio and Roy, 1998).

Reconstituted or step-family households are formed when a single mother and her children live with her partner, and sometimes his children. They can be temporary or long-term arrangements (Chant, 2003).

Embedded households are larger households in which a single mother and her children are contained. Usually this means that a single mother is living at home with her own parents (Chant, 2003); she may be a teenager or adult, and unmarried, widowed or divorced. Some female-headed households are also embedded households. Van Driel's (1994) study of female-headed households in rural Botswana found some families in which three generations of single mothers lived in the same household.

The above household arrangements may be further complicated by the addition of orphans who have lost both parents, or when the children of the mother herself have lost their father to HIV/AIDS. This latter group, "single orphans," risks the loss of their mother as well since she is likely to be infected by the virus too. A recent UNICEF study, *Africa's Orphaned Generations* (2003), shows that female-headed households tend to care for a larger proportion of HIV/AIDS orphans than households headed by men. This may be true for any of the above groupings, although understanding what kind of additional burdens this imposes on specific types of female-headed households is beyond the scope of this study.

As the above classifications illustrate, single mothers do not constitute one homogenous group, but rather reflect a wide range of situations and survival strategies, which result in different outcomes for their children. Moreover, household heads and families are by nature transitory as new relationships are formed and old ones broken. This diversity is not captured by the MICS2 data used in this study. The issue of household diversity is an important one, as previous studies have shown that different types of female-headed households result in different outcomes for the children living in them.

The MICS2 data does not allow us to distinguish between types of single-mother households. Instead, we attempt to analyze the demographic and socioeconomic characteristics and vulnerabilities of single-mother families as a whole and compare them to other broadly-defined living arrangements. These broad categories will inevitably mask some intra-category differences and potentially exaggerate others. These issues are discussed in the next section.

LIMITATION OF SOURCE OF INFORMATION

Using MICS2 data to analyze the relationship between children's living arrangements and development outcomes presents several challenges. Two of these challenges are interrelated. First, the survey does not adequately represent intra-household relationships. Although parents and their biological children are listed, there is no way to identify the relationships between other adults or children living in the same home. Second, the MICS2 attempts to list household heads, but with uncertainty given those families may have good reason to misrepresent this information to the government worker conducting the survey. As a result, this study does not include headship. Information about family relationships and decision makers are particularly important in studying single parent and female-headed households, and the absence of this data in MICS2 greatly limits the kinds of analyses that might be made. Indeed, Quisumbing, et al. (2001), Buvinic and Gupta (1997), Rogers (1996) and others have concluded their studies of female-headed households and poverty with calls for more detailed household categories and greater attention to the processes underlying those living arrangements.

Another challenge pertains to sample size. Children who live with their biological father, for example, may also exhibit vulnerability compared to children in two-parent households, but the sample sizes in this category are generally too small to draw conclusions. Country samples in other categories were also sometimes winnowed away to insignificance by control variables. Finally, differences found between categories may not be significant.

Given these limitations, this study is not able to offer the kind of subtle analysis that has been performed by researchers working with smaller samples but more precise household categories. The categories used here are by necessity more general and undoubtedly mask the differences in vulnerability and inequality that a more nuanced survey might uncover. Thus, the aim of this study is to challenge some of the assumptions about how children fare in different living arrangements and prepare the groundwork for future studies.

Samples are drawn from 41 of the 60 countries surveyed whose MICS2 data indicate child living arrangements. Children in this study are grouped according to which biological parent they are living with, if any. The categories are:

- children living with both parents (LBP);

- children living with their mother only (LM);

- children living with their father only (LF); and

- children living with neither parent (LNP).

These are general categories that do not distinguish between parents who are single because of divorce, separation or widowhood. Likewise, children living with neither parent may or may not be orphans because of the lack of data on family relationships. The categories also do not consider whether other adults living in the household are partners of the parent, as this information is unavailable. The 41 countries are then further narrowed down to those countries in which at least 15% of children are living only with their mother. 17 of the countries that comprise this group are the focus of the bulk of this paper.

The study analyzes the vulnerability and exposure to risk faced by single mothers and their children on two levels. First, it compares the different arrangements in which children live using the four categories mentioned above. Second, it analyzes inequality and vulnerability that children face in the different living arrangements. Variables describing household characteristics include wealth, dependency ratio, mother's age, the highest education level of any household member, and rural or urban residence. Outcomes for children are measured based on indicators of undernourishment, DPT3 immunization, treatment for diarrhea and acute respiratory infections, child labor, early learning and primary education.

FAMILY LIVING ARRANGEMENTS IN 41 COUNTRIES

- 11% of all children studied are living with their mother but not with their father

- Botswana has the highest percentage (39.5%); Albania has the lowest (2.5%)

• Highest regional average is in Latin America and the Caribbean (23%)

• The percentage of children living with both parents varies by region

• These differences are not related to country economic situation (measured by GDP per capita) which suggests that factors other than economic ones determine living arrangements.

Family is one of many elements that contribute to child well-being, and is perhaps the underlying foundation of healthy child development. Families can take on a variety forms ranging from a single parent raising children with the help of a grandparent to an extended family sharing a compound. Children may benefit or face challenges in any of these arrangements, and no single type of family can be equated with a predetermined development outcome. Nevertheless, understanding the types of vulnerability that accompany particular living arrangements can provide a basis for designing policies and interventions to support childcare efforts.

Table 1 presents the regional percentage of children age 14 and under who are living with or without parents. Percentages by region are given in Table 2. The highest percentages of children living with both parents are found in Central and Eastern Europe and the CIS (92.5%) and East Asia and the Pacific (89.2%). Overwhelmingly the second largest category is children living only with their mother, representing 23.2% of children's living arrangements in Latin America and the Caribbean, 18.8% in Eastern and Southern Africa, and 15.5% in Western Africa. These regional averages, however, belie the fact that the highest number of LM children is in Africa, not Latin America: Botswana (39.5%), Swaziland (33.9%) and Sao Tome (32.9%). Botswana and Swaziland also have the largest number of children not living with a biological parent (23.6% and 19.7%, respectively), although regionally the highest incidence of LNP children is found in Western Africa (10.5%). Conversely, only 38.3% of children in Swaziland live with both parents; in Botswana, only 28.1% do so. This means that more children in Botswana live only with their mother than with both parents.

Table 1. Living Arrangements for Children in 41 Countries
(In descending order of 2-parent households, within regions)

Region[2]	Country	% Living w/both parents	% Living w/mother only	% Living w/father only	% Living w/neither parent
CEE/CIS	Albania	96.5	2.5	0.6	0.2
	Uzbekistan	93.2	4.9	0.9	0.8
	Azerbaijan	93.0	5.3	0.6	1.1
	Bosnia and Herzegovina	92.6	5.9	0.6	0.6
	Tajikistan	91.5	6.0	1.3	1.0
	Moldova	83.5	12.8	1.1	1.7
EAPRO	Myanmar	93.2	3.9	1.1	1.6
	Lao	93.1	4.2	1.0	1.5
	Vietnam	90.8	6.3	1.3	1.4
	Indonesia	89.0	5.9	1.3	3.4
	Philippines	86.0	5.9	1.9	6.1
	Mongolia	80.5	16.5	0.9	1.8
ESARO	Somalia	75.1	12.7	2.6	5.1
	Burundi	72.2	15.8	3.8	6.7
	Madagascar	72.2	14.3	4.1	7.6
	Comoros	70.6	15.4	0.9	6.4
	Angola	67.5	19.7	2.9	9.5
	Kenya	65.7	21.4	2.0	6.0
	Zambia	63.5	15.9	2.6	10.3
	Rwanda	57.8	25.8	2.9	11.8
	Lesotho	55.9	25.1	3.3	15.5
	Swaziland	38.3	33.9	3.5	19.7
	Botswana	28.1	39.5	2.5	23.6
MENA	Sudan	84.9	11.3	0.9	1.8
TACRO	Bolivia	80.5	13.0	2.3	3.8
	Guyana	64.9	23.4	2.5	8.5
	Venezuela	63.8	27.3	1.9	6.2
	Surinam	62.2	24.6	2.0	7.8
	Trinidad and Tobago	60.3	28.7	4.7	5.7
	Dominican Republic	58.7	22.2	3.9	13.9
WCARO	Niger	82.6	5.2	3.0	8.4
	Chad	78.9	11.2	2.9	6.8
	Gambia	72.6	12.6	2.9	10.2
	Guinea Bissau	70.7	13.2	3.2	12.4
	DRCongo	68.9	16.6	4.4	9.6
	Senegal	67.0	19.7	2.5	9.6
	Cameroon	65.8	15.6	4.7	11.0
	Togo	63.9	14.8	5.2	12.4
	Cote d'Ivoire	61.2	18.9	4.7	14.4
	Sierra Leone	60.9	13.9	7.2	16.1
	Sao Tome	52.7	32.9	3.3	10.0
Total[3]		**80.5**	**10.9**	**2.2**	**5.5**

Table 2. Percentage of Children in Each Living Arrangement, by Region

Regions	Living with both parents	Living with mother only	Living with father only	Living with neither
CEE/CIS	92.5	5.5	0.9	0.9
EAPRO	89.2	5.8	1.4	3.3
ESARO	66.8	18.8	2.8	8.1
WCARO	68.8	15.5	4.2	10.5
TACRO	66.4	23.2	2.4	7.2

Living with both parents has no clear relation with GNP per capita. As can be observed in Figure 1, countries with GNP per capita less than US$ 500 per year shows the most diverse situations. Children living with both parents ranges from roughly 50 to 95 per cent. However, certain regional patterns can be observed, with African countries presenting the lowest percentages of children living with both parents.

Figure 1. Living Arrangements for Children in 41 Countries

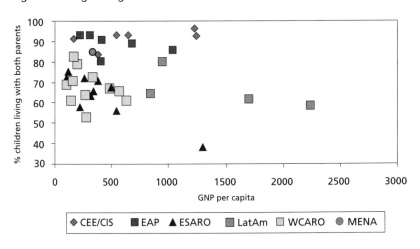

The smallest category of living arrangements is children living only with their father (2.2%). They are never more than a quarter of the children not living with both parents; e.g. in Central and Eastern Europe and the CIS, at less than 1% of all children, they represent 12% of those not living with both parents. The highest number of LF children is in Western Africa (4.5%), which is also the region with the highest number of orphans. At 7%, Sierra Leone exceeds the regional average. Although single fathers are not the subject of this study, it is worth noting the surprisingly small size of this category in terms of single parents. It suggests on the one hand a preference for keeping children in the care of their mothers, and the reasons may be cultural, legal or economic. Little information is available on single-father households in developing countries, and what little can be gleaned from the sparse data provided in this study underlines the need for further research. It may well be that in some cases children in such arrangements may be exposed to greater vulnerability than if they had lived with their mothers. Moreover, given the high numbers of male labor migration in many of the countries in this study, it is also worth exploring what kinds of economic opportunities, if any, single father have had to forego in order to care for their children.

Certainly the fact that so many children in developing countries live with their mother rather than with both parents calls into question traditional assumptions about children's households. It also underscores the need to better understand household coping strategies and the impact that different living arrangements have on children. In other words, knowing what we do about the different forms of gender discrimination that women are exposed to, such as lower wages or access to fewer resources, can we assume that LM children have lower development outcomes? As noted earlier, the current literature on female-headed households suggests that children are not necessarily worse off in these living arrangements. On the contrary, some types of female-headed households protect against vulnerability. If that is the case, then a more appropriate question might be, what are the challenges and opportunities for LM children, and how is that evinced in the MICS2 data? Furthermore, what kinds of policies and interventions might support the efforts of single mothers and strengthen their capacity to achieve better outcomes for themselves and their children?

The remainder of this study will focus on LM children, the largest category of children not living with both parents. Analysis is limited to those countries in which at least 15% of children are living only with their mother. First, some of the characteristics of LM children's living arrangements compared to others are described. It is followed by an assessment of LM children's development outcomes.

LM CHILDREN AND VULNERABILITY

Understanding outcomes for children who live only with their mother requires some understanding of the circumstances and characteristics of the households in which they live. A brief overview is provided in this section.

Women may raise their children without a partner for any number of reasons. They may be divorced or widowed, and an increasing number have not been married at all. Married women sometimes take over sole responsibility for parenting and household management over long periods of time as their husbands migrate to other regions or countries to find work. Such has been the case in Western and Southern Africa and throughout Latin America. Mongolia has a tradition of independent female household heads, and women there continue to run the household while their husbands migrate with their herds (Neupert, 1994). In Sub-Saharan Africa, HIV/AIDS has widowed many young mothers who are in turn infected. The result is an increase in older women raising their grandchildren as their daughters succumb to the virus (UNICEF, 2003). Civil and regional conflict is another reason why high numbers of women raise children on their own and presents other challenges. Rape, genocide and civil war in Rwanda, Burundi, Sierra Leone and the Democratic Republic of Congo have left mothers who are widowed or, as rape survivors, abandoned. Child soldiers in Sierra Leone include girls who fought and sometimes were given as "rewards" to boy soldiers. Many became teen mothers and carry deep emotional scars but are not covered by rehabilitation programs (Mazurana & McKay, 2001). In DRC, women who built new relationships with Ugandan soldiers found themselves left alone with young children after those soldiers were sent home (Puechgirbal, 2003).

Not all forms of single parenting are imposed by social upheaval. Female-headed households have been on the rise since the early to mid-20th century, a phenomena that reflects the choices that individual women make as much as the impact of macro-level social and economic changes. For example, HIV/AIDS is only the most recent contributing factor to Botswana's high number of single-mother households. Van Driel (1994) writes that female-headed households began to increase alongside rising labor migration in the early 20th century and is tied to rapid changes in the organization of traditional society. She observes that nearly 57% of mothers in Botswana are unmarried, preferring independence to unreliable marriage partners. Choice is also at play in Latin America, where a growing number of women prefer serial monogamy over marriage (Chant, 1997; Van Driel, 1994). Yet Van Driel questions whether such choices reflect greater freedom when women are "'compelled' to economic independence" by unreliable partners. Buvinic and Gupta (1997) further note that poor female-headed households reflect a disruption of traditional systems of family governance that enforced income transfers.

Below are some characteristics of households in which children live only with their mother as revealed by the MICS2 data, in comparison to other living arrangements.

HOUSEHOLD CHARACTERISTICS FOR LM CHILDREN

Wealth

A number of studies show that despite the overrepresentation of women among the poor, female-headed households are not necessarily the poorest nor the worst off. Rather, factors other than single motherhood or female headship more accurately predict income poverty, such as whether single mothers receive transfers from male family members or are prevented by discrimination from accessing communal resources (Vecchio and Roy, 1998; Buvinic and Gupta, 1997; Chant, 1997; Quisumbing, et al., 2001; IFAD 2004). The MICS2 household surveys do not collect information on income or transfers, but do construct a wealth index based on assets such as the type of dwelling, number of rooms and other assets that a household has. The shape of the distribution of wealth quintiles for LM and LBP children was practically identical, with a marginally smaller percentage of children living in the richest quintile. A slightly larger percentage of LF and LNP children live in the poorest and richest quintiles.

At the country level, more disparity is seen between the percentage of children occupying the richest and poorest quintiles in Swaziland, Cote d'Ivoire, Comoros and Rwanda, Venezuela and Trinidad and Tobago. Throughout this group, LBP children overwhelmingly occupy the poorest quintile (between 24 and 34%) compared to the richest (as low as 4.3%). While LM children followed similar distributions, their numbers in the richest quintile were much lower. An extreme example is Rwanda, where almost twice (28.5%) as many LM children occupied the first (poorest) quintile compared to LBP children (15%), who largely occupy the second, middle and fourth quintiles.

Not all LM children are poor; in Côte d'Ivoire and Senegal they slightly exceed LBP children in the two wealthiest quintiles. Guyana shows twice as many LBP children in the poorest quintile, whereas twice as many LM children occupy the richest quintile. These numbers may simply point to a growing proportion of women who are better placed economically to choose to live independently with their children, rather than deny that many single mothers live in poverty.

Household Education

Education is another form of asset that can enable a household to take advantage of certain economic opportunities. Higher levels of education are also linked with better development outcomes for children. For the purposes of this study, household education is defined as the highest level of education attained by any household member. At the aggregate level, a slightly larger percentage of LBP children (39%) lived in a household with at least a secondary education compared to LM children (33.3%). 64.6 % of LM children live in a household with a primary-level education. Generally, though, household educational levels were comparable between these two groups of children, with less than a third of households having reached a secondary education in parts of Sub-Saharan Africa. In Burundi, this number is as low as 5 to 6%. Analyzing household education by age group could present a different picture; it may reflect generational changes, in which younger mothers are the product of increasing access to education (Van Driel, 1994).

Age of Mother or Primary Caretaker

Families change in size and composition over time as children are born, grow up and move out, or as new families are started with new partners. The growth in family size can exert additional pressures on households' resources, especially for single parents. This trajectory is not traced within individual families by the MICS2 data, but a look at the distribution of children among mothers of different age groups gives some idea of its pattern. Generally, the percentage of children in households rises with the age of the mother or primary caretaker, and then declines in the mother's 30s and 40s, perhaps as children reach maturity. For LBP children, this slope rises in the mother's early 20s, perhaps as their family is growing, and peaks (27.5%) when the mother is between 25-29 years old. Twice (12%) as many LM children are raised by a teenager aged 15-19 compared to LBP children. Since these numbers are from the perspective of the child, there may be some crossover as single mothers remarry or mothers divorce, separate, or are widowed. Teen caretakers may be an older sibling or the mother herself.

The distribution of LF children among age groups is more even; primary caregivers may not necessarily be the fathers themselves but could also be an older sibling (8.6% of children have a primary caregiver aged 15-19), grandmother or the father's partner (about 33% of children have a primary caregiver in their late 30s or 40s). LNP children (7.8%) might also be raised by an older sibling in their late teens or 20s; the largest number (21.5% and 26.4%) are with older caregivers who are in their early and late 40s.

Rural and Urban Localities

Where families live can play a significant part in the type and amount of material and community resources available. Rural locales may be more advantageous for families who are able to produce their own food or who have strong family and community support networks. On the other hand, urban areas may offer better jobs, schools and hospitals. The perceived advantages differ regionally, as seen by the distribution of children by living arrangement. For example, the majority of LBP children in Sub-Saharan Africa live in the rural areas. The Dominican

Republic and Mongolia showed more equal distributions between rural and urban areas.

Children in other living arrangements largely followed these patterns. LM children, however, seem to gravitate somewhat more to urban areas, possibly as their mothers take advantage of low wage jobs in factories or services. In the Dominican Republic, Cameroon, Côte d'Ivoire, the Democratic Republic of Congo and Senegal, slightly higher percentages of LM children live in cities as compared to LBP children. Guyana showed the greatest contrast, with twice as many LM children living in urban areas. Chant (1997) has reported that in Latin America, women's rural-urban migration is permanent compared to men's and is rising as economic opportunities for women decline in agriculture but rise in the service industry and low-wage manufacturing. This may be true in Western Africa as well, although the higher number of urban LM children might point to relationships formed by urban women with men who migrate to the cities for work during agricultural off-seasons. Thus labor migration could have a double effect on the rate of single motherhood, as urban women seek informal consensual unions with migrant workers and other single mothers arrive seeking low-wage jobs. (Chant, 1997).

OUTCOMES FOR LM CHILDREN

A common assumption is that poverty combined with gender discrimination will translate into lower outcomes for children who live in female-headed households. Several studies, however, have found that this need not be the case. A study conducted in Brazil found that children were no more negatively impacted by their mother's status as household head than they were by gender or racial discrimination (Buvinic & Gupta, 1997). Other studies have found that women tend to invest more of their scant resources on their children, but are prevented from doing so when either it is a matter of survival, or a partner (such as the children's father) controls household resources. For example, a study of food allocation in the Dominican Republic found that despite having fewer resources, female household heads tended to spend more than male heads on higher quality foods. Children living in female-headed households thus tended to be no worse off than other children in terms of height and the speed of recovery from illness. In some cases they did a little better. The women's ability to act on their preferences in allocating limited resources may explain why these children fared as well as they did (Rogers, 1996). Women household heads may also prioritize education for their children but be constrained by school fees or the need for help with domestic chores or even additional earners (Buvinic & Gupta, 1997).

The studies discussed above draw on smaller samples than MICS2, but also rely on more detailed data and break female households down into more succinct categories. The availability of transfers and other forms of support as well as the type of female headship allow for a more subtle analysis than is possible here. Such a level of detail is beyond the scope of MICS2 data collection. Findings are discussed below.

Nutrition

Malnourishment in children under the age of 5 is measured by the MICS in terms of stunting, a long term indicator, and weight, which is more temporary. Overall, about 34% of children experienced stunting regardless of whether they lived with both parents or only their mother. 28% of LM children were underweight, only 2 percentage points higher than if they had lived with both parents.

Health

MICS2 data was used to assess children's health outcomes in terms of immunization coverage and the quality of healthcare sought to treat childhood illness. Maternal and newborn health is included here as antenatal care and birth weight for newborns. Because of small sample sizes, health data is not available for single-father households and orphans.

Antenatal care is low throughout the countries studied, with only 30.2% of mothers of LBP children receiving services. For mothers of LM children it is 5 percentage points lower. Rates of low birth weight were about the same for both groups.

The MICS2 questionnaire asks whether children under the age of five have received the necessary immunizations. DPT protects against diphtheria, whooping cough and tetanus. Because it is administered in three doses at six-month intervals, DPT3 is a fair indication of good immunization coverage. Immunization coverage appeared to be roughly the same among LM and LBP children. LNP children usually had the lowest percentage of immunization coverage, except for LF children in Kenya and Lesotho.

The MICS2 surveys evaluate children's healthcare in terms of what type of treatment children received for diarrhea and acute respiratory infections (ARI) in the two weeks preceding the survey. Both diarrhea and ARI claim high mortality rates among children under the age of 5. Oral rehydration salts (ORS) can save children's lives by replacing the water and electrolytes that are lost through diarrhea. A mixture of water, sodium and a carbohydrate, ORS can be administered at home. ARI can usually be treated with antibiotics under professional medical supervision. UNICEF considers any of the following to be an appropriate healthcare provider: hospitals, health centers, dispensaries, village health workers, MCH clinics, mobile/outreach clinics, and private physicians. The differences in the quality of treatment received by LM and LBP children for ARI and diarrhea were negligible; ORS treatment was higher among LBP children by a mere 3 percentage points.

Child Work & Education

It is not unusual to find children in developing countries helping with chores at home or at the family business regardless of household wealth (Huebler and Loaiza, 2002). Poorer households, however, are more likely to depend on their children for work and an extra income as a matter of survival. The pressure to contribute to the household might be especially felt by children in families with few able-bodied adults present, as when a parent is raising children alone or when one parent is ill or has migrated for work. Working children are less likely to attend school. Using UNICEF's definitions, a child is currently working if during the week before the survey he or she:

- Helped with household chores (such as childcare, cooking, cleaning, shopping or fetching water) for at least 4 hours a day;

- Worked for a family farm or business; or

• Worked for someone who is not a member of the household, paid or unpaid.

Numbers varied by region, but in general roughly the same amount of LM and LBP children worked: 5% helped with domestic work, 14% worked on a family farm or business, and 8 to 9% worked for someone outside the household. Averages among LNP and LF children were higher usually by only a few percentage points, although greater differences were found in some countries such as Mongolia. Rural or urban residence, and not the absence of a parent, seemed to be a determining factor in children's work loads: overall, twice as many rural children worked in a family farm or business as urban children, regardless of living arrangement.

Children who miss school lose out on the skills and education that might gain them broader access to opportunities. Studies of female-headed households have shown that while women recognize education as an investment in the future, they are not always able to keep their children in school when survival is at stake (Buvinic & Gupta, 1997). The MICS2 survey looks at children's attendance in early learning programs and completion rates in primary school. The percentage of children attending early learning programs was similarly low in all four categories, ranging from 6 to 8%. About 63% of LM and LBP children of primary school age attend primary school. (Samples sizes for the other categories were too small to include.) Yet primary school completion rates tell a different story. Completion rates are calculated based on the percentage of children entering Grade 1 who eventually reach Grade 5. The results showed that despite comparable attendance rates, only 66.5% of LM children who entered first grade reached the fifth grade, compared to 74% of LBP children. This may suggest that LM children are missing school out of necessity, and not because of a lower priority placed on education.

FINAL COMMENTS

There is a growing body of literature about female-headed households in developing countries. These studies, however, focus mainly on women themselves with respect to poverty and vulnerability. Few studies actually explore the well-being of the children living without their fathers. A range of questions have been left unanswered by this study: If children living only with their mother are not necessarily worse off than children who live with both parents, then what strategies are their mothers and family members using to compensate for potential inequalities? What toll does this take on women – are women sacrificing their own well-being in order to promote that of their children? How can community and national level policies and programs bolster their efforts? Under what circumstances *are* children who live only with their mother exposed to greater vulnerability, and what kinds of programs and interventions are called for? These issues are best investigated through smaller country or regional studies rather than through large, macro-level surveys. Studies must ask why women and especially single mothers make the choices they do in organizing their households and securing their children's survival. Participatory assessments and other qualitative approaches can offer a deeper understanding of household strategies in single parent families and their impact on children.

It is crucial that future MICS questionnaires provide more detailed information about living arrangements. Identifying relationships between different household members can provide a great deal of information about household coping strategies. Is the primary caretaker of a particular household a sibling or grandparent, rather than the biological mother or father? How many families are living in the same household, and are there internal inequalities? It is strongly recommended that in the future MICS questionnaires incorporate family relationship and educational level for all members of the household. The head of a household should be identified in an accurate way.

In addition to gathering information on household assets, information is also needed about what forms of support are available to parents. Does the household receive remittances or other contributions from family networks, or does it participate in community or government programs? Who determines the allocation of those resources? Is there inequality within the household itself?

Households in which fathers are raising their children without a partner have emerged in this study as an area requiring attention both in terms of research and policy. Little has been written about them, and yet it has been suggested in the findings presented here and elsewhere that children under their care may be more vulnerable than children living with only with their mothers. Further research could provide a better understanding not only of children's outcomes but of what kinds of strategies single fathers use in caring for their children and how their efforts might be supported.

APPENDIX: TABLES

Household Characteristics
(Distributions within each living arrangement)

		Living with both parents	Living with mother only	Living with father only	Living with neither
Age of Mother	15-19	5.4%	12.0%	8.6%	7.8%
or Primary	20-24	20.4%	27.4%	18.7%	9.1%
Caretaker	25-29	27.5%	23.7%	21.0%	12.5%
	30-34	21.2%	16.5%	18.7%	7.9%
	35-39	15.7%	11.9%	14.3%	14.9%
	40-44	7.9%	6.2%	14.0%	21.5%
	45-49	1.9%	2.4%	4.8%	26.4%
Household	Primary or less	58.5%	64.6%	57.8%	62.4%
Education	Secondary	39.0%	33.3%	42.2%	36.4%
	Higher	2.5%	21.1%	0.0%	1.2%
Area	Urban	33.4%	37.8%	59.9%	37.1%
	Rural	66.6%	62.2%	40.1%	62.9%
Wealth	Poorest	22.1%	20.9%	22.4%	19.8%
Quintiles	Second	21.4%	21.1%	17.5%	23.4%
	Middle	20.8%	20.8%	18.3%	20.0%
	Fourth	19.3%	20.0%	19.7%	16.3%
	Richest	16.4%	17.2%	22.1%	20.6%

Outcomes for Children by Living Arrangement
(Distributions within each living arrangement)

Health	Living with both parents	Living with mother only	Living with father only	Living with neither
Stunting, Under Age 5	34.7%	34.3%	46.1%	44.3%
Underweight, Under Age 5	25.9%	28.0%	19.4%	24.3%
DPT3 Vaccination	40.2%	40.5%	44.7%	37.2%
Received ORS	29.8%	28.4%	n/a	n/a
Treatment for ARI	44.7%	47.5%	n/a	n/a
Newborns Under 2500 g	9.5%	10.6%	n/a	n/a

Outcomes for Children by Living Arrangement

(Distributions within each living arrangement)

Education	Living with both parents	Living with mother only	Living with father only	Living with neither
Early Learning	5.4%	6.5%	8.9%	6.5%
Net Primary Education Attendance	63.8%	63.2%	n/a	n/a
Children entering grade 1 who reach grade 5	74.0%	66.5%	n/a	n/a

Household Wealth, by Quintiles

Child's Living Arrangement	Wealth Quintile				
	Poorest	Second	Middle	Fourth	Richest
Two-Parent Household	22.1%	21.4%	20.8%	19.3%	16.4%
Single-Mother Household	20.9%	21.1%	20.8%	20.0%	17.2%
Single-Father Household	22.4%	17.5%	18.3%	19.7%	22.1%
Living w/Neither Parent	19.8%	23.4%	20.0%	16.3%	20.6%

Highest Education Level of Any Household Member, by Child's Living Arrangement (14 Countries)

Child's Living Arrangement	Education		
	Primary or Less	Secondary	Higher
Two-Parent Households	58.5%	39.0%	2.5%
Single-Mother Households	64.6%	33.3%	2.1%
Single-Father Households	57.8%	42.2%	0.0%
Living w/Neither Parent	62.4%	36.4%	1.2%

Note: Data for Single-Father and Neither-Parent Households drawn from 4 and 9 countries, respectively.

Highest Education Level of any Household Member

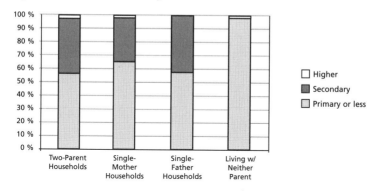

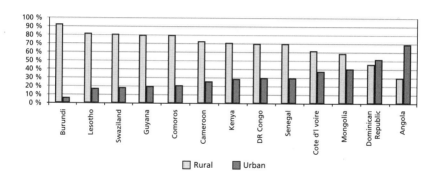

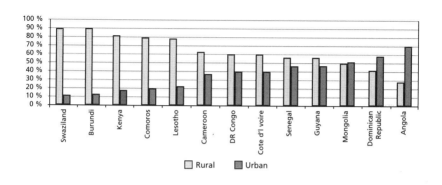

Rural & Urban Distribution
Percentage of children by living arrangement living in rural or urban areas

Region	Country	2-Parent Households		Single Mother Households		Single Father Households		Child Living w/ Neither Parent	
		Rural	Urban	Rural	Urban	Rural	Urban	Rural	Urban
EAPRO	Mongolia	58.7%	41.3%	49.3%	50.7%				
ESARO	Angola	30.3%	69.7%	28.8%	71.2%			33.8%	66.2%
	Burundi	93.0%	7.0%	88.5%	11.5%				
	Comoros	79.0%	21.0%	80.6%	19.4%	80.0%	20.0%	68.5%	31.5%
	Kenya	71.6%	28.4%	82.0%	18.0%			84.1%	15.9%
	Lesotho	81.6%	18.4%	78.3%	21.7%	68.0%	32.0%	83.6%	16.4%
	Swaziland	81.0%	19.0%	89.2%	10.8%	87.0%	13.0%	93.0%	7.0%
TACRO	Dominican Rep.	46.9%	53.1%	41.3%	58.7%			63.2%	36.8%
	Guyana	79.2%	20.8%	54.9%	45.1%			71.0%	29.0%
WCARO	Cameroon	73.0%	27.0%	62.6%	37.4%			66.0%	34.0%
	Cote d'Ivoire	63.3%	36.7%	59.8%	40.2%	41.7%	58.3%	51.3%	48.7%
	DR Congo	70.1%	29.9%	60.3%	39.7%	61.5%	38.5%	60.4%	39.6%
	Senegal	69.6%	30.4%	55.2%	44.8%	74.9%	25.1%	58.7%	41.3%
	Totals	**66.6%**	**33.4%**	**62.2%**	**37.8%**	**59.9%**	**40.1%**	**62.9%**	**37.1%**

Note: Empty cells reflect insufficient data.

Stunting in Children

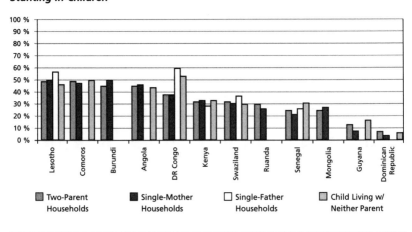

226

Undernourished Children Under Age 5: Stunting
Percentage of under-five children with stunting, 2-standard deviations

Region	Country	Sex	2-Parent Households	Single-Mother Households	Living w/ Neither Parent
EAPRO	Mongolia	Boys	25.2%	27.2%	—-
		Girls	22.9%	27.4%	—-
ESARO	Lesotho	Boys	48.9%	49.8%	50.0%
		Girls	46.7%	48.2%	42.0%
	Comoros	Boys	48.5%	47.7%	45.2%
		Girls	47.0%	47.2%	53.0%
	Burundi	Boys	46.1%	48.2%	—-
		Girls	44.1%	49.4%	—-
	Kenya	Boys	33.7%	32.6%	30.3%
		Girls	30.1%	31.8%	36.1%
	Swaziland	Boys	33.0%	32.4%	33.3%
		Girls	29.6%	28.9%	25.3%
	Rwanda	Boys	32.5%	29.3%	—-
		Girls	27.5%	23.6%	—-
TACRO	Guyana	Boys	13.4%	8.3%	—-
		Girls	11.6%	6.2%	18.3%
	Dominican Republic	Boys	8.1%	2.7%	7.7%
		Girls	5.0%	5.4%	—-
WCARO	DR Congo	Boys	39.9%	40.6%	—-
		Girls	36.0%	34.3%	45.4%
	Senegal	Boys	26.2%	22.4%	26.3%
		Girls	23.3%	20.5%	33.6%
Totals		**Boys**	**35.3%**	**34.7%**	**27.6%**
		Girls	**31.7%**	**31.3%**	**32.4%**

Undernourished Children Under Age 5: Underweight

Percentage of under-five children who are underweight, 2-standard deviations

Region	Country	Sex	2-Parent Households	Single-Mother Households	Living w/ Neither Parent
EAPRO	Mongolia	Boys	12.6%	14.2%	—-
		Girls	11.9%	15.8%	—-
ESARO	Lesotho	Boys	18.4%	20.1%	21.0%
		Girls	15.1%	15.4%	15.3%
	Comoros	Boys	29.9%	26.1%	27.8%
		Girls	24.9%	23.0%	23.2%
	Burundi	Boys	34.5%	42.1%	—-
		Girls	36.8%	41.8%	—-
	Kenya	Boys	21.1%	23.7%	14.8%
		Girls	18.9%	20.4%	18.1%
	Swaziland	Boys	11.8%	9.9%	12.9%
		Girls	11.2%	9.6%	9.3%
	Rwanda	Boys	23.0%	26.1%	—-
		Girls	16.5%	25.7%	—-
TACRO	Guyana	Boys	16.8%	13.4%	—-
		Girls	13.7%	6.7%	18.1%
	Dominican Republic	Boys	5.3%	1.6%	—-
		Girls	5.7%	2.9%	—-
WCARO	DR Congo	Boys	33.5%	38.2%	27.0%
		Girls	29.8%	29.9%	31.1%
	Senegal	Boys	24.0%	20.8%	24.0%
		Girls	21.9%	19.2%	27.3%
Totals		**Boys**	**26.8%**	**29.8%**	**21.4%**
		Girls	**24.1%**	**25.0%**	**17.3%**

Note: Empty cells reflect insufficient data.

DPT3 for Boys and Girls

Percentage of boys and girls, aged 12-23 months, who were vaccinated with a third and final dose of DPT at any time before the survey

Region	Country	Sex	2-Parent Households	Single-Mother Households
EAPRO	Mongolia	Boys	82.8%	81.0%
		Girls	*82.4%*	*79.8%*
ESARO	Comoros	Boys	60.1%	53.3%
		Girls	*61.0%*	*57.4%*
	Rwanda	Boys	62.4%	58.9%
		Girls	*65.2%*	*61.0%*
	Kenya	Boys	69.7%	67.6%
		Girls	*68.4%*	*70.8%*
	Lesotho	Boys	75.4%	72.9%
		Girls	*78.3%*	*72.5%*
TACRO	Trinidad & Tobago	Boys	53.7%	49.6%
		Girls	*53.4%*	*52.2%*
	Venezuela	Boys	54.4%	48.8%
		Girls	*54.9%*	*51.9%*
	Dominican Republic	Boys	58.3%	51.9%
		Girls	*55.0%*	*57.5%*
	Guyana	Boys	85.4%	85.8%
		Girls	*88.9%*	*85.8%*
WCARO	DR Congo	Boys	7.3%	8.8%
		Girls	*6.6%*	*6.9%*
	Cameroon	Boys	39.8%	47.0%
		Girls	*36.2%*	*44.2%*
	Cote d'Ivoire	Boys	54.0%	55.6%
		Girls	*52.5%*	*53.9%*
	Burundi	Boys	67.1%	63.4%
		Girls	*66.6%*	*67.1%*
Totals		**Boys**	**41.4%**	**41.0%**
		Girls	***40.6%***	***41.4%***

Note: Empty cells reflect insufficient data.

Boys & Girls Who Received ORS

Percentage of children with diarrhea in the last two weeks who received oral rehydration solution (ORS)

Region	Country	Sex	2-Parent Households	Single-Mother Households
ESARO	Swaziland	Boys	71.8%	67.8%
		Girls	67.9%	71.1%
	Lesotho	Boys	53.6%	59.2%
		Girls	61.9%	55.7%
	Kenya	Boys	46.3%	41.8%
		Girls	41.9%	39.4%
	Comoros	Boys	20.8%	24.2%
		Girls	21.7%	19.2%
TACRO	Venezuela	Boys	72.6%	51.3%
		Girls	64.3%	55.5%
WCARO	DR Congo	Boys	17.2%	20.8%
		Girls	16.0%	21.2%
	Cote d'Ivoire	Boys	14.1%	16.8%
		Girls	16.3%	14.6%
	Cameroon	Boys	13.9%	12.6%
		Girls	14.1%	23.2%
	Senegal	Boys	13.6%	14.9%
		Girls	12.1%	14.0%
Totals		**Boys**	**30.1%**	**28.2%**
		Girls	**28.0%**	**29.1%**

Note: Empty cells reflect insufficient data.

Newborns Weighing Under 2500 Grams

Percentage of live births in the last 12 months that weighed below 2500 grams at birth, by living arrangement

Region	Country	2-Parent Households	SingleMother Households
EAPRO	Mongolia	4.6%	8.3%
ESARO	Angola	8.5%	7.7%
ESARO	Comoros	16.8%	15.0%
TACRO	Guyana	7.5%	11.0%
WCARO	Cameroon	7.8%	7.4%
WCARO	Cote d'Ivoire	13.7%	13.3%
WCARO	DR Congo	9.4%	11.0%
WCARO	Senegal	7.6%	13.2%
Totals		**9.5%**	**10.6%**

Antenatal Care

Percentage of mothers, aged 15-49, who received antenatal care in the last year, by children's living arrangements

Region	Country	2-Parent Households	Single Mother Households
EAPRO	Mongolia	35.3%	31.7%
ESARO	Angola	27.7%	20.5%
ESARO	Burundi	38.3%	19.3%
ESARO	Comoros	31.3%	20.3%
TACRO	Dominican Republic	36.9%	35.1%
TACRO	Guyana	24.7%	27.5%
WCARO	Cameroon	11.4%	8.9%
WCARO	Cote d'Ivoire	36.1%	38.1%
WCARO	DR Congo	32.4%	25.8%
WCARO	Senegal	35.2%	32.9%
Totals		**30.7%**	**25.5%**

Boys & Girls Treated for ARI

Percentage of children with acute respiratory infection (ARI) in the last two weeks who received treatment from an appropriate healthcare provider

Region	Country	Sex	2-Parent Households	Single Mother Households
ESARO	Kenya	Boys	47.5%	51.1%
		Girls	53.5%	43.2%
	Swaziland	Boys	54.8%	63.2%
		Girls	60.6%	62.7%
TACRO	Dominican Republic	Boys	45.3%	34.0%
		Girls	31.1%	47.2%
	Venezuela	Boys	64.6%	63.2%
		Girls	71.2%	79.8%
WCARO	Senegal	Boys	28.2%	36.0%
		Girls	20.5%	26.6%
	Cote d'Ivoire	Boys	31.9%	45.3%
		Girls	38.7%	40.0%
	DR Congo	Boys	34.7%	43.4%
		Girls	37.5%	35.1%
Totals		**Boys**	**41.5%**	**47.8%**
		Girls	**44.5%**	**43.7%**

Note: Empty cells reflect insufficient data.

Early Childhood Education, 16 Countries

Percentage of children, aged 36-47 months, who are attending some form of organized early childhood education program

Region	Country	2-Parent Households	Single-Mother Households	Single-Father Households	Living w/ Neither Parent
EAPRO	Mongolia	8.2%	6.7%	—-	5.1%
ESARO	Angola	2.4%	2.5%	—-	3.9%
ESARO	Burundi	3.6%	2.8%	—-	5.6%
ESARO	Comoros	5.8%	6.2%	6.1%	9.1%
ESARO	Kenya	5.8%	5.9%	16.7%	8.7%
ESARO	Lesotho	10.1%	10.2%	2.0%	13.2%
ESARO	Swaziland	5.8%	4.1%	8.1%	5.3%
TACRO	Dominican Republic	22.5%	22.4%	—-	11.8%
TACRO	Guyana	12.7%	18.1%	—-	21.3%
TACRO	Trinidad & Tobago	32.4%	36.8%	—-	—-
TACRO	Venezuela	12.9%	16.7%	22.5%	12.2%
WCARO	Cameroon	5.1%	7.1%	—-	11.3%
WCARO	Cote d'Ivoire	2.2%	1.2%	1.4%	1.9%
WCARO	DR Congo	1.0%	1.2%	3.4%	3.5%
WCARO	Senegal	2.8%	4.1%	3.3%	5.2%
Regional Totals:					
	ESARO	4.8%	4.7%	15.4%	7.2%
	TACRO	15.8%	18.7%	—-	12.3%
	WCARO	2.8%	4.1%	3.0%	4.6%
Totals		**5.4%**	**6.5%**	**8.9%**	**6.5%**

Note: Empty cells reflect insufficient data.

Primary School Attendance & Completion

Percentage of children of primary school age attending primary school, and percentage of children entering grade 1 who eventually reach grade 5

		% Attending Primary School		% 1st Graders Reaching Grade 5	
Region	**Country**	2-Parent Households	Single Mother Households	2-Parent Households	Single Mother Households
ESARO	Kenya	74.3%	75.0%	96.4%	95.2%
	Burundi	50.5%	40.9%	82.8%	72.5%
	Swaziland	70.0%	70.6%	81.9%	91.0%
	Lesotho	65.7%	66.3%	79.2%	80.8%
	Comoros	35.1%	33.1%	23.1%	19.3%
TACRO	Guyana	87.2%	87.7%	98.8%	94.7%
	Venezuela	83.7%	86.0%	98.3%	91.8%
	Dominican Republic	91.9%	92.4%	—-	—-
	Trinidad & Tobago	97.9%	95.6%	93.6%	94.8%
WCARO	Rwanda	60.6%	61.0%	85.0%	89.1%
	DR Congo	52.4%	47.3%	55.2%	39.4%
	Senegal	44.7%	53.5%	52.3%	49.4%
	Cote d'Ivoire	57.0%	55.9%	71.5%	70.3%
	Cameroon	71.3%	79.7%	—-	—-
Regional Totals:					
	ESARO	69.2%	68.1%	91.8%	89.4%
	TACRO	86.2%	87.8%	98.2%	92.0%
	WCARO	55.7%	54.7%	60.3%	50.2%
Totals		**63.8%**	**63.2%**	**74.0%**	**66.5%**

Note: Empty cells reflect insufficient data.

Regional Summaries: % Children Working, by Living Arrangement

Domestic work, 28 hrs+/week	Sex	2-Parent Households	Single Mother Households	Single Father Households	Living w/ Neither Parent
ESARO	Boys	3.9%	4.8%	7.0%	4.6%
	Girls	*5.8%*	*6.5%*	*5.5%*	*7.2%*
TACRO	Boys	0.5%	0.8%	1.1%	1.6%
	Girls	*1.4%*	*0.8%*	*2.0%*	*4.3%*
WCARO	Boys	13.4%	15.5%	21.9%	15.8%
	Girls	*22.8%*	*23.4%*	*23.4%*	*34.2%*

Work for family business or farm, 1 hr+/week	Sex	2-Parent Households	Single Mother Households	Single Father Households	Living w/ Neither Parent
ESARO	Boys	9.7%	10.3%	11.2%	9.5%
	Girls	*8.5%*	*9.0%*	*21.7%*	*8.1%*
TACRO	Boys	4.7%	4.7%	6.1%	5.6%
	Girls	*2.4%*	*2.7%*	*2.8%*	*2.7%*
WCARO	Boys	20.6%	19.7%	23.9%	23.7%
	Girls	*18.8%*	*19.3%*	*17.4%*	*20.3%*

Work for non-household member, 1 hr+/week	Sex	2-Parent Households	Single Mother Households	SingleFather Households	Living w/ Neither Parent
ESARO	Boys	3.2%	3.9%	3.2%	3.4%
	Girls	*3.3%*	*3.6%*	*3.9%*	*9.1%*
TACRO	Boys	5.1%	8.4%	8.2%	8.2%
	Girls	*2.6%*	*4.6%*	*2.9%*	*4.4%*
WCARO	Boys	11.6%	12.4%	13.9%	14.2%
	Girls	*11.9%*	*13.1%*	*12.8%*	*13.1%*

NOTES

[1] The difficulty has been in finding terms that are clear, descriptively accurate and respectful. Describing living arrangements that included only one parent was especially challenging. Earlier drafts of this paper have experimented unsuccessfully with terms such as children living with "single mothers" or "single fathers", "unaccompanied mothers" or "unaccompanied fathers", and children living "without a mother" or "without a father." "Single" implied a judgment about the parent's marital status; "unaccompanied" suggested that a lone parent requires a partner, and "without" suggested that the family structure itself was lacking by not having two biological parents. "Lone mother", used in some studies, is likewise unappealing. Finally, the oft-used term "female-headed household" is not useful for our study for reasons described in the text. For an in-depth discussion of attitudes and biases reflected in the language used in studies on mothers who raise their children on their own, see Chant 1997.

[2] Regional acronyms are as follows: CEE/CIS (Central and Eastern Europe and the Commonwealth Independent States; EAPRO (East Asia and Pacific); ESARO (Eastern and Southern Africa); MENA (Middle East and North Africa); TACRO (Latin America and the Caribbean); WCARO (Western and Central Africa).

[3] All total averages are weighted by population of children under the age of 18.

REFERENCES

Asian Development Bank (2004). "Country Assistance Plan - Mongolia. 2003". January 1. <www.adb.org/Documents/CAPs/MON/0102.asp>.

Akinsola, Henry A. and Judith M. Popovitch (2002). "The Quality of Life of Families in Female-Headed Households in Botswana: A Secondary Analysis of Case Studies," *Health Care for Women International* 23, pp. 761-772.

Bruce, Judith, et al. (eds.) (1988). *A Home Divided: Women and Income in the Third World.* Stanford: Stanford University Press.

Buvinic, Marya and Geeta Rao Gupta (1997). "Targeting Women-Headed Households and Woman-Maintained Families in Developing Countries," *Searching for security: women's responses to economic transformations*, Isa Baud and Ines Smyth (eds.), London-New York: Routledge, pp. 132-154.

Chant, Sylvia H. (1997) *Women-Headed Households: Diversity and Dynamics in the Developing World*, consultant editor, Jo Campling, New York: St. Martin's Press.

— (2003). "Gender, Families and Households," *Gender in Latin America*, Sylvia Chant with Nikki Craske (eds.), New Brunswick: Rutgers University Press.

— (2004). "Female Headship and the 'Feminization of Poverty'," In *Focus*, UNDP International Poverty Centre, May, pp. 3-5

Chant, Sylvia H. and Matthew Gutmann (2000). *Mainstreaming Men into Gender and Development: Debates, Reflections, and Experiences.* Oxford: Oxfam.

DESIPA (1995). *Living Arrangements of Women and Their Children in Developing Countries: A Demographic Profile*. New York: United Nations, Dept. for Economic and Social Information and Policy Analysis. Population Division.

Donovan, Cynthia, et al. (2003). "Prime-Age Adult Morbidity and Mortality in Rural Rwanda: Which Households Are Affected and What are Their Strategies for Adjustment?". Contributed paper selected for presentation at the 25th International Conference of Agricultural Economists, Durban, South Africa, August 16-22, 2003.

Harris, Betty J. (1997). "Swazi Women Workers in Cottage Industries and Factories," *African Feminism: The Politics of Survival in Sub-Saharan Africa*, ed. Gwendolyn Mikell. Philadelphia: University of Pennsylvania Press.

IFAD (2004). "The Issue of Poverty among Female-Headed Households in Africa," n.d., January 3, <www.ifad.org/gender/learning/challenges/women/60.htm>.

Iken, Adelheid (1999). *Woman-Headed Households in Southern Namibia: Causes, Patterns, and Consequences*. Frankfurt: IKO in Kooperation mit Gamsberg Macmillan.

Joint United Nationals Program on HIV/AIDS (2002). *Report on the Global HIV/AIDS Epidemic*. Geneva: UNAIDS.

Mazurana, Dyan and Susan McKay (2001). "Child Soldiers: What about the Girls?", *Bulletin of the Atomic Scientists* 57:5, pp. 30-35.

Mernissi, Fatima (1987). *Beyond the Veil: Male-Female Dynamics in Modern Muslim Society*, rev. ed., Bloomington: Indiana University Press.

Moser, Caroline (1993). *Gender Planning and Development: Theory, Practice and Training*, New York: Routledge.

Nain, Gemma Taing (1997). "The Retreat of the State in the English-Speaking Caribbean," *Searching for Security: Women's Responses to Economic Transformations*, Isa Baud and Ines Smyth eds., London-New York: Routledge, pp. 24-44.

National Statistical Office of Mongolia (2004). "Status and Trends." 2003. January 1, <www.nso.mn/mdg/eng_goals3.htm>.

National Statistical Office of Mongolia and World Bank (2001). "Mongolia: Participatory Living Standards Assessment, 2000". Summary report prepared for Donor Consultative Group Meeting, Paris, May 15-16.

Neupert, Ricardo F. (1994). "Fertility Decline in Mongolia: Trends, Policies and Explanations," *International Family Planning Perspectives* 20:1, March, pp. 18-22.

Puechguirbal, Nadine (2003). "Women and War in the Democratic Republic of Congo," *Signs* 28:4, Summer, p. 1271.

Quisumbing, Agnes R. et al. (2001). "Are Women Overrepresented among the Poor? An Analysis of Poverty in 10 Developing Countries," *Journal of Development Economics* 66, pp. 225-269.

Rogers, Beatrice Lorge (1996). "The Implications of Female Household Headship for Food Consumption and Nutritional Status in the Dominican Republic," *World Development* 24:1, pp. 113-128.

Schoepf, Brooke, Grundfest and Walu Engundu (1991). "Women's Trade and Contributions to Household Budgets in Kinshasa," *The Real Economy of Zaire: The Contribution of Smuggling and Other Unofficial Activities to National Wealth*, eds. Janet MacGaffey et al. Philadelphia: University of Pennsylvania Press.

UN (1995). "Copenhagen Declaration on Social Development", <www.un.org.esa/socdev/wssd /agreements/decparta.htm>.

UN Habitat (1995). *Women in Human Settlements Development: Getting the Issues Right,* Nairobi: United Nations Centre for Human Settlements (Habitat).

UNFPA (2004). "Women as Food Producers," *Interactive Population Center: Food for the Future,* n.d., January 3, <www.unfpa.org/intercenter/food/womenas.htm>.

UNICEF HIV/AIDS (2003). Unit. *Africa's Orphaned Generations.* November, New York: UNICEF.

Van Driel, Francien Th. M. (1994). *Poor and Powerful : Female-Headed Households and Unmarried Motherhood in Botswana.* Saarbrücken: Verlag für Entwicklungspolitik Breitenbach.

Vecchio, Nerina and Kartik C. Roy (1998). *Poverty, Female-Headed Households, and Sustainable Economic Development.* Westport: Greenwood Press.

World Bank and National Statistical Office of Mongolia (2001). "Mongolia. Participatory Living Standards Assessment 2000". Summary report prepared for Donor Consultative Group Meeting, Paris, May 15-16.

Chapter 12

Child Work and Schooling in Niger*

Mamadou Thiam

INTRODUCTION

Education is increasingly recognized as essential for economic growth and social development. Unfortunately in Africa, particularly in sub-Saharan Africa, many children are not in school and the number out of school children has increased by 17 percent over the last decade (UNESCO 2003/2004). Research on education in developing countries has shown that low levels of school participation are not completely explained by the lack of school supply. Although governments are the primary providers of schooling in Africa, parents and other family members play a part in the decision as to whether children attend school (Lloyd and Blanc, 1996) and some children do not attend despite the availability of schooling. Indeed, education is only one of the activities in which children engage: economic employment and domestic work are competing alternatives (Shapiro et al. 2003). Children contribute to household welfare through significant participation in the running of the home, for example by caring for younger children or fetching water and woods, or by working in the family farm or business, or through external employment. In some African societies parents may consider work as an important training and means of socialization for children.

It is important to identify factors that might influence households' schooling decisions. Many studies have concluded that parents' education is one of the most important determinants of children's participation in school. Educated parents are more likely to perceive the benefits of schooling and thus enroll their children in school. As with parents' education, household wealth also influences the demand for schooling perhaps because poor households are not able to bear the cost of sending their children to school. Children's participation in

* Many thanks to my colleagues for suggestions that have led to improvements in the manuscript.

economic employment and domestic work is a common survival strategy for poor families. The low enrolment of girls has long been a concern to policymakers. In some developing countries, girls perform more home-related work than boys and thus may be less likely to attend school. In addition to gender inequalities, there are many disparities between urban and rural areas in developing countries with rural areas tending to be poorer and thus having lower school enrolment rates. Using data from the MICS-2 survey conducted in 2000, this paper examines children's work and participation in school in Niger, the impact of children's work on school attendance, grade repetition and school dropout. The determinants of schooling and child work considered in the paper are the educational attainment of the mother or person responsible for the child's care, household wealth and residence, the number of young children living in the household, and child's age and gender.

It is worth noting that the literature distinguishes child labour from child work. Child labour is defined as the regular participation of school age children in the labour force for economic reasons. As such, child labour prevents children from receiving schooling and may also be harmful to their health. On the other hand, child works refers to children's participation in light work that does not negatively affect their health and development or interfere with their education.

BACKGROUND INFORMATION ON NIGER

With a population of about 10 million people and a gross national income per capita of US $190 in 1999 (World Bank, 2001), Niger is one of the poorest countries in the world. Eighty percent of the population live in rural areas and about half of the population is under age 15 (UNDP, 2001). According to official data from the education system, the primary school net enrolment ratio for year 2000/2001 is 32 percent with more boys being enrolled than girls (39% versus 25%). There are also disparities in school enrolment between regions and between urban and rural areas. The net enrolment ratio was 42 percent for urban compared to 28 percent for rural. Official statistics also indicate that between 1995 and 2000, the gross enrolment rate in primary school increased slowly from 30 percent to 34 percent while public education expenditure as percentage of total government expenditure dropped from 16 percent to 12 percent. In year 2000[1] the percentage of repeaters in primary school was 10 percent while the survival rate to final grade (grade 6) was 65 percent.

The MICS-2 national report found that in Niger only 20 percent of adults aged 15 and over reported they are able to read, write and understand a short and simple statement about everyday life. Moreover, there are marked differences in literacy rates between men and women (30% versus 11%, respectively) and between adults living in urban and rural areas (51% versus 14%, respectively).

The current annual population growth rate of 3.6% (UNDP, 2001) greatly exacerbates the problem of achieving universal primary education by year 2015.

DATA

The MICS-2 survey in Niger was a nationally representative survey of all households, designed to obtain data on key indicators for assessing progress towards the goals of the World Summit for Children. The survey instruments include 3 separate questionnaires for households, individual women aged 15-49, and for children under 5 years of age. This paper analyses data collected from the 4,321 households that were interviewed. Data collection took place from April to August 2000. The household questionnaire covers modules relating to child labour and education as well as gathering information on individual and household characteristics.

The child labour module was administered to the mother of each child living in the household aged between 5 and 14. If the child's mother was not living in the household, the person responsible for the child's care was interviewed. For each child, the survey asked if, during the week before the survey, the child was employed by someone other than a household member, helped with housekeeping chores, or performed any other work for the family (on the farm or in a business). For each type of work, the survey collected the number of hours worked during the week before the survey.

For each household member aged 5 and over, the education module collected information on whether the member had ever attended school and the highest level attended and grade completed at that level. For each household member aged 5 to 17, the survey gathered information on school attendance, level and grade attended for both the current and previous school years. It is worth noting that in Niger, the school year starts in October and ends in June, and the official primary school ages are 7 to 12 years.

The survey also asked for information on water and sanitation, the main material of dwelling floor, number of rooms, main cooking fuel, availability of electricity, assets owned by households (e.g., radio) or by household members (e.g., bicycle, car). The information was used to derive a wealth index for households based on the method of principal components as described in Filmer and Pritchett (1998a). This wealth index serves as a proxy for the socioeconomic status of households.

The survey employed a complex probability sample design featuring disproportionate sample allocation, stratification and clustering. In order to take this complexity into account, some of the analyses in this paper were performed using SUDAAN 8.0.

RESULTS

Child work

The definition of child work used in the analysis is that of UNICEF which considers a child to be currently working if during the week before the survey, the child worked for someone other than a member of the household (paid or unpaid), or did household chores for 4 or more hours per day, or worked in a family farm or business.

During the week before the survey, about 69[2] percent of children 5-14 in Niger were engaged inchild work as is shown in table 1 and graph 1. Children were heavily engaged in domestic activities: about 89 percent of children helped with household chores of whom 17 percent spent 4 hours or more per day on these chores. The proportion of children who worked for someone who is not a member of the household is similar to the proportion of children who worked in a family farm or business: 43 and 44 percent, respectively. The data show that the work burden differs among children. In order to identify which children are spending more time on work, an ordinary least square (OLS) regression model of the number of hours children work was estimated separately for each type of work. The following explanatory variables were used in each model: age, sex and schooling status of the child, the number of children under 5 residing in the household, household wealth and residence, and the educational attainment of the mother or person responsible for the child's care. In the text, the word caretaker is used to refer to the mother or person responsible for the child's care. The results of the regression analyses are reported in table 2. As expected, these results show that the number of hours children work increases with their age.

It has been shown in some studies (see for example Canagarajah and Coulombe, 1997) that boys and girls carry out different types of work; girls do more household chores while boys are more likely to be in the labour force. The data presented here confirm this conclusion with respect to household chores. While girls do on average 6 more hours of domestic work, boys spend 6 more hours on the farm or in a business.

Children who are not in school spend 3 more hours on the farm or in a business than children who are currently attending school. However, the regression model indicates that after controlling for other variables in the model, the difference between the children attending school and the others in relation to the time spent in domestic activities is barely significant ($p = 0.0494$). This last result is an indication that schooling does not prevent children from doing domestic work for the household.

Research on child labour in the African context shows that more rural children engage in work than children living in urban areas (see for example Canagarajah and Coulombe, 1997; Grootaert, 1998). Our analysis confirms this finding. Indeed, in Niger a child living in a rural area spends on average 3 more hours on domestic work and 7 more hours on the farm or in the family business compared to a child living in an urban area.

It is commonly believed that household poverty drives children into work. The data certainly show that children from the poorest households work more hours than children from the richest households; the difference in the number of hours worked being on average 2 and a half hours for domestic activities and 3 and a half hours for other family work. However, the data reveal no significant difference in the work burden between children from the poorest households and children from households in the middle categories. This might be due to there being little difference in wealth between the poorest and middle categories because of the depth of poverty in Niger or it might indicate that the wealth index is an inadequate proxy for socio-economic status. As mentioned earlier, in the absence of data on household consumption and expenditures, household characteristics and assets owned by households and household members are used to derive the wealth index. Inevitably the choice of the variables affects the quality of the index.

The educational attainment of the mother or person responsible for the child's care is also associated with the amount of time the child works. Children cared for by someone with primary level education work on average 2 hours less on the farm or in a business than those cared for by someone with no education. When the caretaker's educational attainment is secondary and higher, the time children spend in domestic

Graph 1. Proportion of children 5-14 who are currently working

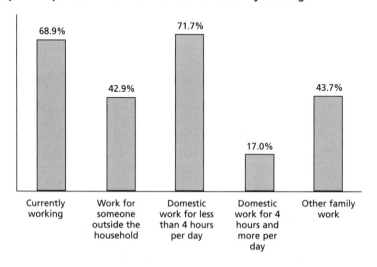

activities and work for someone other than a household member decreases by 3 and a half hours and one and half hour, respectively.

The number of children under 5 residing in the household influences only the number of hours children work for someone outside the household.

School attendance

About one third of children 5-14 (32%) were reported in the survey as currently attending school. As expected, the data confirm that there are marked differences between sub-groups of population. While 38 percent of boys were in school, the proportion was 26 percent for girls. The proportion of urban children attending school is 63 percent compared to 26 percent for rural children.

Much of the literature on the determinants on schooling (Lloyd and Blanc, 1996; Filmer and Pritchett 1998) shows that the educational attainment of the household head and household wealth are important determinants of children's participation in school. As can be seen in graph 2 and table 3, the proportion of children attending school increases from 27 percent of those with uneducated caretakers to 82 percent of those with caretakers who have secondary education and higher. School attendance also increases with household wealth from 20 percent in the poorest households to 58 percent in the richest households.

A straightforward examination of the data seems to show that working children and non-working children do not differ significantly with respect to school attendance ($p=0.1320$). However, in order to better assess the relationship between child work and school attendance, a logistic regression model of school attendance was employed. The explanatory variables used in the model were: the child's age, sex and work status, the educational attainment of the caretaker, the number of children under 5 residing in the household, household wealth and urbanization. The logit being linear in age, age was used as a continuous variable in the model. The results of the logistic regression analysis are presented in table 4 in the form of odds ratios, which represent the change in the odds of attending school associated with a one-unit change in the explanatory variable.

Older children are more likely to attend school than younger ones, all things being equal. Although the analysis included children 5-14 and schools cater for children 7 and over, the proportion of children currently attending school still increases with age among children 7-11 and then dropped for children ages 12-14 as is shown in graph 5. Boys and urban children are twice as likely to attend school as girls and rural children, after controlling for other variables in the model. However the logistic regression analysis confirms that even after adjusting for other factors, working children and non-working children still don't significantly differ on school attendance. Children from the wealthiest households are nearly 3 times more likely to attend school than children from the poorest households. However, there is no difference in school attendance between children from the poorest households and children from households in the middle wealth categories.

As expected, the more educated the caretaker the higher the probability of children 5-14 attending school. When the caretaker has attained primary education children are nearly twice as likely to attend school as those with a caretaker with no education. This likelihood increases to nearly 5 times when the caretaker has education at the secondary level and higher. The data also show that children are better off even when the caretaker has non-standard education with the odds of school attendance being 2.46 times that for children with an uneducated caretaker.

A common but not undisputed opinion is that, in the African context, the presence of young siblings in the household has an effect on children's schooling, particularly girls' education. In studying school enrolment and attendance in rural Botswana, Chernichovsky (1985) concluded that the presence of very young siblings was detrimental to children's schooling. However, (Canagarajah and Coulombe, 1997) did not find such an effect in a more recent study of child labour and schooling in Ghana. In our analysis the number of children under 5 residing in the household in Niger is not related to children's likelihood of attending school.

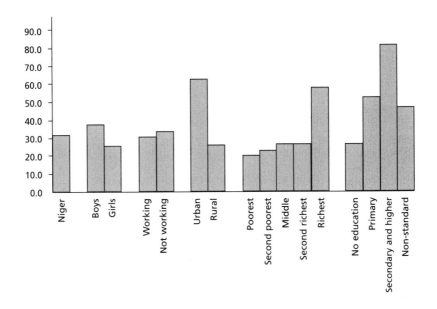

Grade repetition

A high number of children repeating grades represents a serious drain on education system capacity (UNESCO 2002), particularly in countries with a shortfall of schools or school places due to limited resources. Table 5 shows that among children 5-14 who were currently attending school or attended school at any time during the current school year,[3] about 29 percent were repeating the grade they attended in the school year preceding the survey. Table 5 also shows that the proportion of repeaters varies between different sub-populations.

Not surprisingly, grade repetition is more common among working children. Overall, 34 percent of working children were repeating their grade versus 19 percent for nonworking children (p<0.001). Despite the gender disparity in school access, boys and girls are equally likely to repeat their grade: 30 percent of girls were repeating their grade compared to 28 percent of boys. For both sexes, grade repetition is higher among working children.

Grade repetition is also higher among rural children than urban children (34% versus 16%). Moreover, the difference in grade repetition between working children and nonworking children is more pronounced in rural areas.

Table 5 shows that after controlling for household wealth, working children and nonworking children differ significantly on grade repetition only for households in the middle wealth category. In households from the middle wealth category, 44 percent of working children were repeating their grade compared to 23 percent for nonworking children.

In households where the caretaker has received no education or non-standard education, child work significantly increases children's likelihood of repeating their grade. However, child work has no statistically significant effect on grade repetition when the caretaker has attained primary education or higher.

Graph 3. Proportion of children 5-14 currently repeating their grade

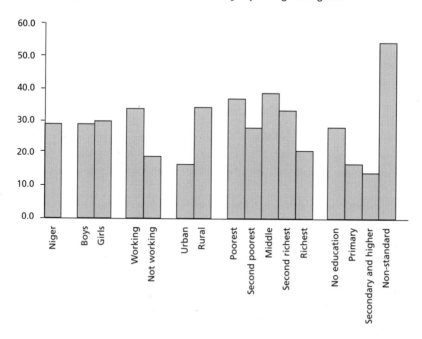

School dropout

Table 6 shows that among children 5-14 who attended school in the school year before the survey, 11 percent have dropped out at the time of the survey. Like grade repetition, the proportion of children who dropped out of school is higher among working children than nonworking children (13% versus 6%). Although boys are twice more likely than girls to attend school there is no gender difference on school dropout: 11 percent of girls dropped out of school versus 12 percent of boys. For both sexes, dropout remains higher among working children.

Dropout is also higher among rural children: 13 percent compared to 7 percent for urban children. Overall, the proportion of children who dropped out of school decreases with rising levels of the caretaker's educational attainment: from 12 percent when the caretaker has no education to about 5 percent when the caretaker has secondary education or higher. The data also reveal that after controlling for the caretaker's educational attainment, working children and nonworking children differ significantly on dropout only when the caretaker is uneducated. For other levels of education of the caretaker, child work has no statistically significant effect on children's school dropout. This last result is not surprising since uneducated parents are less likely to recognize the benefits of schooling and their children are more likely to drop out of school.

Our analysis shows that after controlling for household wealth, the relationship between child work and school dropout disappears for all levels of household wealth except for the middle wealth category.

CONCLUSION

This paper examined child work and schooling in Niger focusing on the impact of child work on school attendance, grade repetition and school dropout. The data reveal that about 3 out of 10 children 5-14 attend school in Niger and 2 of these 3 children are engaged in work at the same time. During school year 1999/2000, about 29 percent of children 5-14 were repeating the grade they attended in the previous school year. Among those who attended school in the previous school year, 11 percent have dropped out. The analysis shows that child work does not affect school attendance but significantly increases grade repetition and school dropout. The survey didn't collect information on the nature of work children do for someone other than a household member. Such information would help understand why child work is not related to school attendance because fostering, which is common in many African countries is often seen as an opportunity for schooling and fostered children, particularly girls are expected to carry out domestic activities. Our analysis shows that children are heavily engaged in domestic activities and less than 3 percent of children working for someone other than a household member were paid. Older children do more work but are more likely to attend school than younger ones.

Although boys are twice more likely to attend school than girls, there is no gender difference in grade repetition and school dropout. This result suggests that, once enrolled in school, girls tend to progress as well as boys. Girls and boys work nearly the same amount of time but contribute

Graph 4. Proportion of children 5-14 who have dropped out of school

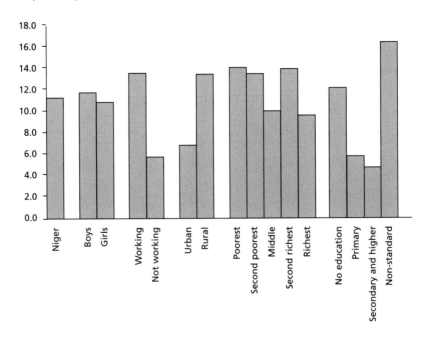

to different types of work; girls are more likely to carry out domestic work while boys are more likely than girls to work more for the family on a farm or in a business.

The data show that rural children experience a higher work burden and are more likely to repeat their grade and drop out of school. In sub-Saharan Africa, the quality of education is often poor in rural areas and children may drop out due to the lack of a local school or because the only school is far from the household. Equity concerns in Niger, as in many countries in sub-Saharan Africa, should not be limited to gender. With 80 percent of the population being rural, the urban-rural parity in school access and learning performance should also be given priority in policy intervention.

As expected, children are less likely to work and more likely to attend school when their caretaker is educated. Child work significantly increases the probability of grade repetition and school dropout only when the caretaker is uneducated; it has no effect on repetition and dropout when the caretaker has primary education or higher. The presence of young children (up to 5 years) in the household reduces only the time children work for non members of the household but it does not affect time spent in domestic work and work for the family on the farm or in a business.

The analysis confirms that children from poor households do more work and are less likely to attend school. However, after controlling for household wealth, working children and nonworking children don't differ significantly on grade repetition and school dropout for all levels of household wealth except for the middle wealth category.

In a review of research on education and inequality in developing regions, Buchmann and Hannum (2001) found that the relationship between schooling and child work differs across countries. Comparisons between different sources of data within and across countries are difficult to do because of the variation in the definition of child work and children's age group used in different studies. The MICS-2 surveys having applied essentially the same survey instrument overcome these difficulties and therefore, provide an excellent opportunity for comparative research. One limitation of the MICS-2 surveys is that the education module does not include questions on the reasons why children are not attending school. Building an understanding of these reasons would help in the examination of the impact of child work on children's progression in school.

Graph 5. School attendance by age. Currently attending school

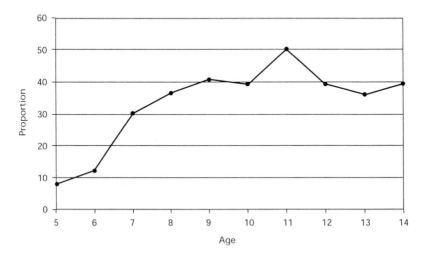

Table 1. Proportion of children 5-14 currently working, by background characteristics

Background characteristics	Work for someone who is not a household member (%)		Domestic work (%)		Other family work (%)	Currently working (%)	Number of children sampled
	Paid	Unpaid	Less than 4 hours per day	4 hours or more per day			
Age							
5 – 9	1.6	38.4	77.3	8.6	32.5	59.1	4172
10 – 14	3.9	42.9	64.0	28.3	59.0	82.3	3061
Gender							
Boys	3.2	40.4	74.7	9.9	52.3	72.6	3595
Girls	2.0	40.3	68.7	24.1	35.3	65.2	3637
Currently attending school							
Yes	3.1	42.2	75.9	13.2	40.1	67.1	2253
No	2.4	39.4	69.8	18.9	45.6	70.1	4821
Residence							
Urban	4.2	34.9	72.5	11.3	17.0	52.4	1164
Rural	2.2	41.4	71.5	18.1	48.9	72.0	6069
Household Wealth							
Poorest	2.3	41.0	70.6	20.0	51.9	73.9	1393
Second poorest	1.8	45.1	71.9	16.2	48.2	71.9	1198
Middle	2.6	38.6	70.6	20.1	47.9	69.2	1582
Second richest	2.7	40.2	69.3	18.8	47.0	74.1	1400
Richest	3.2	38.2	75.4	10.7	27.0	57.8	1660
Caretaker's educational attainment							
No education	2.5	39.6	70.9	18.3	45.8	70.4	5915
Primary	3.7	36.8	73.7	11.2	31.4	60.9	537
Secondary and higher	1.2	31.0	79.3	4.7	16.5	44.3	211
Non-standard	2.3	55.0	74.6	13.7	44.0	70.2	56.6
Niger	2.6	40.3	71.7	17.0	43.7	68.9	7233

Table 2. OLS regressions of the number of hours children worked during the week before the survey

Variables	Number of hours worked for who is not a household member		Number of hours someone spent on domestic work		Number of hours spent on other family work	
	Coefficient	p	Coefficient	p	Coefficient	p
Age	0.39	0.0000	1.79	0.0000	2.06	0.0000
Gender (reference = boys)						
Girls	-0.27	0.2013	5.89	0.0000	-6.27	0.0000
Currently attending school (reference = yes)						
Non	-0.10	0.7553	1.14	0.0494	3.12	0.0001
Residence (reference=urban)						
Rural	0.86	0.1012	2.81	0.0068	7.08	0.0000
Household wealth (reference=poorest)						
Second poorest	0.43	0.3386	-0.19	0.8410	-1.81	0.2301
Middle	0.30	0.4846	1.18	0.1400	-1.48	0.1476
Second richest	0.67	0.2903	0.18	0.8292	-0.83	0.6387
Richest	-0.06	0.9100	-2.58	0.0061	-3.55	0.0429
Caretaker's educational attainment (reference= no education)						
Primary	-0.54	0.1957	-1.32	0.0542	-1.84	0.0380
Secondary and higher	-1.44	0.0047	-3.34	0.0001	-1.48	0.1613
Non-standard	0.18	0.7819	-1.06	0.2951	0.90	0.4713
Number of children under 5	-0.32	0.0056	-0.14	0.4808	0.08	0.7780

Table 3. Proportion of children 5-14 currently attending school, by background characteristics

Background characteristics	Percentage	Number of children
Gender		
Boys	37.8	3517
Girls	26.0	3557
Currently working		
Yes	30.9	4892
No	34.0	2181
Residence		
Urban	63.1	1135
Rural	25.9	5939
Household wealth		
Poorest	20.0	1377
Second poorest	22.5	1172
Middle	26.7	1538
Second richest	26.3	1361
Richest	58.1	1626
Caretaker's educational attainment		
No education	26.7	5790
Primary	52.3	529
Secondary and higher	81.9	207
Non-standard	47.2	544
Niger	31.8	7073

Table 4. Logistic regression of school attendance

Variables (OR)	Odds Ratio	p Limit OR	Lower 95% Limit OR	Upper 95%
Intercept	0.03	0.0000	0.02	0.04
Age	1.20	0.0000	1.17	1.23
Gender				
Boys	2.01	0.0000	1.73	2.34
Girls	1.00	——	1.00	1.00
Currently working				
Yes	1.00	——	1.00	1.00
No	1.25	0.0379	1.01	1.54
Residence				
Urban	2.13	0.0000	1.47	3.09
Rural	1.00	——	1.00	1.00
Household wealth				
Poorest	1.00	——	1.00	1.00
Second poorest	1.13	0.5164	0.78	1.64
Middle	1.40	0.0402	1.02	1.92
Second richest	1.34	0.0864	0.96	1.86
Richest	2.90	0.0000	1.95	4.31
Caretaker's educational attainment				
No education	1.00	——	1.00	1.00
Primary	1.95	0.0000	1.52	2.50
Secondary and higher	4.72	0.0000	3.10	7.19
Non-standard	2.46	0.0000	1.74	3.50
Number of children under 5	1.04	0.2186	0.97	1.12

Table 5. Proportion of children 5-14 currently repeating their grade, by background characteristics

Background characteristics	Working children (%)	Nonworking children (%)	p*	All children(%)	Number of children
Gender					
Boys	31.9	17.2	0.0000	28.1	1447
Girls	36.2	20.4	0.0000	30.0	1002
Residence					
Urban	18.8	13.8	0.0334	16.4	743
Rural	37.9	23.1	0.0007	34.3	1705
Household wealth					
Poorest	39.9	22.7	0.0587	36.6	305
Second poorest	30.5	17.6	0.0990	27.9	290
Middle	44.2	22.5	0.0022	38.7	455
Second richest	37.7	19.4	0.0109	33.1	387
Richest	23.4	17.4	0.1035	20.8	1011
Caretaker's educational attainment					
No education	31.4	19.7	0.0002	28.1	1694
Primary	20.0	11.9	0.0757	16.7	285
Secondary and higher	15.5	12.9	0.6331	14.0	174
Non-standard	61.8	32.1	0.0018	54.4	293
Niger	33.5	18.8	0.0000	28.9	2449

* p-value for testing the association between child work and grade repetition.

Table 6. Proportion of children 5-14 who dropped out of school, by background characteristics

Base: children 5-14 who attended school in the previous school year

Background characteristics	Working children (%)	Non working children (%)	p*	All children (%)	Number of children
Gender					
Boys	13.6	4.9	0.0006	11.6	1246
Girls	13.1	6.5	0.0001	10.7	860
Residence					
Urban	8.9	4.0	0.0108	6.7	660
Rural	14.8	7.5	0.0063	13.3	1447
Household wealth					
Poorest	14.4	11.0	0.5444	13.9	255
Second poorest	15.0	5.8	0.0245	13.3	260
Middle	12.4	0.0	0.0073	9.9	389
Second richest	14.9	9.5	0.2754	13.8	327
Richest	12.3	5.7	0.0278	9.5	876
Caretaker's educational attainment					
No education	14.2	5.4	0.0000	12.0	1461
Primary	6.6	4.0	0.4373	5.6	240
Secondary and higher	9.5	0.7	0.0922	4.6	153
Non-standard	15.7	18.6	0.6611	16.4	251
Niger	13.4	5.7	0.0000	11.2	2106

* p-value for testing the association between child work and school dropout.

NOTES

1   UNESCO Institute for Statistics database.

2   In this analysis a small number of children were excluded because a clear answer was not obtained to questions.

3   Attendance at any time during the current school year was only asked of children who were not currently attending school. The majority of repeaters (92%) are children who were currently attending school.

REFERENCES

Buchmann, C. and Hannum, E. (2001). "Education and Stratification in Developing Countries: A Review of Theories and Research", *Annual Review of Sociology*, vol. 27, pp. 77-102.

Canagarajah, S. and Coulombe, H. (1997). *Child Labor and Schooling in Ghana*, Working Paper No. 1844, Washington, D.C.: The World Bank.

Chernichovsky, D. (1985). "Socioeconomic and Demographic Aspects of School Enrollment and Attendance in Rural Botswana", *Economic Development and Cultural Change* 33, pp. 319-332.

Direction des Etudes et de la Programmation, Niger (2001), *Annuaire Statistique 2000-2001.*

Filmer D. and Pritchett L. (1998a). *Estimating wealth effects without expenditure data –or tears: An application to educational enrolments in States of India*, World Bank Policy Research Working Paper No. 1994, Washington, D.C.

Filmer D. and Pritchett L. (1998). *The Effect of Household Wealth on Educational Attainment Around the World: Demographic and Health Survey Evidence*, World Bank Policy Research Working Paper No. 1980, Washington, D.C.

Grootaert, C. (1998). *Child Labor in Côte d'Ivoire: Incidence and Determinants,* Washington, D.C.: The World Bank.

Huebler, F. and Loaiza E. (2002). *Child labor and School Attendance in Sub-Saharan Africa: Empirical Evidence from UNICEF's Multiple Indicator Cluster Surveys (MICS)*, New York: UNICEF.

Lloyd, C. B. and Blanc, A. K. (1996). "Children's Schooling in sub-Saharan Africa: The role of Fathers, Mothers, and Others", *Population and Development Review*, vol. 22, issue 2, pp. 265-298.

Shapiro, D., Nankhuni, F., and Findeisa, J. (2003). "Women's and Children's Work,

Environmental Stress, and Children's Education in Malawi," Paper prepared for presentation at the Quebec Inter-university Centre for Social Statistics and the UNESCO Institute for Statistics workshop on "New approaches to assessing the determinants of demand for primary education in Africa," Montreal, Quebec, September 3-4, 2003.

UNESCO (2002), "EFA Global Monitoring Report," *Education for All, Is the World on Track?*

UNESCO (2003/4). "EFA Global Monitoring Report," *Gender and Education for All, The Leap to Equality.*

United Nations Children's Fund (2000). *Enquête à indicateurs multiples de la fin de la décennie (MICS2)*, Niger.

United Nations Development Programme (2001). *Human Development Report*, New York.

World Bank (2001). *World Development Indicators*, Washington, D.C.

Chapter 13

The Working and Education Status of Children in India: An analysis based on the Multiple Indicator Survey, 2000

*Robert Jenkins**

BACKGROUND OF THE SITUATION

Under the Constitution of India, no child below 14 years of age shall be employed to work in any factory or in any hazardous employment (article 24). The Constitution also states that "Childhood and growth are to be protected against exploitation and against moral and material abandonment" (article 39F) and "the state shall endeavor to provide... free and compulsory education for all children until they complete the age of 14 years" (article 45). Article 39 of the Directive Principle of State Policy pledges that:

> the state shall, in particular, direct its policy towards securing ... that the health and strength of workers, men and women, and the tender age of children are not abused, and that citizens are not forced by economic necessity to enter vocations unsuited to their age or strength, that children are given opportunities and facilities to develop in a healthy manner, and in conditions of freedom and dignity, and that childhood and youth are protected against exploitation, and against moral and material abandonment...

While the global discussion on definitions of child labour continues, figures related to child labour in India from various sources show conclusively that child labour exists and remains a significant challenge to eradicate. Based on a definition of a worker as a person who is engaged in any economic activity, 5.4% of 5-14 year old children are "working" according to the Census of 1991 compared to 4.1% according to the 55th round (1999-2000) of the National Sample Survey Organization (NSSO).[1]

* The views expressed are those of the author and do not necessarily represent the views of UNICEF. Robert Jenkins is Chief, Strategic Planning, Monitoring and Evaluation Section, UNICEF, India. The author would like to express appreciation for the contributions from V. Jayachandran and Malti Gandhi of UNICEF India.

A comparable indicator from the Multiple Indicator Survey 2000 (MICS 2000) is the percentage of 5-14 year old children working for others, which was found to be 5.2%. However, the MICS 2000 collected additional data related to the working status of children, including whether a child works for others (for pay or unpaid and the number of hours per day); does household chores (including number of hours per day); and does other economically productive work at home. Adopting a broader definition of child labour such as "those who work for someone else, and/or engage in household chores for more than four hours a day, and/or do economically productive work at home", it is found that 14 % of children aged 5-14 years of age are engaged in child labour.[2] The extent of child labour however varies significantly among different population subgroups (see table A1 in the annex).

Regarding the education sector in India, there has been a significant increase in gross enrolment in primary schools, from 87.3% in 1991 to 95.7% in 2001 (Department of Education, 2003). A number of factors have contributed to the rising enrolment including the introduction of mid-days meals, opening of alternate schools, active participation of Parent Teacher Associations (PTAs) and massive enrolment drives. According to MICS 2000, more than three-fourths (77%) of children in the age group of 5-14 years are currently attending school. However, girls are disadvantaged compared to boys, with 82% of boys attending school compared to only 72% of girls (MICS 2000). Similarly, the gross enrolment ratio in 2001 was higher for boys (104.9%) than girls (85.9%) (Department of Education, 2003).

A constitutional amendment was passed in 2002 making free and compulsory education a fundamental right for children aged 6-14 years. The national and state governments continue to deliver the programme *Sarva Shiksha Abhiyan* (SSA), which aims to achieve universal elementary education by 2010. However, the modest increase in financial allocation to the SSA programme is not sufficient to meet the targets of the programme, with Rupees 15,120 million (approximately US$350 million) allocated in 2002-03 increasing to Rupees 19,000 million (approximately US$441 million) in 2003-04. The percentage of GDP expenditure on education has only slightly risen over the past decade, from 3.8% in 1991-92 to 4.1% in 2000-01 (Government of India, 2002).

Contrary to conventional wisdom that poor parents are not interested in education, the 1990s have seen an upsurge in the demand for basic education. The Probe Report (1999) concluded that 98% of parents answered yes to the question "is it important for a boy to be educated?" and 89% answered yes to "is it important for a girl to be educated?" While these figures indicate gender discrimination against girls, it is clear that parents recognize the importance of education for their children.

While enrolment and attendance in primary school has increased, the quality of education remains a major concern. Little emphasis has been placed on making education more relevant and in encouraging learning by doing and learning by observation. Activity based and child centered learning arrangements are still very weak. There are situations where children mechanically go through five years of primary education and emerge barely literate, leading to community apathy towards schooling. The continued poor quality of elementary education remains one of India's major areas of development failure, having implications for social development more generally including issues related to child labour.

BACKGROUND ON MICS 2000 IN INDIA

The Multiple Indicator Survey (MICS 2000), undertaken in 2000, was one of the largest socio-demographic household surveys conducted in India. Developed in collaboration with the WHO, UN Statistical Division, the London School of Hygiene and Tropical Medicine, and the Centers for Disease Control and Prevention; the MICS was customized and applied to the Indian context. Conducted at the state level, this survey involved all States and Union Territories and collected information from 119,305 households in 3,260 clusters in rural and urban areas.

MICS 2000 in India was designed to provide estimates at the national and state/UT's level, and for larger states separately for urban and rural areas. A two stage stratified sampling design was adopted, with sampling done independently for each stratum. The modus operandi of MICS 2000 was to interview, on the basis of uniform questionnaires, mothers and principal caregivers of children below the age of 15 and women aged 15-49 years from selected households.

MEASURING CHILD LABOUR

The continuing global debate on the definition of child labour sheds light on the difficulty of measuring this phenomenon. The challenge of arriving at a precise and accurate estimation of child labour was observed by the Committee on Child Labour of the National Commission on Labour in India which observed:

> The precise estimate of the overall magnitude of child labour in India is admittedly difficult on account of the predominance of the informal and unorganized nature of the labour market, and also due to multiplicity of concepts, methods of measurement and the sources of data (Kulshreshtha, 1994: 152).

Recognizing that in India, the majority of child labour is "concentrated in the urban informal sector and unorganized rural sectors, its exact size is not easily ascertainable" (Singh, 2004: 37). Therefore, to compliment the information from labour and economic surveys, a household survey, such as MICS, has proven to be an effective methodology to assess the working status of children and measure the extent of child labour in the country.

In MICS 2000, specific questions were canvassed to obtain the extent of child labour among children aged 5-14 years and also the education status of these children. At the time MICS 2000 was undertaken, there was very little information related to number of hours a child works in household chores or in an economically productive work, whether inside or outside the household. Regarding education, the MICS 2000 also assessed whether the child was ever enrolled, dropped out, or is currently attending school. The survey also asked care-givers for reasons why a child was never enrolled or dropped out.

The MICS 2000 complements and augments existing data from other sources such as the Census of India (every ten years), the National Family Health Survey (every five years), and the annual surveys from the National Sample Survey Organization (particularly the larger one which is undertaken every five years). Taken together, the information provides important insights for policy makers and programme managers on issues related to the situation of women and children.

While the data for the 2001 Census related to child labour has not been released, the 1991 Census has published information regarding children in the 5-14 age group who are employed fully or partially.

The categories of work according to the 1991 Census are as follows:

- "Main workers": in which the time criterion of engagement in work is the major part of the year, i.e. - at least 183 days in the preceding one year.

- "Marginal workers": those who worked for a certain period during the last year but not for the major part of the year.

- "Non-workers": those who have never worked in the last one year.

The total working population constitutes both main and marginal worker categories. According to the 1991 Census, 5.4% of children (5-14 years) are "working", which is an increase from 5.2% from the 1981 Census. The percentage of boys working decreased from 6.0% in 1981 to 5.7% in 1991, while the percentage of girls working increased from 4.3% in 1981 to 5.1% in 1991. According to the preliminary data from the Census 2001, more than 12 million children aged 5-14 years are working (percentage not yet available), of which 54% live in the five states of Andhra Pradesh, Bihar, Madhya Pradesh, Rajasthan and Uttar Pradesh.

The Multiple Indicator Survey 2000 included a variety of different questions which generated information related to the working status of children, including whether inside or outside the home, whether paid or unpaid, in what sector, how many hours per week, and whether the child does household chores and for how many hours. In India, 5.2% of children aged 5-14 years are working for someone outside the home, with slightly more than half (2.8%) of them receiving pay (see table A1). Almost 2 % of children in this age range are engaged in household chores for more than four hours a day (3% of female children as compared to less than 1% of male children).

CHILD LABOUR AND EDUCATION

There are many determinants of child labour, including poverty, illiteracy of the care-givers, migration, unemployment, social exclusion and discrimination, and poor quality or lack of access to education. There are also many reasons why children enroll, regularly attend or drop out of school. Based on the experience of analyzing the causes of malnutrition by UNICEF in the early 1990s, it is often useful to categorize these causes into structural, underlying and immediate causes in order to better understand the cause and effect relationships. However, this detailed analysis is beyond the scope of this paper.

MICS 2000 indicates a significant correlation between a child's working status and their education status. Table 1 compares the education status of children with their working status.

The education status of children who are working (by the various types of work) is significantly poorer than the education status of children who are not working. For example, nearly half (47%) of children who are working for someone else are currently attending school, whereas 79% of children who are *not* working for someone else are attending school. The data also indicates that working outside the home *for pay* is even more detrimental to the education status of children, perhaps indicating that the working conditions for children who are paid are more rigid or demanding (in terms of hours) and therefore, children working for pay are less likely to be able to successfully balance work and education.

Table 1 also highlights the implications of working for more than 28 hours a week (i.e. more than 4 hours per day) on school attendance. While the difference in the education status of children who are "doing household chores" compared to those who are not was limited, of the children engaged in household chores for more than 28 hours per week, only 30% are currently attending school whereas 78% of children who were doing less chores (or none) were attending school. MICS data therefore clearly indicates that children who work outside the home, particularly when for pay, and the children who work for more than 28 hours a week are disadvantaged in their access to education.

Table A2 illustrates the correlation between certain characteristics of a household and the education status of the child. For example, the following characteristics correlate with relatively poor education outcomes of children compared to the mean: rural households, caste/scheduled tribes, illiterate father or mothers. Recognizing that

Table 1. Children age 5-14 years by work and schooling status

	Never attended school (%)	Dropped out from school (%)	Currently attending school (%)	Number of children
Working for someone outside home*				
Yes	24	29	47	5,647
No	15	6	79	130,472
Working for someone outside home for pay				
Yes	37	46	17	2,838
No	15	6	79	133,281
Doing household chores				
Yes	15	11	73	56,027
No	15	5	80	80,222
Doing household chores > 28 hrs a week				
Yes	35	35	30	1,870
No	15	7	78	134,405
Children in economically productive work at home				
Yes	23	20	57	10,998
No	14	6	80	125,252
Child Labour**				
Yes	24	24	52	17,042
No	14	5	81	119,006
Total	15	8	77	136,339

Note: Sub totals may not add to the total because missing cases are not shown separately.

* For pay or without pay; ** Working for someone else outside home or doing household chores for more than 28 hours a week or engaged in economically productive work at home.

there are many other factors which influence the working status of children, a logistic regression analysis was undertaken in order to better understand the relationship between the education status of children and their working status, after controlling for certain other correlates (see Table A5 in the Annex). The logistic regression analysis was done separately for the various characteristics of working status, and has controlled for rural/urban, parent's literacy, and type of house (as a proxy for poverty). The exponential beta of the logistic regression gives the likelihood of children attending school by working status compared to those who are not working. The most striking results of this analysis is that while children who work for someone outside the home are more than 4 times less likely to attend school (than those who do not work for someone else), the influence of working for someone outside the home *for pay* is significantly greater –with children being more than 15 times less likely to attend school if they work outside the home for pay. Similarly, while children involved in any work are 2-3 times less likely to be in school, the children who are working for more than 28 hours are more than 7 times less likely to be currently in school (see table A5).

The MICS included a question to the mothers on why a child dropped out or was not enrolled in school. Table A4 (annex) summarizes the responses. It is clear that while there are many reasons why children dropout, "no time for school, child busy with household work" was cited 20.1% (11.9% for boys and 26.8% for girls) and "child busy with wage labour" was cited 8.9% (11.3% for boys and 6.9% for girls). Therefore, adding these two figures, 29% of parents with children who have dropped out or never attended school have cited working as one of the reasons for dropping out. Recognizing the social stigma of providing such an answer to the enumerator, such a high figure provides further evidence of the relationship between working and the education status of children. This data also indicates an important gender differential in the reasons given for leaving school: with more than twice as many girls than boys leaving school for household work; and almost twice as many boys than girls leaving school due to wage labour. Further analysis is required on the reasons children do not attend school, but based on MICS data, is clear that work is one important factor for lack of attendance and that gender disaggregated analysis is required in order to better understand the different realities of boys and girls.

CONCLUSION: CAUSE AND EFFECT?

The inter-linkages between the work status of children and their corresponding education status as reflected in school enrolment, attendance and dropouts are significant and telling. The data generated by MICS 2000 statistically demonstrates that children working for someone else, particularly for pay, and/or involved in family work for more than 28 hours per week, are less likely to be enrolled or currently attending school.

It cannot necessarily be concluded, however, that children are not going to school in order to work –that is, they are being "pulled" from school for work. With many children still having limited access to school; high level of teacher absenteeism; poor quality of education; the clash of school timings and agricultural operations; and the cost of schooling; there is also a certain "push" factor for leaving the school system which may result in children entering the labour market. Based only on the MICS data, it is not conclusive on whether child labour causes poor education outcomes (i.e. a child starts working and therefore never enrolls or drops out of school), or whether the poor quality or inaccessibility of the school system results in children dropping out, which puts them on a path towards becoming child labourers. That is, it is unclear whether it is the "pull factor" of work (out of necessity due to more structural causes such as poverty and discrimination) or the "push factor" of a poor quality or inaccessible education system which results in children working.

It should be noted that of the 5-14 year old children who are not attending school (the three categories are not mutually exclusive)

- 12% work for someone else

- 16% do economically productive work at home

- 30% work for someone else or are engaged in household work for more than four hours a day or do economically productive work at home.

Therefore, a significant portion of children who are not attending school are also *not* involved in work, which would indicate that there are other reasons for children to drop out or never enroll in school other than out of necessity to work (i.e. the "push factor" out of school). However, it should also be considered that there would be a strong tendency for care-givers to under-report child labour due to the social stigma of the issue.

While the MICS 2000 provides important information on the association between child labor and education status, further information and analysis is required in order to shed light on the cause and effect relationship between these two important social issues. Further disaggregating the information and undertaking more additional primary data collection to inform an analysis by rural/urban, male/female, by age, by level of exploitation, by characteristics of the school, by caste, and by economic group would be useful inputs to the policy-making and planning process. This disaggregated analysis would inform policy and programme formulation, including the development of distinct strategies to reach girls and boys, and also to address the negative influence of children doing household chores for more than 28 hours per week and children working outside the home (either pay or unpaid).

Furthermore, the reality of a child regarding their choices (or lack thereof) and the reasons behind these choices will remain difficult to capture in nationwide quantitative surveys. Qualitative processes including case studies and participatory methodologies such as participatory learning for action (PLA) would compliment surveys such as the MICS 2000 to gain a better understanding of the reality of disadvantaged children and the necessary policies and plans required to enhance the realization of their human rights.

Throughout the world, education and work during childhood are widely seen as incompatible. Work is generally viewed as preventing children from obtaining an education; providing good quality education to all children is often cited as a solution to child labour. Improving the quality of education and enhancing access will present further choices to children which will discourage child labour. Furthermore, recognizing that one of the structural causes of child labour is poverty and illiteracy of care-givers (particularly mothers), investing in education will also contribute to breaking the cycle of poverty which will enable future generations to be less likely to become child labourers. Therefore, interventions which improve the education system will have an immediate influence and long-term positive impact on reducing child labour. However, recognizing the various characteristics which correlate with education outcomes and with working status, a multiplicity of policy and programmatic interventions are necessary and must work in tandem in order to improve education indicators and also eliminate child labour.

Beginning with principles of Human Rights in which all children have a right to education and to be free from exploitation, policy-makers and planners should frame related policies and programmes towards improving access and quality of education and addressing the structural, underlying and immediate cause of child labour. Recognizing the interrelationship between these two issues, and also the unique experiences of each child, a multiplicity of policy and programme options should be explored depending on the local and perhaps even individual context. This would require emphasis on local solutions being developed within a broader enabling policy environment. The MICS 2000 clearly indicates an intimate relationship between child labour and education, and therefore policies and programmes will need to address both issues within a coherent framework.

ANNEXURE A

Table A 1. Summary of Data on Child Labour by Various Characteristics

Percent children aged 5-14 years engaged in different 'activities' by type of activity, according to selected background characteristics, India, MICS 2000

| Background characteristics | Percent children working for others[1] | | | Percent children engaged in | | | |
	For pay	As unpaid	Total	H.hold chores[2]	Econ prod. Work in home[3]	Child labour[4]	Number of children
Age of the child							
5-9 years	0.6	2.1	2.7	0.5	3.8	6.6	69261
10-14 years	5.2	2.8	8.0	3.2	13.4	22.4	67078
Sex of the child							
Male	2.7	2.6	5.3	0.5	8.7	13.6	69638
Female	2.9	2.3	5.2	3.1	8.1	14.8	66701
Place of residence							
Rural	3.0	2.3	5.3	2.0	9.5	15.3	92379
Urban	2.2	3.0	5.1	1.1	4.8	10.6	43960
Religion							
Hindu	2.8	2.5	5.3	1.8	8.7	14.5	88397
Muslim	2.7	2.1	4.7	1.7	6.7	12.3	20873
Christian	2.2	7.0	9.3	1.0	9.0	18.3	18166
Other	1.8	1.2	3.0	1.1	8.0	11.2	8797
Caste/tribe							
Scheduled Caste	3.7	2.2	5.9	2.1	8.3	14.7	20603
Scheduled Tribe	4.6	1.3	5.9	2.6	15.7	21.9	30272
Other	2.3	2.7	5.0	1.6	7.6	13.1	85346
Attending school							
Yes	0.6	2.6	3.2	0.7	6.2	9.6	113341
No	10.2	2.0	12.1	5.4	15.9	29.5	22938
Survival of parents							
Both alive	2.6	2.4	5.0	1.7	8.2	13.6	127833
Father not alive	6.3	3.9	10.2	2.7	12.2	23.2	4857
Mother not alive	4.8	2.5	7.3	4.1	11.8	20.3	2442
Both not alive	13.6	4.4	18.1	5.4	12.5	29.9	423
Total	**2.8**	**2.5**	**5.2**	**1.8**	**8.4**	**14.1**	**136339**

[1] Not a member of the household where the child live.

[2] Doing household chores for more than four hours a day.

[3] Engaged in any economically productive work at home.

[4] Working for others or doing household chores for more than four hours a day or engaged in any economically productive work at home.

Table A 2. School attendance by characteristics

Percent of children aged 5-14 years by school attendance, according to selected characteristics, India, MICS 2000

Characteristics	Never attended school	Dropped out from school	Currently attending school	Number of children
Age of the child				
5-9 Years	18.4	2.9	78.6	69261
10-14 Years	11.8	12.6	75.6	67078
6-10 Years	13.6	4.0	82.3	70719
11-13 Years	11.4	12.3	76.2	39426
6-13 Years	12.9	6.8	80.2	110145
Sex of the child				
Male	11.5	6.6	81.9	69638
Female	19.2	8.6	72.2	66701
Place of residence				
Rural	17.7	7.9	74.3	92379
Urban	7.5	6.3	86.1	43960
Religion				
Hindu	15.2	7.6	77.2	88397
Muslim	17.9	8.1	74.0	20873
Christian	8.9	5.0	86.1	18166
Other	5.9	4.0	90.1	8797
Caste/tribe				
Scheduled Caste	19.6	9.0	71.3	20603
Scheduled Tribe	25.9	9.0	65.1	30272
Other	12.9	7.0	80.1	85346
Household literacy				
No literate	61.4	10.4	28.1	7703
Some literate	13.2	8.4	78.3	94570
All literate	0.2	2.3	97.5	34066
Education of father				
Literate	8.0	5.0	87.0	83029
Illiterate	27.2	10.9	61.8	36873
Father not in HH1	15.2	9.8	74.9	16437
Education of mother				
Literate	3.7	2.6	93.7	58729
Illiterate	21.0	9.7	69.2	67597
Mother not in HH1	16.7	10.7	72.5	10013
Total	**15.2**	**7.5**	**77.2**	**136339**

[1] These refers to cases where either parent is not staying with the child or information is missing.

Table A 3. Children working outside and inside the home

Percent children aged 5-14 years working both outside and inside the home; and doing household chores or other family work by selected characteristics, according to sex of the child, India, MICS 2000

Characteristics	Percent children working both outside and inside the home			Percent children engaged in household chores for more than four hours a day or doing other family work		
	Male	Female	Total	Male	Female	Total
Age of the child						
5-9 years	0.2	0.3	0.2	4.1	4.2	4.1
10-14 years	1.4	1.6	1.5	14.6	17.2	15.9
Place of residence						
Rural	0.9	1.1	1.0	10.3	11.7	11.0
Urban	0.3	0.5	0.4	5.2	6.6	5.8
Religion						
Hindu	0.8	1.0	0.9	9.4	10.9	10.1
Muslim	0.7	0.6	0.7	7.8	8.5	8.2
Christian	1.0	0.5	0.7	8.8	10.8	9.8
Other	0.6	0.6	0.6	8.0	9.8	8.8
Caste/tribe						
Scheduled Caste	0.8	1.2	1.0	8.6	11.1	9.9
Scheduled Tribe	1.3	1.9	1.6	16.8	18.5	17.6
Other	0.7	0.7	0.7	8.3	9.4	8.9
Attending school						
Yes	0.4	0.4	0.4	7.0	6.4	6.8
No	2.6	2.4	2.5	18.2	21.0	19.9
Survival of parents						
Both alive	0.7	0.9	0.8	8.8	10.1	9.5
Father not alive	1.3	1.7	1.5	13.4	15.8	14.5
Mother not alive	1.9	1.8	1.9	13.7	16.1	14.9
Both not alive	5.0	5.6	5.3	12.7	21.0	17.1
Total	**0.8**	**0.9**	**0.9**	**9.1**	**10.5**	**9.8**

Table A 4. Reasons for dropout

Percent distribution of children aged 5-14 years who have dropped out by reason for dropout according to sex, India, MICS 2000

Particulars	Rural			Urban			Total		
	M	F	Total	M	F	Total	M	F	Total
Reasons for dropout[1]									
School far away	2.6	6.1	4.6	2.2	5.9	4.1	2.5	6.0	4.5
Time of school inconvenient	0.2	0.5	0.4	0.7	1.5	1.1	0.3	0.6	0.5
No time for school, child busy with household work	13.5	29.3	22.5	6.2	15.7	10.9	11.8	26.8	20.1
Child busy with wage labour	10.3	7.0	8.4	14.6	6.8	10.7	11.3	6.9	8.9
Child unwell/sick	4.1	3.2	3.6	3.2	4.9	4.1	3.9	3.6	3.7
Child is disabled	1.3	0.9	1.1	2.3	1.8	2.1	1.6	1.0	1.3
Did not consider schooling important	2.0	2.6	2.3	2.6	3.7	3.1	2.1	2.8	2.5
School not necessary for girls	NA	4.8	2.8	NA	7.4	3.7	NA	5.3	2.9
Child not interested	48.0	32.0	38.9	46.6	31.8	39.3	47.7	32.0	39.0
Birth certificate not available	0.3	0.2	0.3	1.4	0.7	1.1	0.6	0.3	0.4
Child scared of corporal punishment	4.7	3.6	4.1	2.3	2.0	2.2	4.2	3.3	3.7
Quality of schooling very poor	1.9	1.9	1.9	1.4	1.1	1.2	1.7	1.8	1.8
Teacher comes rarely or does not come at all	3.0	2.8	2.9	0.8	0.5	0.7	2.5	2.4	2.4
Caste factor	0.2	0.3	0.2	0.1	0.9	0.5	0.2	0.4	0.3
Teacher is male	0.1	0.4	0.3	0.0	0.0	0.0	0.1	0.4	0.2
Lack of toilet facilities	0.2	0.1	0.1	0.3	0.2	0.2	0.2	0.1	0.1
Others	36.9	39.5	38.4	45.5	43.0	44.3	38.9	40.2	39.6
Total percent	100.0	100.0	100.0	100.0	100.0	100.0	100.0	100.0	100.0
Number of children	2357	2954	5311	930	954	1884	3287	3908	7195

[1] Total percent may add to more than 100.0 due to multiple responses. NA: Not applicable.

Table A5. Logistic regression analysis of "currently attending school" and various working characteristics after controlling for selected background variables*

Variables	Beta coefficient	Standard error of beta	Exponential beta
Child working for someone outside home	1.165	0.030	4.328
Child working for someone outside home for pay	2.732	0.050	15.367
Child doing household chores for mare than 28 hours a week	2.014	0.053	7.490
Child engaged in other family work	0.797	0.023	2.219
Child engaged in economically productive work at home	1.236	0.021	3.442

* Separate logistic regressions were carried out after controlling for urban/rural, mother and father's literacy, and type of house (Kuchcha, pucca or semi-pucca).

NOTES

[1] While a detailed analysis of these two sources is beyond the scope of this paper, the difference in figures between these two sources (Census 1991 and 55th Round of NSSO (1999-2000)) may relate to certain methodological differences between them and/or is due to a reduction in the prevalence of child labour during the 1990s.

[2] Further analysis of the MICS data on the implications for children of working for more than 4 hours a day should be undertaken in order to better understand the merits of including this in the definition of child labour.

REFERENCES

Aggarwal, S. C. (2004), "Child Labour and Household Characteristics in Selected States", *Economic and Political Weekly*, January 10, pp.173-185.

Chakravarty, B. (1989). *Education and Child Labour*, Allahabad: Chugh Publications.

Department of Women and Child Development (DWCD) & United Nations Children's Fund (UNICEF) (2001), *Multiple Indicator Survey: India Summary Report*, New Delhi: DWCD & UNICEF.

Department of Women and Child Development & United Nations Children's Fund (2002), *Multiple Indicator Survey 2000: All India Report (draft),* New Delhi: DWCD & UNICEF.

Government of India (2002), *Selected Educational Statistics 2000-20001,* New Delhi: Department of Education.

Huebler, F. & Loaiza, E. (2002), *Child Labour and School Attendance in Sub-Saharan Africa: Empirical Evidence from UNICEF's Multiple Indicator Cluster Surveys (draft),* New York: Strategic Information Section & Division of Policy and Planning, UNICEF.

Jain, M. (1996), "Child Labour: A Growing Phenomenon in India", in Raghavan, K. & Sekhar, L. (eds), *Poverty and Employment: Analysis of the present situation and strategies for the future,* New Delhi: New Age International Publishers.

Kulshreshtha, J. C. (1994), *Indian Child Labour,* New Delhi: Uppal Publishing House.

Mustafa, M. & Sharma, O. (1996), *Child Labour in India: A Bitter Truth,* New Delhi: Deep & Deep Publications.

Probe Team (1999), *India Education Report*, New Delhi: Oxford University Press.

Registrar General of India (1991), *Census of India 1991: a Study Report on Working Children in India,* New Delhi: Registrar General.

Singh, K. (2004), "Child Labour in India: Dimensions, Issues and Concerns", *Man & Development*, Vol. XXVI, No.1, pp. 37-46.

Tripathy, S. N. (ed.) (1996), *Child Labour in India: Issues and Policy Options,* New Delhi: Discovery Publishing House.

United Nations Children's Fund (2002), *Implementation Handbook for the Convention on the Rights of the Child*, Geneva: UNICEF.

Weiner, M. (1994), *Compulsory Education and Child Labour*: Proceedings no. 4 from the Rajiv Gandhi Institute for Contemporary Studies, New Delhi.

Chapter 14

Urban-rural Differentials in Child Labor: How Effective is the Multiple Indicator Cluster Survey in Informing Policies that Promote the Human Rights of Children in Urban Areas? An Example of Kenya

Frederick Mugisha

INTRODUCTION

There is fairly widespread agreement that the cornerstone of pro-poor growth strategies is investment in human capital. This investment occurs largely in children, in building their health and educational capital. International organizations of varied persuasions (such as the ILO, UNICEF and the World Bank) have adopted the goal of reducing child labor as a human right violation and currently have fairly large programs directed at this goal. While research is now fairly active, this is an area in which policy has run ahead of research. There is now an urgent need to identify which of a number of intuitively plausible policies is likely to be most effective, and this depends on understanding the nature and causes of child labor.

In setting out an analytical structure for thinking about why children work, it is useful to go down to the level where parents are faced with a choice between sending a child to work or to school. This choice can be structured in terms of constraints, incentives and agency. The common presumption is that it is the constraints of poverty that drive children into work. If this is so, the appropriate policy will attempt to relax this constraint by, for example offering cash transfers to very poor households. However, if schools are costly, unavailable or of poor quality then, even when the household is not very poor, it may be more beneficial to send the child to work. This is the case where incentives dominate: the rewards to work exceed the rewards to schooling.

It is recognized that the trend towards extending human rights polices beyond civil and political rights and embracing social and economic rights, including the right to development necessitates a new strategy that rests on evidence-based and science driven approach, and this requires more disaggregated data that goes beyond the "one size fits all" policy. The Multiple Indicator Cluster Surveys (MICS) was setup in part to provide such evidence and established a unique approach of clusters. Other than provide national and regional estimates of child labor, the MICS data provides a possibility of understanding the role of neighborhoods–across cluster variations in child labor.

The MICS data for Kenya is used to explore the extent of inequities in child labor in urban and rural areas –making a distinction in urban areas between urban slum and urban non-slum areas. The argument is that these inequities demonstrate the fact that urban areas have distinct groups in respect of how they are affected by child labor with varying reasons, and these need to be addressed to inform policies better.

CHILD LABOR AS A HUMAN RIGHT VIOLATION

A child working is not necessarily a violation of his/her human rights. It becomes a violation of human rights under at least two conditions; when children are working in hazardous and dangerous jobs in which they are in danger of injury, even death and when their right to schooling is violated. Now consider who today's children will become in the future. Between today and the year 2020, the vast majority of new workers, citizens and new consumers –whose skills and needs will build the world's economy and society– will come from developing countries. Over that 20 year period, some 730 million people will join the world's workforce –more than all the people employed today in the world's developed nations. More than 90 percent of these new workers will be from developing nations, according to research by Population Action International. How many will have had to work at an early age, destroying their health, or hampering their education?

WHY FOCUS ON RURAL-URBAN DIFFERENCES IN CHILD LABOR?

The African continent is facing an urbanization challenge; increasing urbanization, which unlike the rest of the world is associated with increasing urban poverty (United Nations Population Fund 1996). The African urban population was 15 percent in 1950, 32 percent in 1990, and is projected at 54 percent for 2030 (United Nations Population Fund 1996). While urbanization in the developed and some developing countries were accompanied by economic development, it has been the reverse in Africa. For example, while the urban population grew by 4.7 percent between 1970 and 1995, the Gross Domestic Product dropped by 0.7 percent (World Bank 2000). As a result the local economies have not been able to cope with the increasing rate of urbanization and are unable to provide basic services such as water, housing, electricity, sanitation and employment opportunities. Due to the inability of local economies to provide basic services and employment opportunities, increasing proportions of urban dwellers will continue to live in poor conditions, mainly in slums or informal settlements with poorer social outcomes than their rural counterparts. These slums or informal settlements accommodate more than 60% of the Nairobi residents yet constitute only 5% of the residential land, and thrive along relatively well organized and economically better of neighborhoods. In addition, these communities have had to bear the blunt of the economic decline with increasing unemployment and low school enrollment and high dropout rates for adolescents. Their health indicators are also known to be worse than their rural counterparts (APHRC 2002). This has at least two implications; income inequalities are wide and visible which creates a sense of hopelessness, and the economic conditions have challenged many would be breadwinners.

In the face of this, families are increasingly faced with tough choices for themselves and their children –should children go to school or look for money in form of employment? These choices are made easier in favor of children going to work for at least two reasons. First, schools accessible to slum communities are of poor quality, informal and only have limited number of classes, which makes progression into higher levels of school difficult. Those schools situated outside the slum communities are unaffordable to the slum dwellers. Second, high levels of unemployment among urban slum communities means that every penny that can be brought into the household is preferred to sending the child to school –whose benefits are unlikely to accrue in the near future. As such, decisions at the household level to send children to work are much easier due to the above constraints.

Examining child labor focusing on the traditional distinction between urban and rural divide hides considerable disparities within the urban areas. If the majority of those affected by child labor are living in areas considered slums, every effort to understand how they are affected ought to be exerted.

METHODS

Introduction

Using the Multiple Cluster Indicator Survey data, rural-urban differentials were explored for four types of work in which children 5-17 years were involved in the preceding 7 days of the survey. In addition to general rural-urban differentials, an index of whether an urban household is in the slum or non-slum was constructed to further explore the slum and non-slum differentials in the four types of work.

Construction of slum residence

The UN-HABITAT in close collaboration with the United Nations Statistic Division and the Cities Alliance Organized a gathering of experts and other stakeholders from around the globe in Nairobi (October 2002). The purpose of the Expert Group Meeting (EGM) was to reach a consensus on operational definition for slum dwellers that would be applied to monitoring the Millennium Development Goal 7, target 11 " achieve significant improvement in lives of at least 100 million slum dwellers, 2020".

Resulting from the EGM, a *slum household* is defined as a group of individuals living under the same roof lacking *one or more* of the conditions below:

- access to improved water
- access to improved sanitation facilities
- sufficient-living area, not overcrowded
- structural quality/durability of dwellings
- security of tenure.

This operational definition was supposed to be locally adapted. For example, in Rio de Janerio living area is insufficient for both the middle classes and the slum population and is not a good discriminator. It could either be omitted, or it could be formulated as two or more of the conditions such as overcrowding and durability of housing. This operational definition has been applied to estimating the number of slum population across the globe by country (UN-Habitat 2003).

In the MICS survey, two important indicators exist: water and sanitation. Information on source of water for a household was categorized as either of the following; a) piped into dwelling, b) piped into yard or plot, c) public tap, d) tubewell/borehole with pump, e) protected dug well, f) protected spring, g) rainwater collection, h) bottled water, i) dug well/unprotected spring, j) pond, river or stream, k) tanker truck vendor, and l) other. Based on these categories, access to improved drinking water was taken to be a) to g) in urban areas.

Information on type of toilet facility for a household was categorized as either of the following; a) sewage system/septic tank, b) pour flush latrine, c) improved pit latrine, d) traditional pit latrine, e) open pit, f) bucket, g) other, and h) no facilities/bush/field. Based on these categories, access to improved sanitation was taken to be a) to c) in urban areas.

An urban non-slum household was therefore defined as having either improved drinking water or improved sanitation. The slum household was thus defined as having neither improved drinking water nor improved sanitation.

RESULTS

Introduction

The results exploring urban-rural differentials in child labor are presented in tables 1-4. Table 1 presents background characteristics, table 2 urban-rural differentials, table 3 provincial differentials and table 4 urban slum-urban non-slum and rural differentials.

Working for pay

The results suggest that more children in urban were more engaged in work for pay in the preceding seven days. This is consistent even across provinces which are considered predominantly urban; Nairobi, the coast and North Eastern. Only the urban areas were surveyed during the Multiple Indicator Cluster Survey.

In addition to more urban children working for pay, they also spend substantially more hours at work. For example, the urban children spend more than twice the number of hours working compared to the rural children. The North Eastern province is exceptional with 5.14 percent of the children working for pay. The children also work much longer hours than children in other provinces of the country.

School dropout is also associated with paid work. Twenty nine percent of children that have ever attended school and dropped out were in paid work compared to 1.52 percent of those who did not have discontinuity in their schooling –that is, were in school the preceding year and are still in school. Those who drop out of school between the preceding year and the time of the survey were about 9 times more likely to have been engaged in paid work.

The results in table 2 showing regional differences by sex point to the fact that in provinces that are predominantly urban, girls are more likely to be in paid work than boys. In Nairobi, it is almost exclusively girls. In North Eastern, girls are 3 times more likely than boys and in Coast province it is about one and half times. From table 3 which provides a distinction between urban slum, urban non-slum and rural areas, the difference by sex is widest – girls are four times more likely to engage in paid work compared to boys. The girls also spend about twice the time the boys spend working in the slum areas.

Household chores

Generally rural children are more engaged in household chores (see table 1). Also children in provinces that are predominantly urban are less likely to be engaged in household chores. Schooling disruption also does not seem to have an effect on whether children are engaged in household chores as compared to paid work. Actually those that did not have any disruption in schooling –that is, they were in school the preceding year and are still in school are more likely to be engaged in household chores. In all cases the time allocated to household chores is quite little to have a negative effect on say schooling.

Looking at urban slum, non-slum and rural distinction in respect to male-female distinction, in all cases females are more likely to be involved in household chores. Also the older they become, the more they are involved in household chores. This observation that females are more in household chores points to gender roles that society has prescribed to men and women in most of the world. As will be explained in more detail in the discussion, females were traditionally supposed to work in the home, and that seems to have largely persisted even in urban slum areas of Kenya.

Family farm work

Family farm work is opposite of household chores when it comes to the male-female divide. In general however, similar to household chores, the rural children are more engaged in farm work (see table 1). Also children in provinces that are predominantly urban are less likely to be engaged in farm work, which is largely expected due to the agricultural nature of most rural areas of Kenya. Unlike the case with household chores, schooling disruption does seem to have an effect on whether children are engaged in farm work. Those out of school spend more hours in the farm than those going to school. In all cases, urban slum, non-slum and rural areas males are more likely to be involved in farm work compared to females. Also the older they become, with the exception of urban non-slum, the more they are involved in family farm work. This could be explained by the fact that at older ages, they join secondary schools, most of which are either boarding schools or at a distance from home such that their participation in farm activities is limited. Again the observation that males are more involved in family farm work points to gender roles that society has prescribed to men and women in most of the world. These traditional roles have largely persisted even in all areas –urban slum, non-slum and rural areas.

Family Business

Like with paid work, family business is more in urban areas than in rural areas, although not as much different. The pattern is also less clear across provinces although the coast has a higher prevalence –probably due to higher number of families with their small businesses. School disruption, like with paid work has an effect on whether the children are involved in family businesses (see table 1). Unlike other work involving children, the male-female divide is not well pronounced. In respect to urban slum, urban non-slum and rural distinction, more children in non-slum urban areas than in slum and rural areas in that order are involved in family business. Considering also the hours worked, this seems more to do with "child work" rather than child labor. Children seem to support their families marginally.

DISCUSSION

Regional differences in Kenya

The results show that provinces that are predominantly urban such as Nairobi, Coast and North Eastern (urban sample only), more children in these provinces work for pay. More children in North Eastern province are in paid work. North Eastern is a semi-arid area which relies mainly on cross-border trade with neighboring countries of Somalia and Ethiopia. The urban area under consideration has the least primary school completion rates compared to other provinces.

Rural-urban differentials

Girls in urban areas are more likely to engage in paid work than boys. This is true across provinces that are predominantly urban and across urban areas. There are three possible explanations to this observation. First, most of these girls could be involved in work as housemaids. Many housemaids at least in Nairobi work and live outside their work place. The salaries available to them cannot afford the rents charged in other parts of the city other than in slum areas. Second, they could be working in activities such as weaving, sorting – which either the employers prefer ladies or are best suited for such jobs. Third, as the difference is highest among what is considered slum areas, these ladies could be employed in prostitution. Prostitution is quite high in the slum areas, and girls stream the streets of major urban centers to earn a living (Mugisha *et al.* 2003).

GENDER AND DIVISION OF WORK

The facts that female children are more involved in paid work mainly in the slum communities and household chores in all communities point to gender differences in allocation work. There are at least two gender related factors that are either protective or predispose male or female children to work; traditional division of labor and style of child upbringing. In the African tradition, there was a division of labor between males and females. Women were supposed to take up mainly household chores such as cooking, take care of the children; the sick and household farming, and that explains why female children are more involved in household chores. The men on the other hand were supposed to go hunting, work in shambas (till the land), look after animals and carry out construction work (Arinaitwe-Mugisha 1999). This is largely still practiced in most rural areas of Africa where it is still feasible, and that explains why significantly more males in rural areas are involved in family farm work.

Does this gender difference then explain why more female children are working in slums than their male counter parts? Part of the explanation lies in the nature of work available to them. As explained, most of the work available to the slum children is either being house maids, working in factories or prostitution. Being a house maid means taking care of children while their bosses leave for work, cooking food and doing other household chores, which clearly according to gender roles falls in the docket for female children. They work outside the slums but live in the slums because their salaries can only afford the rent in the slums. At their age, working in factories means doing work that is not extremely energy consuming but requires great patience such as sorting of grain for export, needling etc. Women are taught from childhood how to be submissive while men are taught how to exercise authority. This affects the way they behave in different circumstances (Bisilliat 2001). In this case, female children are more patient and resilient and are able to cope with the work.

The other work available to the slum children is casual work, which in most cases requires muscle power that children have not developed.

Unfortunately, this is likely to take these boys to other social ill such as alcohol and drug abuse (Bisilliat 2001;Mugisha, Arinaitwe-Mugisha, & Hagembe 2003).

Multiple indicator surveys

One of the strong attractions of the Multiple Indicator Cluster Surveys is the availability of clusters that would help explain factors that affect child health. An easier example is poor sanitation in urban slums. The other example is concentration of child labor in specific neighborhoods either in urban areas or in rural areas. Although the cluster sizes do not allow independent estimates, they allow analysts to explore their influence on key factors.

The question this paper set out to answer is whether the Multiple Cluster Indicator Surveys can effectively inform policies that promote the human rights of children in urban areas. The results revealed that girls in urban slum areas are more likely to work and work for much longer hours than their male counter parts. Although this can be taken as a process of women emancipation in working, it also raises some questions on why the slum communities who have less job-connection networks than urban non-slum areas are getting on to the jobs. They could be missing out on their schooling –in the actual fact, the same MICS data and other studies suggest that children in the slums are more likely to have had their schooling interrupted than the urban non-slum and rural children (APHRC 2002). They also work twice as hard as the boys in the slums, girls in the non-slum and rural areas. The fact that these ladies are more exposed and in varying conditions of work, and more people in sub-Saharan Africa will live in urban areas, with the majority in slum areas suggests that identifying them is critical to reducing the incidence of child labor in these communities. While the Multiple Indicator Survey data provides good estimates for countries with respect to rural and urban populations, the large inequities in urban areas and incidence in slums suggest that the data may be limited in understanding child labor issues facing the urban slum communities. However, for purposes of providing slum specific estimates or understanding slum specific child labor issues such as parent child-labor decisions, the surveys will have to be modified to generate slum data or supplemented by specific slum studies.

ANNEXURE

Table 1. Percentage of children 5-17 years working in the last 7 days

	For pay		Household Chores		Family Farm		Family Business		Number
	Percent	Hours	Percent	Hours	Percent	Hours	Percent	Hours	
Residency									
Rural	3.26	25	71.81	12	41.81	7	1.97	8	14,629
Urban	4.51	63	46.52	8	2.57	6	2.33	12	2,530
Province									
Nairobi (Urban)	4.54	66	40.76	7	0.25	1	0.45	28	422
Central	4.41	24	72.37	10	36.14	6	2.08	8	2,066
Coast	4.47	21	57.10	12	28.35	8	3.99	12	2,126
Eastern	4.10	49	74.34	13	34.92	7	0.74	12	2,400
North eastern (urban)	5.14	84	43.92	14	13.08	14	2.23	22	147
Nyanza	2.53	14	77.66	8	42.32	6	2.49	6	2,933
Rift valley	2.43	40	62.68	14	37.84	8	1.57	7	5,181
Western	3.38	24	75.26	12	49.40	7	3.65	9	1,884
Age									
5-9 years	0.87	14	56.31	10	21.82	7	0.97	7	7,202
10-14 years	3.48	28	76.31	12	42.47	7	2.49	7	6,882
15-17 years	9.64	48	73.15	14	49.14	8	3.46	14	3,075
In school last year, in school now									
No last year, no now	29.10	56	67.62	20	42.21	18	3.83	32	11,798
Yes last year, no now	13.77	42	71.36	20	45.85	14	3.07	16	670
Yes last year, yes now	1.52	14	72.86	10	38.48	6	2.11	7	615
Total	3.61	34	67.48	11	35.14	7	2.03	8	17,159

Table 2. Percentage of children 5-17 years working in the last 7 days by provinces in Kenya

		For pay		Household Chores		Family Farm		Family Business		Number
		Percent	Hours	Percent	Hours	Percent	Hours	Percent	Hours	
Nairobi	Male	0.00		33.31	4	0.00		0.95	28	208
	Female	8.74	66	47.66	10	0.48	1	0.00		214
Central	Male	5.16	27	66.83	8	40.36	6	2.37	8	1051
	Female	3.61	21	78.3	10	31.65	6	1.77	14	1015
Coast	Male	3.63	12	48.46	10	28.65	10	3.23	16	1087
	Female	5.35	35	66.47	14	28.03	8	4.8	10	1039
Eastern	Male	4.52	36	72.18	14	38.4	7	0.68	8	1187
	Female	3.68	68	76.39	13	31.61	6	0.79	12	1213
North Eastern (Urban)	Male	3.11	42	34.85	10	15.51	14	3	24	65
	Female	6.83	84	51.6	14	11.06	28	1.59	15	82
Nyanza	Male	2.82	8	71.89	7	44.11	6	2.25	6	1440
	Female	2.24	21	83.31	10	40.57	6	2.73	6	1493
Rift Valley	Male	2.52	24	53.15	14	42.45	10	1.44	10	2569
	Female	2.35	42	71.85	14	33.39	8	1.69	4	2612
Western	Male	3.08	25	69.61	11	52.6	8	2.96	7	964
	Female	3.7	20	81.2	14	46.04	6	4.38	9	920

Table 3. Percentage of children 5-17 years working in the last 7 days, by urban slum, non-slum and rural classification

	For pay		Household Chores		Family Farm		Family Business		Number
	Percent	Hours	Percent	Hours	Percent	Hours	Percent	Hours	
Urban slum	4.58	60	51.36	10	4.37	6	3.70	8	2213
Male	1.70	36	45.70	8	4.89	7	3.90	9	1,058
Female	7.30	65	56.62	12	3.89	4	3.52	8	1,155
5-9 years	0.50	19	38.28	7	2.76	4	1.55	7	994
10-14 years	4.08	55	61.28	10	5.30	6	4.82	7	823
15-17 years	15.89	63	63.31	14	6.46	7	6.76	13	396
Urban non-slum	3.27	35	56.81	12	12.04	6	4.35	14	316
Male	4.69	39	46.81	10	13.57	6	4.29	18	153
Female	2.04	30	65.63	14	10.69	6	4.40	14	163
5-9 years	0.00	0	39.17	7	8.47	6	2.54	8	126
10-14 years	4.35	35	70.31	14	17.97	6	4.69	16	134
15-17 years	8.00	33	64.15	21	5.66	6	7.55	14	56
Rural	3.26	25	71.81	12	41.81	7	1.97	8	14,629
Male	3.55	24	65.55	10	45.13	7	1.78	7	7,360
Female	2.97	28	78.10	12	38.47	6	2.17	8	7,269
5-9 years	1.03	14	61.35	10	26.26	7	0.97	7	6,082
10-14 years	3.52	16	79.80	12	49.66	7	2.44	7	5,924
15-17 years	7.79	35	77.01	14	58.92	8	3.17	14	2,623

REFERENCES

APHRC (2002). *Population and health dynamics in Nairobi's informal settlements.* Nairobi: African Population and Health Research Center.

Arinaitwe-Mugisha, J. (1999). "The changing traditional roles of men and women, and the coping mechanisms". *Gender Alert News* 3.

Bisilliat, J. (2001). *Introducing the gender perspective in national essential drug programmes,* Department of Essential Drugs and Medicine Policy, World Health Organization.

Mugisha, F., Arinaitwe-Mugisha, J. & Hagembe, B. (2003). "Alcohol, substance and drug use among urban slum adolescents in Nairobi Kenya". *Cities* 20, 231-240.

UN-Habitat (2004). "Slums of the world: the face of urban poverty in the new millennium? Monitoring the Millennium Development Goal", Target 11 - Worldwide slum dweller estimation.

United Nations Population Fund (1996). *The state of the World Population 1996. Changing places: population, development and the urban poor,* New York: United Nations.

WHO (1998), "Gender and Health: technical paper", Geneva: World Health Organization.

World Bank (2000). *Entering the 21st century: World Development Report 199/2000.* New York: Oxford University Press.

Chapter 15

Child Labour in Bolivia: A Comparison of Estimates from MECOVI and MICS Survey Instruments

Lorenzo Guarcello and Scott Lyon *

INTRODUCTION

World Bank multipurpose household surveys,[1] UNICEF MICS surveys,[2] and ILO SIMPOC surveys[3] are particularly important instruments for generating information on child labour in developing countries. Datasets from these surveys, based on comprehensive interviews with a stratified sample of households, provide information on the incidence and key characteristics of children's work, as well as the links between children's work, child age and sex, household income levels, mothers' education and a range of other factors (see Table 1).

How do the results generated by these survey instruments compare? And to what extent are child labour estimates survey-dependent? This paper compares the results of a World Bank multi-purpose survey and a UNICEF MICS survey in Bolivia in an attempt to address these questions. It builds on a previous comparison of World Bank and ILO survey results in Zambia,[4] and constitutes part of a broader effort to improve the quality and consistency of child labour data collected through the agencies' main survey instruments.

Bolivia provides a good opportunity for this survey comparison because a World Bank Living Standards Measurement Study[5] and a UNICEF MICS survey were both conducted there during 2000, meaning that discrepancies in the survey findings are likely due to methodological differences rather than to longitudinal changes in the actual child labour situation.

---

* This paper is a result of the Interagency (ILO/World Bank/UNICEF) Project on Child Labour "Understanding Children's Work". The views expressed here are those of the authors and should not be attributed to the ILO, the World Bank, UNICEF or any of these agencies' member countries.

This paper looks specifically at the degree to which the findings on child labour are consistent across the two Bolivia surveys, and therefore have similar implications for policy. The paper focuses on the 7-14 years age group. The upper bound of 14 years is consistent with the ILO Convention No. 138 on Minimum Age,[6] which states that the minimum age for admission to employment or work should not be less than 15 years (Art. 2.3), and is the age at which compulsory schooling ends in Bolivia.[7] The lower bound of seven years was that used in the employment module of the MECOVI survey.[8]

The paper is structured as follows. Section 1 provides background information on the two surveys and the sampling methodology employed for each. Sections 2, 3 and 4 then examine survey findings relating to the incidence, characteristics and impact of children's work. For each, the two surveys are compared in terms of how key variables are constructed and in terms of results generated. Section 5 looks at key correlates of children's work, and their consistency across the two surveys. Section 6 discusses the results of the survey comparison and areas of future research.

SURVEY CHARACTERISTICS

The Bolivia Living Conditions Survey (*Encuesta continua de hogares, MECOVI)* was carried out in 2000 by the National Statistical Office. The survey, part of the regional MECOVI programme,[9] was aimed at improving and extending information on household living conditions, information needed for the effective formulation and evaluation of poverty reduction programmes. The survey questionnaire covered a wide range of socio-economic and demographic variables in an effort to capture the various dimensions of poverty and living conditions.

The MECOVI survey sample comprised 4,875 households and 20,815 persons, representing 1,906,668 households and an expanded population of 8,274,803 individuals. The survey was addressed to all households, excluding people living in collective housing (hospitals, etc.). A stratified sample design was used, based on the Probability Proportional to Size method for the PSU (primary sample unit) and for the households in the second stage, building a sample representative at the national as well as regional, urban and rural levels. Questions relating to children aged seven years and older were addressed directly to the children.

The Bolivia Multiple Indicator Cluster Survey, referred to hereafter as MICS, was also carried out in 2000 by the National Statistical Office. The survey was undertaken as part of the UNICEF global MICS programme,[10] and was designed to assess progress on the end-decade goals set at the 1990 United Nations World Summit for Children. These goals related to nutrition, health and education, as well as to birth registration, family environment, knowledge of HIV/AIDS, and child labour.

The Bolivia MICS survey followed the design, planning and implementation methodologies of the global MICS survey programme. A stratified sample design was employed, building a national probabilistic sample, stratified by geographic area, department and residence (urban-rural).[11] The survey sample comprised 4,312 households. The survey questionnaire targeted male and female children under 17 years of age (household questionnaire module), women of child-bearing age (women questionnaire module), and children aged less than five years (child questionnaire). Questions in the household module relating to children were addressed to caretakers rather than to children themselves.

As illustrated in Table 1, the two surveys differed somewhat in terms of scope and variables examined. While both surveys collected information on children at work in economic activity, only MICS looked at child involvement in household chores. Although international labour standards provide for exceptions for household chores performed in a child's own household, household chores can pose risks to children's health, and can affect children's ability to attend and benefit from schooling, in the same ways as work in economic activity. Consideration of household chores is therefore also important to a general understanding of child labour.

Both surveys provided information on the intensity and modality of work, but only MECOVI looked in detail at the type (i.e., sector and sub-sector) of work performed by children, and children's specific work functions. MECOVI was also unique in collecting information on illness and injury among the 7-14 years age group. These variables are all

Table 1. Availability of data relating to child labour

Indicator area	MICS	MECOVI
Work in economic activity	•	•
School attendance	•	•
Work in household chores	•	x
Hazardous work	x	x
Unconditional worst forms	x	x
Work modality	•	•
Work sector	x	•
Work intensity (hrs. worked)	•	•
Learning achievement	x	x
Reported illness/injury	x	•
Mothers' education	•	•
Schooling expenditures	x	•
Household income/wealth	•	•
Water availability	•	•
Electricity availability	x	•
Exposure to shock	x	x
Access to credit	x	x
Access to land	x	x
Employment of HH head	x	•

critical to assessing the hazardousness of work, and the extent to which children's work constitutes child labour for elimination. Neither survey offered information concerning children's involvement in unconditional worst forms of work, an area for which large-scale household surveys are ill-suited.[12]

MECOVI provided a much wider range of background household and community variables for use in analysing the determinants of child labour. In addition to the background variables provided by MICS (i.e., mothers' education, water availability and household wealth), MECOVI collected information on electricity access, schooling costs, electricity availability, household expenditures and employment of household head, all of which are potentially important to understanding household decisions concerning children's work.

MEASUREMENT OF CHILDREN'S ACTIVITIES

How common is children's work Bolivia? The estimates generated by the MICS and MECOVI surveys offer somewhat different answers. As illustrated in Table 2, the MICS survey results suggest a much higher rate of children's work than those of the MECOVI survey. Indeed, for the 7-14 age group as a whole, the MICS-based estimate of children's involvement in economic activity is almost one-third higher than the MECOVI-based estimate. This gap in the estimates across the two surveys holds for all ages and for both sexes. The MICS results also indicate a higher proportion of children attending school, again across all ages and for both sexes, than the MECOVI results, although the gap in attendance estimates across the two surveys is less large (Table 2).[13]

Table 2. Percentage of children involved in economic activity, school and child labour, by age and data source

Age	At work in economic activity		Attending school		Involved in child labour	
	MICS	MECOVI	MICS	MECOVI	MICS	MECOVI
7	19.1	10.9	99.3	95.8	19.1	10.9
8	20.3	12.1	99.1	96.1	20.3	12.1
9	23.9	15.5	99.0	97.8	23.9	15.5
10	27.2	15.7	98.6	96.5	27.2	15.7
11	26.9	18.1	98.4	94.1	26.9	18.1
12	34.1	24.4	93.5	90.5	17.0	18.5
13	34.0	26.2	91.9	88.3	17.0	21.8
14	38.8	31.8	87.2	82.4		
Total	27.7	19.2	96.1	92.8	21.6	16.1

Not all child economic activity constitutes child labour for elimination,[14] and it is therefore also important to compare survey estimates of child labour.[15] In the absence of detailed information on work characteristics and work hazards, minimum working age as defined by ILO Convention No. 138 must be used as the main criterion for estimating child labour.[16]

Bolivia, upon ratifying ILO Convention No. 138 in 1997, set the general minimum working age at 14 years. Therefore, all economically active children below the age of 14, with the exception of 12- and 13-year-olds in "light work",[17] may be thought of as being in child labour.[18]

Table 2 also presents the estimates of the proportion of children in child labour according to this criterion. The MICS estimate is again higher that the MECOVI estimate, for both sexes and all ages. The difference in the child labour estimates across the two surveys, however, is smaller than that for economic activity, because MICS indicates a much higher proportion than MECOVI of 12-13 year-old working children in light work (and therefore not in child labour). Fifty-nine percent of 12-13 year-old working children are in light work according to MICS, but only 22 percent are in light work according to MECOVI (see discussion below on estimates of hours worked).

Breaking children down into four non-overlapping activity categories – those that work, those that attend school, those that do both, and those that do neither – is another way of comparing the results across the two surveys. This breakdown shows that the higher overall economic activity and school attendance estimates yielded by the MICS survey stem entirely from the group of children that both work and attend school (Table 3). The MICS estimate puts this group at 25 percent of total children aged 7-14 years, and the MECOVI estimate at only 15 percent.

MECOVI, on the other hand, generated higher estimates of children working exclusively, children attending school exclusively, and children neither attending school nor working (Table 3). This last group, reportedly "idle" children also constitute an important policy concern – they not only do not go to school but are also the category of children most at-risk of entering work when households are exposed to individual or collective shocks.[19]

What might account for these differences in estimates across the two surveys, and in particular the higher estimate for child economic activity generated by the MICS survey? Differences in the design of the survey questionnaires might provide at least part of the answer (Table 4). The fact that the MICS questionnaire, unlike that for MECOVI, specifically targeted children's work, might have helped focus respondents' attention

Table 3. Child activity status, by sex and data source

Activity status	% Children aged 7-14 year					
	MICS 2000			MECOVI 2000		
	Male	Female	Total	Male	Female	Total
Working[1]	30.1	25.1	27.6	20.4	18.0	19.2
Attending school	96.7	95.4	96.1	94.4	91.2	92.8
Working, not attending school	2.1	2.4	2.2	3.0	4.6	3.8
Attending school, not working	68.7	72.7	70.7	77.0	77.8	77.4
Working and attending school	28.0	22.7	25.4	17.4	13.4	15.4
Not working, not attending school	1.3	2.2	1.7	2.6	4.2	3.4

Notes: [1]refers to work in economic activity.

on the *children* in the household at work, leading to less under-reporting of children's involvement in work.[20] On the other hand, the absence of follow-up questions in the MICS questionnaire to control for factors such as temporary absence from work due to vacation or illness meant that some economically-active children were likely missed in the MICS survey.

Survey respondents were different in the two surveys, also possibly influencing the survey results. As noted above, the survey respondent in the MICS survey was the caretaker, while MECOVI was administered directly to children aged seven years and older. But any bias in responses would presumably be in the same direction for these two groups, i.e., towards overstating school attendance and understating work involvement.

Seasonality likely played the largest role in explaining the differences in the survey estimates. Fieldwork for the MICS survey took place from mid-August to mid-September, a period overlapping with the sugar cane harvest. Other studies indicate that children are frequently used in this harvest.[21] Fieldwork for MECOVI took place in November and December,

Table 4. Questions used to determine work status of children

MICS	MECOVI
During the past week, did (NAME) do any kind of work for someone who is not a member of this household? 1 yes, for pay (cash or kind); 2 yes, unpaid 3 no	During the past week, did (NAME) do any other family work (on the farm or in a business)? 1 yes; 2 no
At any time during the past year, did (NAME) do any kind of work for someone who is not a member of this household? 1 yes, for pay (cash or kind); 2 yes, unpaid 3 no	During the past week, did (name) work at least one hour? 1 yes; 2 no
	During the past week, did (name) work for at least one hour in 1: Agriculture or livestock 2: Help in the family business 3: Street vendor 4: Cooking, spin the wool, weave, sew or other activities for selling 5: Work for someone who is not a member of the household for pay 6: Other activities for pay 7: No Activities
	Although (name) did not work during the past week, did you have a job or an enterprise where you were absent for one of the following reasons? 0: Not applicable 1: Holiday 2: Illness or injury 3: Lack of materials customers 4: strike 5: Personal problems 6: Bad Weather 7: suspended 8: None

outside the harvest season for sugar cane and other crops.[22] The fact that the MICS survey was conducted earlier in the school year[23] also may at least partially account for the different school attendance estimates generated by the two surveys.

CHARACTERISTICS OF CHILDREN'S WORK

Both surveys collected data on work modality, an important indicator of the nature of children's work. MICS data permitted a breakdown of child workers by those in paid work, those in non-paid work and those that work for their family. MECOVI provided greater detail, distinguishing between children that are in wage work, self-employed, employers (paid and unpaid), part of a cooperative, and working within the family unit. Both MICS and MECOVI indicated that by far the largest proportion of working children –nine out of 10– work for their families.

Data on children's total labour supply (i.e., average total hours worked) were also collected by both surveys. These data are critical to determining how much children's labour contributes to household income and welfare. They are also very important to determining the intensity of work, and offer insight into its possible health and developmental consequences. A limited amount of time spend on light work is not necessarily bad for a child's health, and need not interfere with formal education. Long working hours, on the other hand, are likely to have more serious health and developmental consequences on the child.

Both surveys indicate that older children work longer hours than younger children (Table 5), and that working hours differ little by sex. Both also indicate, not surprisingly, that children combining school and work put in fewer hours than those working exclusively, though the hours logged by the former group are by no means insignificant.

The two surveys, however, generate dramatically different estimates of total hours worked. According to MICS, working children put in an average of only about 14 hours per week, while according to MECOVI, by contrast, they put in an average of over 27 hours per week. Estimates of hours worked differ both for children that work exclusively (38 hours per week according to MECOVI and 25 hours per week according to MICS),

Table 5. Average weekly working hours, by age, school attendance status and data source

Age	Economically active but not attending school		Economically activite and also attending school		All economically active children (regardless of school attendance)	
	MICS	MECOVI	MICS	MECOVI	MICS	MECOVI
7	14.0	20.7	10.1	19.8	10.4	19.9
8	11.3	45.3	10.9	20.2	11.4	22.4
9	10.2	41.7	10.9	21.1	10.8	22.2
10	23.8	50.4	12.1	20.9	12.6	23.9
11	18.3	39.4	13.0	19.8	13.1	22.3
12	29.1	49.5	14.3	22.5	15.7	27.2
13	24.7	38.9	13.7	29.5	15.3	32.2
14	24.6	46.3	17.3	28.9	19.3	35.8
Total	**24.5**	**43.7**	**13.0**	**23.3**	**14.1**	**27.4**

and for children that combine school and work (23 hours per week according to MECOVI and 13 hours per week according to MICS). This has important implications for estimates of child labour for elimination (see previous section), for which hours worked is an important criterion.

The reasons for this large discrepancy are not clear and require further investigation. But again, at least part of the explanation likely lies in the way the survey questions were formulated (Table 6). MICS asked only about the number of hours worked during the reference week in family and non-family work, while MECOVI asked more specifically about the number of days worked in the reference week, and hours worked for each. These formulations, though similar, could nonetheless have led to different interpretations on the part of respondents. The frequency distribution for hours worked for the two surveys is shown in Figure 1.

Only MECOVI goes beyond work modality and intensity to provide detailed data on work sector, as well as occupation (primary and secondary), work functions, previous activity status, and level of remuneration. Neither questionnaire collected information concerning the strenuousness of work, exposure to potential risks such as machinery

Table 6. Questions used to determine the working hours of children

MICS	MECOVI
Since the last day of the week, about how many hours has he/she worked for someone that is not a member of the household? (if more than one job include the total hours)	How many days did you work last 7 days? On average, how many hours per day did you work in the week of reference?
Since the last day of the week, about how many hours has he/she spend on family work (on the farm or in a business)?	

Figure 1. Distribution of working hours, MICS and MECOVI

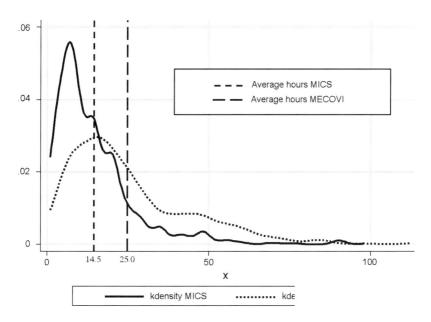

and chemicals, relationship with employer, workplace abuses, and work benefits, all critical for a more complete picture of the nature and characteristics of children's work, and for assessing its harmfulness.

EFFECTS OF INVOLVEMENT IN ECONOMIC ACTIVITY

The effect of work on children's health and education are an important consideration in determining whether work constitutes child labour for elimination.

Looking first at health, only MECOVI provides information on reported illness and injury among children in the 7-14 years age group. The MECOVI results do not provide clear evidence that working children are worse off health-wise than other groups of children. Children working exclusively have a lower rate of reported illness/injury than children that are reportedly idle. But this is a finding that comes up frequently in household surveys, and likely stems in large part from difficulties in measuring the work-health link.[24]

Turning to education, the two surveys offer somewhat different pictures of the ability of working children to attend school. MICS results indicate that 92 percent of working children attend school, while MECOVI indicates that the attendance rate of working children is only 80 percent (Figure 2). The MICS school attendance estimates for working children are higher across the entire 7-14 age spectrum, but the gap in estimates is largest for working children aged 12-14 years.

Again, the reasons for these discrepancies in school attendance estimates are not immediately apparent and merit further investigation. Both estimates are based on similar survey questions, and both surveys control for the possibility that the survey subject is on holiday. The surveys did, however, take place at different times during the school year, as noted

Figure 2. School attendance rate of working children, by age and data source

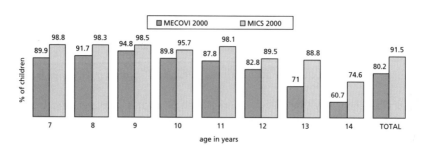

above. Only MICS looked at the regularity of attendance, relevant because children reported as currently attending school may actually be frequently absent from class. This indicator was not, however, considered in the calculation of the school attendance rate.

The impact of work on schooling of course extends beyond attendance. The data from both surveys suggest that working children who attend school must nonetheless cope with long working hours, leaving little time or energy for studies, and undoubtedly affecting their ability to derive educational benefit from schooling. MICS indicated that children combining school and work put in an average of 13 hours of work per week, and MECOVI indicated that this group works 23 hours per week. Data on links between work and learning achievement, however, were not collected for either survey.

FACTORS ASSOCIATED WITH CHILDREN'S WORK

The results from the two surveys point to similar broad correlates of child work and schooling. Both surveys indicate that children's work prevalence rises steadily with age, reflecting the higher opportunity costs of school in terms of earnings forgone, as the child gets older (Table 2). For school attendance, on the other hand, the surveys indicate that attendance rates remain relatively constant for the 7-11 age group but fall off thereafter (Table 2), as students reach the end of the second cycle of the eight-year compulsory education stage.[25]

Both surveys also show that boys work in economic activity in greater proportion than girls, though for MECOVI the gap by sex is narrower and not consistent across all ages. It is worth noting, however, that girls are much more likely than boys to perform household chores. Indeed, according to MICS (MECOVI did not collect data on household chores), the proportion of girls carrying out household chores for at least 28 hours per week is twice that of boys.

The two surveys indicate that children's work is closely related to place of residence (i.e., urban or rural). According to MICS, 47 percent of rural children are at work in economic activity, against only 11 percent of urban children. MECOVI indicates that 38 percent of rural children are economically active, compared to just seven percent of urban children.

Table 7. Children's activity status by household income, mothers' education, household water access and data source, children aged 7-14 years

Activity status	Household income level										Mothers' education level						Household water access[1]			
	MICS (wealth index)					MECOVI (expenditure quintiles)					MICS			MECOVI			MICS		MECOVI	
	1	2	3	4	5	1	2	3	4	5	None	Primary	2ndary+	None	Primary	2ndary+	Access	No access	Access	No access
Working, not attending school	5.0	3.1	1.2	0.5	0.1	10.5	4.1	2.6	1.1	1.4	4.5	2.6	0.1	10.1	2.3	0	1.5	4.2	2.1	7.6
Attending school, not working	42.3	66.2	77.9	89.4	88.5	53.6	74.9	84.4	83.6	88.5	53.4	66.0	89.7	58.4	80.2	95.9	77.8	49.9	83.8	63.2
Working and attending school	49.4	28.6	19.4	9.2	11.2	33.8	17.1	10.9	9.2	8	39.1	29.6	9.5	28	14.1	0.9	19.6	42.1	10.6	26.0
Not working, not attending school	3.3	2.1	1.5	0.9	0.2	2.0	3.9	2.1	6.1	2.1	3.0	1.9	0.8	3.4	3.4	3.2	1.0	3.8	3.5	3.2
Total	100	100	100	100	100	100	100	100	100	100	100	100	100	100	100	100	100	100	100	100

Notes: [1] 'Water access' is defined as households with water either pumped into home or into yard/plot.

The survey results thus underscore the fact that children's work in Bolivia, as in most South American countries, is primarily a rural phenomenon.

A strong relationship between household wealth, on the one hand, and children's work and school attendance, on the other, is also apparent from the two surveys (Table 7). The survey results indicate that children who mainly work come from low-wealth households, whereas children who mainly attend school come from households with higher levels of wealth, evidence for the oft-cited role of poverty in the decision to make children work. The results show child work decreasing, and schooling increasing, as household wealth rises. MICS data, however, permit only construction of a wealth index based on housing characteristics, while MECOVI data also permit the measure of household wealth based on household expenditures.[26]

The education level of mothers appears to be another important correlate of children's work prevalence and school attendance (Table 7). Both surveys indicate that children's work is most common in households in which the mother has no schooling, and least common in households in which the mother has at least a secondary education. The surveys indicate that the relationship between school attendance and education of the mother is the reverse, i.e., attendance is highest in households in which the mother is educated, and lowest in households in which the mother is not educated.

This pattern is likely in part the result of a disguised income effect.[27] It is also possible that education confers on the mother greater weight (moral authority or, if education translates into income, bargaining power) in family decisions, or that mother's time is an input into the education (production of human capital) of their children, and that the mother's own level of education raises the productivity of this input.[28]

Finally, the two surveys suggest a close relationship between involvement in work, school attendance and household water access (Table 7). The results from both surveys indicate that the rate of children's work is much higher, and the rate of school attendance slightly lower, in households without ready water access. This undoubtedly reflects the fact that a lack of water access can raise the value of children's time in non-schooling activities, as children are needed to undertake responsibility for water collection or to help cover the cost of purchasing water.[29]

DISCUSSION

This study compared and contrasted the World Bank MECOVI 2000 survey and the UNICEF MICS 2000 survey, and assessed the extent to which findings relating to child labour were consistent across the two surveys.

The study uncovered large differences in the estimates of several key variables relating to children's work across the two surveys, with concomitant differences in implications for policy. In particular, the MICS-based estimate of children's work prevalence was almost one-third higher than that based on MECOVI, while the MICS-based estimate of weekly hours worked was just half of the estimate yielded by MECOVI. The MICS survey also generated significantly higher estimates of school attendance than the MECOVI survey, both for 7-14 year-old working children and for the overall 7-14 years age group. The differences were statistically significant at the five percent level (Table 8). As the surveys were conducted in the same year, these differences cannot be explained by longitudinal changes in actual work and school attendance rates between the survey dates.

Table 8. Test of hypothesis of the difference of sample mean

	MECOVI	MICS	Significance of the difference
Economically Active Children	19.2	27.7	-7.5*
Working, not attending school	3.8	2.2	3.46*
Attending school, not working	77.4	70.7	5.69*
Working and attending school	15.4	25.4	-9.25*
Not working, not attending school	3.4	1.7	3.97*
Average weekly working hours	27.4	14.1	12.1*
School attendance rate of working children	80.2	91.5	-11.95*

*Significant at 5% level.

The study found that the correlations between children's work and key background variables (i.e., child age and sex, residence, house socio-economic level, mothers' education and household water access) were consistent across the two surveys. The study did not, however, include a bivariate estimation of child labour and schooling, owing to the limited number of variables in the MICS dataset for inclusion in such estimation. Causal links between children's work and various background variables, and the relative strength of these links across the two surveys, were therefore not examined.

The reasons for the large differences in estimates of children's work, school attendance and hours worked across the two surveys are not immediately clear and merit further investigation. There is also a need to examine whether these differences in the World Bank and UNICEF survey estimates are unique to Bolivia or also occur elsewhere, in which case they would likely reflect underlying differences in the survey instruments. The fact that World Bank multi-purpose household surveys and UNICEF MICS surveys are the two most common sources of information on child labour makes understanding the differences in their results especially important.

NOTES

[1] Principally, the Living Standards Measurement Study/Integrated Survey series and the Priority Survey series.

[2] Multiple Indicator Cluster Surveys.

[3] Statistical Information and Monitoring Programme on Child Labour.

[4] Blunch N.H., Dar A., Guarcello L., Lyon S., Ritualo A.R. and Rosati F.C. (2002), "Children's Work in Zambia: A Comparative Study of Survey Instruments", World Bank SP discussion paper, December.

[5] Entitled: "Encuesta continua de hogares (programa MECOVI)", referred to hereafter as MECOVI 2000.

[6] In countries where the economy and educational facilities are insufficiently developed the Convention sets a minimum age of not less than 14 years for general work, and 12 years for light work, for an initial period. In Bolivia, the minimum working age is 14 years, with the exception of apprentices. Children less than 18 years of age are prohibited from work that could retard their physical growth, that requires great strength, or that is dangerous (Ley General del Trabajo, del 8 de diciembre de 1942, Decreto Supremo del 4 de agosto de 1940).

[7] It should be noted that the stipulations contained in ILO Conventions Nos. 138 and 182 relating to hazardous work, excessively long work hours and unconditional worst forms,

also extend to children aged 15-17 years. The two surveys, however, do not collect information on these issues.

8   MICS, on the other hand, collected information on child labour for the 5-14 years age group.

9   A regional programme of technical assistance for statistical capacity building to improve household surveys to measure living conditions and poverty in Latin America and the Caribbean region. a joint initiative of IDB, World Bank and UN-ECLAC.

10 With in mind the purpose of obtaining comparable information at international level, the division of Evaluation, Policy and Planning of UNICEF, in cooperation with UNESCO, USAID, OMS and DHS, has developed the Multiple Indicator Cluster Survey (MICS) programme, for implementation in a wide numbers of countries.

11 Due to inaccessibility were excluded from the sample the rural areas of the departments of Beny and Pando, accounting for 1.5 percent of the National population.

12 It is very unlikely, for example, that unconditional worst forms of work would be reported by a household member to a survey interviewer, even if the child in question were still part of the household. And frequently the concerned children do not belong to a household, having run away or been abandoned, orphaned, displaced or even sold. Alternative survey tools and methodologies are needed for generating statistical information on these children.

13 As noted above, only MICS collected information on household chores. The survey indicated the five percent of 7-14 years put in at least 28 hours on household chores per week, with the proportion of girls performing household chores for at least this amount of time twice that of boys.

14 Child labour is the subset of children's work that is injurious, negative or undesirable to children and that should be targeted for elimination in accordance with international child labour norms. The UN Convention on the Rights of the Child (CRC) recognises the children's right to be protected from forms of work that are likely to be hazardous or to interfere with the child's education, or to be harmful to the child's health or physical, mental, spiritual, moral or social development. In order to achieve this goal, the CRC calls on States Parties to set minimum ages for admission to employment, having regard to other international instruments. ILO Conventions No. 138 (Minimum Age) and No. 182 (Worst Forms) target as child labour 1) all forms of work carried out by children below a minimum cut-off age (at least 14 years in less developed countries), with an exemption for children in "light work" carried out by children above a second lower cut-off age (at least 12 years in less developed countries); and 2) all 'worst forms' of child labour carried out by children of any age under 18 years, where worst forms include any activity or occupation which, by its nature or type has, or leads to, adverse effects on the child's safety, health, or moral development.

15 Determining where, and how, to draw the statistical line between benign forms of work, on one side, and child labour for elimination, on the other, is complicated. For a discussion of the measurement challenges associated with estimating rates of child labour, see UCW Project, *Towards an inter-agency consensus on child labour indicators: A discussion note*, draft project working paper, October 2003.

16 ILO Convention No. 138 (or Minimum Age Convention) stipulates that ratifying states must establish a general minimum working age (at least 14 years in less developed countries).

17 ILO Convention No. 138 provides an exemption for younger children (at least 12 years in less developed countries) performing only "light work". Following the approach of ILO in its revised global estimates of child labour, "light work" is defined as work that is carried out for less than 14 hours per week. The concept of "light work", however, in reality extends beyond hours worked to include the type and hazardousness of work.

18 This estimate does not take into account children working in non-economic activities, i.e., household chores, as information on this group of children was not collected by MECOVI.

19 See, for example, UCW Project, *Understanding Children's Work in Guatemala*, Guatemala, April 2003.

20 But a Zambia study comparing the results of another survey specifically targeting child labour (SIMPOC) with those of a more general living conditions survey (LSMS), did not show a similar difference in estimates of child economic activity. For further details, see Blunch N.H., Dar A., Guarcello L., Lyon S., Ritualo A.R. and Rosati F.C., *Children's Work in Zambia: A Comparative Study of Survey Instruments*, UCW Project working paper, September 2002.

21 See, for example, Dávalos G., *Child Labour in Sugarcane: A Rapid Assessment*, International Labour Organization, International Programme on the Elimination of Child Labour (IPEC), Bolivia, May 2002, Geneva.

22 However, neither survey overlapped with harvest seasons for other major crops. Wheat, barley, maize, rice, soybeans and potatoes are harvested from March to May, and sweet potatoes from mid-May to mid-August (FAO, 1999). The brazil nut harvest, also reportedly involving children, begins in January.

23 The school year runs from March to December in Bolivia.

24 The health consequences of work, for example, may be obscured by the selection of the healthiest children for work, or by the fact these health consequences may not become apparent until a later stage in a child's life. Different levels of reported health problems may also be a reflection of different health perceptions rather than of differences in actual health status. It may also be that it is not child work per se that is damaging to health but rather certain kinds of work, a fact that is concealed when looking at prevalence of health problems averaged across all categories of child workers. For a more detailed discussion, see O'Donnell O., Rosati F.C., and van Doorslaer E., *Child Labour and Health: Evidence and Research Issues*, Understanding Children's Work (UCW) Project, 12 December 2001.

25 As part of the education reform of 1994, compulsory education was defined as eight years and was divided into three cycles: three years of basic learning; three years of essential skills; and two years of applied learning.

26 Several studies call into question the relevance of an asset index as a proxy for living standards and poverty. For further information on the construction of the wealth index, see: Filmer D. and Pritchett L., *Estimating wealth effects without expenditure data – or*

tears: An application to educational enrolments in States of India, World Bank Policy Research Working Paper No. 1994, Washington, 1998; Filmer D. and Pritchett L., *The effect of household wealth on educational attainment: Evidence from 35 countries*, Population and Development Review, vol.25, no.1, pages 85-120, March 1999; and Filmer D. and Pritchett L., *The effect of household wealth on educational attainment around the world: Demographic and Health Survey evidence*, World Bank Policy Research Working Paper No. 1980, Washington, 1998.

[27] I.e., mothers with higher levels of education are also likely to have higher levels of income, and therefore less need to involve their children in work.

[28] For a more complete discussion of the role of mothers' education in decisions concerning children's work, see Cigno A., Rosati F.C., and Tzannatos Z., *Child Labor Handbook*, World Bank SP Discussion Paper No. 0206, May 2002.

[29] For a more detailed discussion of the role of basic infrastructure availability in household decisions concerning children's work, see Guarcello L., S. Lyon and Rosati F.C., *Child labour and access to basic services: Evidence from five countries*, Understanding Child Work Project, unpublished draft, November 2003.

REFERENCES

Blunch, N. H., Dar, A., Guarcello, L., Lyon, S., Ritualo, A. R. and Rosati F. C. (2002). *Children's Work in Zambia: A Comparative Study of Survey Instruments*, SP Discussion Paper, December, World Bank.

Cigno, A., Rosati, F. C., and Tzannatos, Z. (2002). *Child Labor Handbook*, SP Discussion Paper No. 0206, May, World Bank.

Dávalos G. (2002). *Child Labour in Sugarcane: A Rapid Assessment*, Geneva: International Labour Organization, International Programme on the Elimination of Child Labour (IPEC), Bolivia, May.

Filmer, D. and Pritchett L. (1998). "Estimating wealth effects without expenditure data –or tears: An application to educational enrolments in States of India", Washington: World Bank Policy Research Working Paper No. 1994.

— (1998). "The effect of household wealth on educational attainment around the world: Demographic and Health Survey evidence", Washington: World Bank Policy Research Working Paper No. 1980.

— (1999). "The effect of household wealth on educational attainment: Evidence from 35 countries", *Population and Development Review*, vol. 25, No.1, March, pp. 85-120.

Guarcello, L., S. Lyon and Rosati, F. C. (2003). "Child labour and access to basic services: Evidence from five countries", Understanding Child Work Project, unpublished draft, November.

O'Donnell O., Rosati F.C., and van Doorslaer E. (2001). *Child Labour and Health: Evidence and Research Issues*, Understanding Children's Work Project, 12 December.

Chapter 16

MICS in Pakistan: A Tool for Disparity and Poverty Reduction

Abdul Alim

STATISTICAL INFORMATION, SOCIAL DEVELOPMENT AND POLITICS IN PAKISTAN

Pakistan, the sixth most populace and the second largest Muslim nation in the world, has undergone serious internal and external upheavals since the events of 9/11 in 2001. Unlike many developing countries, however, what makes Pakistan unique is its direct role at the international level, through its involvement in Afghan conflict during the 1980s, in shaping and bringing this (external) upheaval upon itself. Security concerns, which shaped the doctrine of strategic depth (*Daily Times*, 2003)[1] and necessitated Pakistan's involvement in the Afghan conflict, still consume a large part of nation's resources (World Bank, 2003).[2]

The preoccupation with security concerns has come at a huge cost characterized by a widening gap between economic and social performance. With a burgeoning population of close to 150 million, seventy percent of who are below 18 years of age, and a fertility rate of 4.7 (NIPS, 2001), Pakistan sits on top of a demographic deluge. A big youth bulge; stagnant enrollment and malnutrition rates (graph 1) for over a decade (UNICEF, 2003); low functional literacy rates (CRPRID, 2003);[3] failure to eradicate Polio (WHO-GoP, 2004) and growing poverty (UNDP, 2003),[4] despite recent economic gains, characterize a rapidly evolving social emergency, which may not be silent for long. A large cohort of children, consisting of millions (SBP, 2004)[5] has already lost the chance of going to school. The mix of illiteracy and malnutrition with rising disparity and militancy, which has shown no signs of abetting until recently, may already have set into motion events, "fundamentally compromising the long term ability of the country to grow economically" (World Bank, 2002, p. xvii).

National figures mask the persistent (UNICEF, 2003),[6] and in some cases, rising (UNICEF, 2002)[7] regional (graph 2), gender,[8] and economic (UNDP, 1999) disparities. Locked in the ever-growing poverty cycle, the poor populace of Pakistan is increasingly discriminated against for access to basic services (World Bank, 2002). The birth place of child, its gender and ethnicity largely determines the probability of its survival and future social class. Rising poverty has affected some regions more than others (UNICEF, 2003).[9] Persistent disparities have also fueled the centrifugal tendencies in the provinces challenging the very basis of the federation (Richard, S., Rose, L., 1991).[10] The investment in education and health sectors has hovered around 2% and 0.7 of the GDP respectively for the whole the decade of 1990s (SPDC, 2000). The resources for social development are projected to increase by a meager 0.2% of the GDP in the Poverty Reduction Strategy Paper (GoP-Ministry of Finance, 2003). At this level of investment targets for the MDG are unlikely to be met (Planning Commission, 2004).

In this resource poor context of growing poverty and persistent social disparity among the federating units, statistical information, particularly the census and estimates of provincial population size, have held special significance for the politics[11] of resource distribution between the federation and among the provinces. There is no doubt that statistical information is a powerful tool (Santos-Pais, 1999) when it is used to analyze, not only policy options, since these can result in good or bad governance practices, (Komarecki, 2003) but to also make critical political decisions. Given the political importance and complexity of the issue, the 1973 Constitution (under Article 160)[12] established a basic framework for the management of public finance and provides for periodically setting up a National Finance Commission (NFC) to make recommendations on the criteria and award for distribution of national resources. The center, until 2001, had a monopoly over this statistical information, as all surveys including the census were conducted under a government controlled centralized unit (CRPRID, 2004).[13] While social indicators, until now, have not been explicitly included as a part of the criteria for resource distribution by the NFC, provinces[14] and development economists have consistently argued for inclusion of other criteria like social underdevelopment (Ahmad, N., Wasti, S., 2000).[15]

Statistical information on social indicators, however, has already acquired a special significance for sub national resource distribution, and will be dealt with, in detail, later in the paper.

Two conclusions can be drawn from the above. One, that quantitative information based on surveys like MICS and census hold significant importance for policy making and the politics of resource distribution at the national and sub national levels in Pakistan. Two, that well informed and objective debate on resource distribution, is a critical element in the dynamics of holding Pakistan together as a federation.

It can be argued that a large sample survey, like MICS, with information that can be disaggregated for gender, location and regions is "potentially" politically sensitive since it highlights disparities and rights violations. This is inherent in the design of MICS (Komarecki, 2003). The most vulnerable are often the least politically empowered. Any attempt to collect, use or make information available and speak on behalf of the vulnerable is, and can be construed as non "neutral" and taking a particular political stance. For UNICEF, this is a well considered risk, since without making information available on the most sensitive issues it is often difficult to get to the "real" problems in a society.

As a politically sensitive tool, MICS can evoke a range of responses from the state structures, especially, if they are highly politicized as is the case in Pakistan (World Bank, 1998). The response of these structures to statistical information can range from a complete denial of its existence, to benign ignorance leading to disuse. A change in the government can also bring about a radical change in these responses as illustrated later in the paper. Statistical rigor or validity of a survey, in this context, is therefore, only of relative importance. What is critical, however, is; whether a government is interested in objective information on its performance in the social sector; whether institutions that rely on information are functioning and are willing to use it for transparent decision making; how relevant is the survey to the interests of major political stakeholders in the country, especially the different levels of the government, and how well has it been socially marketed to the development community.

The use of a survey then depends on, how well the survey managers are tuned in to the political and policy making needs of a government. This is truer for an international instrument like MICS, which may be seen by a host government, as the agenda of an international organization, rather than a sincere effort to alert these governments, to the necessity of measuring social progress and addressing rights violations. This may also partly explain the lack of use of MICS in several countries (Komarecki, 2003). An optimum balance must, therefore, be reached between technical rigorousness of a survey and the political decision and policy making needs of a government, if, a survey is to be fully utilized. To reach this optimum balance it is critical to understand not only the significant political issues that may be impacted by a survey but also how socio-economic information is used for policy and political decision making process in a country. By comparing the two rounds of MICS, especially their political context, this paper attempts to tease out factors that allow the survey managers to reach this optimal balance.

The two rounds of MICS in Pakistan represent two important landmarks in the history of the country. The first round was undertaken in 1995-96, to measure the mid decade progress of end decade goals, committed to by Pakistan at the World Summit for Children (WSC) in 1991. While the first one was a national survey, the second is being conducted on a provincial level from mid 2001 to early 2004. The first round in the mid 1990s reflects a particular set of circumstances shaped by the decisions taken in late 1970s and 80s, the second round, post 9/11, is being undertaken at a major watershed in the recent history of Pakistan and poses a completely different set of challenges to the relevance and use of MICS in the country.

THE 1995-1996 MICS AND THE DECADE OF THE NINETIES

Until 1990, when Pakistan went to the WSC as one of the six initiator countries, it had led many other low-income countries in economic growth but without a commensurate change in the social indicators (ADB, 2002). After Zia's death, in 1988 in an air crash, Pakistan entered a phase of serious political and economic instability. The country saw four governments fall within a span of eleven years.[16] Political instability led to poor economic management and deterioration of governance. Between 1988 and 1998, Pakistan negotiated three programs with the International Monetary Fund(IMF), but was unable to implement them.

Lack of macro economic reforms in the 1980s had led to a weakening of institutions especially the financial sector. The fiscal deficit continued to average over seven percent of the GDP and public debt expanded rapidly (ADB 2002, MOWD 2000). Political instability was at its peak when MICS was being undertaken in 1995-96. Benazir Bhutto's government, which had once again come to power in 1993, was sacked in 1996 mainly due to the unrest[17] in the southern port city of Karachi and charges of corruption.[18] The End Decade Review[19] for Pakistan (MOWD, 2000) showed that, except for the coverage of safe drinking water, none of the other goals of the National Plan of Action for children, formulated in 1991, were met (NPA).

The problems that affected the 1995 MICS reflect, in part, the political crisis prevalent in the country at that time. It is important to note that several other institutional arrangements to collect and use data were also deeply affected during this period, especially from 1990-1998. The population census due in 1991, could not take place, since the population size of the federating units, by virtue of being a major criterion for resource distribution in the NFC, had become a politically divisive issue. Pakistan Integrated Household Survey (PIHS), a government and DFID sponsored survey, which held its first round in 1991 and was to be an annual feature, could not be conducted until 1996-97. Pakistan Demographic and Household Survey (PDHS) that was carried out in 1991 ran into technical problems. A delayed evaluation showed that "majority of the variables were not reported consistently" (Curtis, S.1994 p. 51). Due to the lack of information from census, most of the surveys,[20] including MICS, were faulted for sampling errors (CRPRID 2004).[21] Finally, the NFC, constitutionally mandated to meet every four years, did not meet between 1990 and 1997.

Given the backdrop of this political and economic crisis in the country, UNICEF's interest in conducting the MICS[22] was met with, at best, by a benign indifference by the decision-makers. The survey was seen more as pursuance of UNICEF agenda rather than an initiative on part of the government. Ministry of Health was the given the actual charge of the survey. National Institute of Health[23] was made the secretariat (MoH-GoP, 1995). A consultant was hired to liaise between UNICEF and government ministries. The Planning Commission recalls its inadequate representation in the steering committee and a lack of public sector interest in the backdrop of the political instability and governments' preoccupation with economic issues. Despite some provincial involvement in the early discussions, the way survey was managed, did not allow the governments to become major stakeholders.

The 1995-96 MICS was commissioned to the private sector. It was done on a national basis with a sample of approximately 15,000 households with allowance for appropriate weights for urban rural, gender and provincial dis-aggregation (MoH-GoP, 1995). The private sector firm that managed the survey from the federal capital had sublet provincial components to other private sector parties. The survey results were challenged by allegations of inaccurate sample design and fictitious data. Even within UNICEF, staff was skeptical of the data quality, due to an inadequate involvement in the monitoring of the survey by UNICEF's provincial based field staff.

In normal business practices, the interest of client is the main factor determining the quality of a product. The quality of a survey (product) is compromised if a major stakeholder like the government is disinterested or taken up by other issues. Rights based instruments like MICS, which make objective data available, holding the government accountable (Fukuda-Parr, 2001)[24] for failing to govern well or to attend to the rights of its people, can and do pose athreat to unstable governments. Given the lack of progress on social issues (MoWD-GoP, 2000) and the state of crisis in governance institutions in Pakistan during these years, it would have been surprising if MICS 1995-96 would have been received well. Other than the use of information for policymaking on IDD, there is little evidence to show a significant impact of 1995-96 MICS on the political or policy making process in the country.

It can be safely concluded that the major reasons for the challenge to the statistical validity and the relative lack of use of MICS 1995-96 were the unstable political and economic conditions and inconsistency in the policy direction attributable to the frequent change of the governments during these years. The disinterest of the central and provincial governments was thus more reflective of a governance crisis diverting their attention to the more emergent issues, than the quality or use of the survey. Paralysis of institutions, such as NFC; UNICEF's inability to understand and pitch the survey to the right decision makers and creating a complementarity or constructive relationship with a government owned competing instrument like PIHS also contributed to the underutilization of the survey.

INTER-GOVERNMENTAL RELATIONS, DEVOLUTION AND MICS 2001-2004

In 1998, when post-nuclear-test-economic-sanctions heralded the beginning of a full-blown economic crisis, Pakistan's debt indicators were worse than most heavily indebted poor countries (ADB, 2002). Regional tensions had escalated due to the Kargil conflict and India and Pakistan were on the verge of a full blown nuclear war. Three critical developments in 1999, when the second round of MICS was initiated, played a significant role in ensuring that statistical information is used in the political decision and policy making process in the country.

First, following a blood less coup, in October 1999, General Parvez Mussharaf came to power. He has remained in power since, allowing for the return of political stability. His constructive initiatives on the foreign policy front[25] have earned praise internationally and have played a key role in stabilizing the region.

Second, initiation by the administration, of comprehensive reform programmes to address outstanding macroeconomic and structural problems. In October 2000, Pakistan began implementing a far-reaching macroeconomic stabilization and restructuring program under an International Monetary Fund (IMF) standby arrangement (SBA) and implemented it successfully despite the adverse impact of 9/11 event. Over the last five years, Pakistan's macroeconomic indicators have improved steadily. The fiscal deficit has declined, inflation has been low, exports have grown, the balance-of-payments deficit has declined, and foreign exchange reserves are at a record high (SBP, 2003).

Third, to diffuse the centrifugal pressures and harmonize relations between the federation and the provinces, the government initiated a set of governance reforms. This included devolution with an emphasis on fiscal decentralization (Ahmad, N., 2001)[26] to the lowest tier of the government; the reconstitution of the NFC to revitalize and open the national and sub national dialogue on resource distribution; and a renewed interest in outcome driven social development through writing of a comprehensive PRSP (IMF, 2001). One of the most significant developments on this front was the Local Government Ordinance (LGO) issued in October 2001 (NRB, 2001) and the formation of Provincial Finance Commissions (PFC)[27] on the pattern of the NFC (NRB, 2001) to distribute resources between the districts in each province, through declaring a provincial award. Provinces were encouraged to define and use transparent criteria for these awards.

The current round of MICS was initiated in 2001 riding on these positive political and economic developments The first provincial governments to take initiative was the North-West Frontier Province government (GoNWFP). In contrast to the 1995-96 MICS, where UNICEF itself had taken the initiative, request for this survey came from the highest policy making body of the provincial government. UNICEF was requested to provide assistance to the Planning and Development Department (P&DD) of the province in undertaking this survey. The major objectives of the NWF provincial MICS were to establishes a credible baseline for monitoring the socioeconomic status of the districts; develop ranking of the districts to highlight the inter -district disparities; provide information on the situation of children and women, as well as child-focused benchmarking; rectify the data gaps in the information systems from national surveys and sectored databases; build capacity of the relevant government institutions, especially the provincial Bureau of Statistics, through their active involvement in all the phases of the survey (NWFP PRSP, 2003).

A traditional MICS, conforming to the international design to fulfill the provincial and district needs was used with an emphasis on poverty-related indicators (see annex B for poverty module) ensuring adequate proportionate coverage of all districts of NWFP. MICS was conducted from September to December 2001. A total of 13, 076 households drawn from 873 primary sampling units of which 223 were urban and 650 were rural were interviewed (P&DD, 2003). This survey was the first attempt to get district-level representative estimates in any of the four provinces of the country.

Major difficulties encountered during the survey were the sustenance of the ownership process at the provincial and district level; covering a large sample in a short time frame with limited budget; addressing technical capacity in the government, which had its own competing priorities, and coordination among key actors. One of the key features of the survey report was the ranking of the districts in an order of social development (P&DD MICS, 2002, Annex C).

Two major uses of MICS in NWFP highlight how it has contributed to the planning and policy initiatives of the Government of NWFP to better target resources and shape policy instruments like the PRSP to the advantage of the vulnerable.

One, historically in Pakistan, the official planning practices in the provinces have led to the preparation of constituency driven development plans, with the implicit intention of the political leadership to cultivate patronage. These are then collated and presented as the Annual Development Plans (ADP) from each district and aggregated to the provincial level to be called a provincial ADP. In a major deviation from these routine planning practices, under the devolution initiative, the NWFP-PFC award gave a 25 percent weight to the social development indicators (termed backwardness in the award document) based on the composite ranking in the MICS, as a part of the criteria to distribute resource to the districts (P&DD, 2003). This allowed for the pegging of one-line budgets (block allocations) to the districts to an indexing process. This was the first time in the history of the country that a survey was planned, conducted and used to make regional disparity a determinant of allocations for a particular geographic or administrative jurisdiction.

This has two significant aspects. First, while the NWFP MICS was not specifically designed to fully deal with poverty and to do justice to the poverty diagnostics for a PRSP, it did carry a new module on poverty to address the oft cited shortcoming of this instrument (Komarecki, 2003). The indexing process also allows for a more holistic diagnosis of poverty, which according to UNICEF is not just lack of income but a lack of access to basic services or "loss of dignity" (UNICEF, 2002). Second, it allowed for higher allocations to the more vulnerable districts. This fulfills the conditions of a rights based, disparity reduction approach confirming the principle of progressive realization of the rights of the vulnerable (Green, 2001; Garonna & Balta, 2002). MICS had, therefore, led to a rights based decision process that was sensitive not only to gender concerns but also to geographic disparity by being able to disaggregate social information to lower levels of governance (Komarecki, 2003).

Two, Pakistan had agreed on a Poverty Reduction Growth Facility with the IMF in October 2001 (IMF, 2001). This was based on an Interim PRSP (I-PRSP). The government had committed to writing a full PRSP as a part of qualifying for the facility. One distinguishing feature of Pakistan PRSP was the commitment of the federal government to make the Poverty Reduction Strategy (PRS) process as participatory as possible (MoF-GoP, 2003). While a federal PRSP was being written, the provinces also initiated the process of writing provincial PRSPs. The provincial PRSP s are meant not only to facilitate the borrowing process from the International Financial Institutions (IFIs) but are also a comprehensive policy package for poverty reduction. An important part of this document is the Medium Term Expenditure Framework (MTEF) (IMF, 2001) outlining the three year provincial resource position and its investment in different sectors including the social sectors.

The Go-NWFP had started to address poverty in the province as early as 2000. In order to address resource issues the Go-NWFP had also committed to a Structural Adjustment Credit Programme (SAC) with the World Bank to bolster its medium term plan. Following the successful completion of the MICS in NWFP and its use by the PFC to distribute resources to the districts, the NWFP Government also took lead in requesting UNICEF's assistance for writing the Provincial Poverty Reduction Strategy (PPRS).

UNICEF's assistance to the province on the PPRSP aimed at influencing the PRS for achieving three major outcomes. One was to ensure that the rich analysis available in MICS on gender and geographic disparity was used as a benchmark for poverty diagnostics and policy development for the social sectors. Two, encourage a broad based participatory process focused on the most vulnerable and representation of all tiers of governance and civil society in the discussions on strategy and, three, obtain a firm policy and political commitment at the provincial level on social outcomes and targets for the province. Once these outcomes were achieved, UNICEF also highlighted successfully, the mis-match between the social commitments, and the resources allocated to achieve them in the MTEF.

In short, the MICS catalyzed not only a better disparity reduction planning and resource allocation process in NWFP but also helped to lay down the foundations of a good analysis for the PRSP by providing social benchmarks. It also enabled UNICEF to advocate with the provincial government the allocation of higher resources for the most vulnerable.

Following the elections in October 2002, a religious alliance[28] of political parties took over the government in NWFP. Two interesting developments have since taken place. One, the MICS was challenged for its validity of results mainly on the ranking of the districts, two, the provincial government, while having acknowledged the final draft of PRSP and having endorsed it at the chief ministerial level, is still to bring it to the provincial parliament for an open debate and final approval. This should be seen within the context of political developments and negative incentives (Komarecki, 2003) that have led to a tension between the federal, provincial and district governments with different political agendas. Without going into the detail of this, it is clear that the change of political leadership has brought about a change in how MICS and PRSP are being perceived in NWFP.

The stipulations of the LGO and SAC signed by the NWFP government with the World Bank has however, tied the hands of the current leadership from making any drastic changes in the PFC award. The districts are bound to spend 70% of the resources on social sectors. While this may be in contravention to district autonomy, its does mean a consistency of social targeting and a higher focus on rights.

In conclusion, NWFP MICS experience demonstrates that despite high level of acceptability, successful integration in planning and use of a statistical tool in a political decision and policy making process for poverty reduction, a change in the government can lead to a complete reversal of an earlier position about a survey.

MICS AND REGIONAL POVERTY REDUCTION STRATEGIES

Having seen the practical uses of the NWFP MICS at the Pakistan Development Forum (PDF)[29] in 2002, where it was presented as a landmark survey and planning tool for poverty and disparity reduction, all other provinces initiated negotiations with UNICEF to provide assistance for conducting the MICS. Two major reasons account for the continuation of the current round of MICS as a stand alone survey in each of the other three provinces.

One, fiscal situation of all the provinces has been worsening for over a decade. Their debt to the federal government runs into billions of rupees. Delays in the NFC awards and in subsequent release of provincial allocations (Ahmad, N., 2000) have necessitated, that the federating units, borrow from the federation at very high interest rates. Growing poverty, worsening fiscal constraints and higher responsibility to meet social sector needs under the devolution initiative has tremendously increased the pressure on the, already stretched, provincial financial resources. The main contention of the provinces is that the incidence of poverty in the federating units is higher than the one declared by the federal government (CRPRID 2003) under its centrally administered surveys like Household Income and Expenditure Survey (HIES). They argue that the federal government must forego some of the provincial debt as the federation gets a relief in its domestic and foreign debt through rescheduling.[30] Establishing baseline for poverty is also critical to the PPRSPs and discussions in the NFC to advocate for higher allocation of national resources to the province and diversify the NFC criteria. It will also empower the districts to negotiate a better share of resources from the provincial government.

Two, the keen interest of the provinces also emanates from their desire to use MICS as a tool for improving the allocation process through the respective PFCs but also to acquire independent statistical information to establish an independent database to monitor poverty reduction and bring a reliable alternative view to the federal perspective. They see that this will also facilitate both devolution and fiscal decentralization by better equipping them in monitoring their own performance and that of the district governments under their jurisdiction.

The special features of the MICS being undertaken now in the three provinces is its unique institutional framework that allows for participation of public, private and civil society institutions in all aspects of the survey; its focus on local and provincial capacity building, and enhanced poverty diagnostics with full ownership by the provincial policy and planning institutions. Using the flexibility of MICS, provincial governments have been encouraged to choose the type and number of indicators. All technical details have been endorsed by a high powered committee of the provincial governments. With the approval of the government, civil society institutions have been engaged in the monitoring of the survey. A full poverty module has been included which focuses on several dimensions.

Following the NWFP example, where UNICEF moved swiftly to provide technical assistance to help with the NWFP PRSP, all three remaining provinces requested technical assistance for their respective PRS. The first drafts of the provincial PRSPs have already been completed and endorsed by the provincial executive while the MICS is still in the process of being completed. UNICEF's assistance allowed for district and provincial level consultation aimed at participation of the different stakeholder in the PRS process. Without the availability of primary statistical information at the district level to focus on disparity, UNICEF has attempted to ensure that human development remains a major focus of the PRS. Other sources of information have been used to strengthen the gender dimensions of the poverty and the need the most vulnerable. Since PPRSPs will be rolling documents, provinces have already voiced their intention to use MICS as a benchmark for detailed poverty plans, as soon as the data becomes available.

The PFC awards of all the provinces in 2003 included multiple criteria (see table 1). As in the case of NWFP where "backwardness or developmental lag" of the districts is measured through the MICS, in all the provinces a weight is assigned to this criteria, except for Balochistan. For the PFC awards in 2003, MICS data was not available, therefore, secondary data or census (SPDC 2000) was used to assign district ranking. It is expected that once MICS data becomes available for the districts in all the provinces, it will be used for resource allocations to the districts. This will be true also for Balochistan, which is the most data poor province.

Since statistical information in MICS is an important determinant in the PFCs, the districts in Pakistan have woken up to the crucial importance of statistical data. They have great enthusiasm for not only assisting in carrying out the survey, monitoring its quality, but also its results. This is sea change in the attitude towards statistics in the country and carries promise for the future.

It is important to note that while both provincial level MICS and the PPRSPs facilitate the devolution process, they do not necessarily find favor with policy makers, politicians and civil society (ICG, 2004) at all levels. The National Reconstruction Bureau (NRB), the official think tank, while designing the initiative, bypassed the federating units. This may have been intended to diffuse the centrifugal forces from the provinces. The political leadership, mainly representing the provincial level has been against this reform. The implementation of the reform has been full of difficulties due to capacity and resource constraints at the district level.

It should be clarified that UNICEF's assistance to the provincial governments for MICS and PPRSPs was not intended to take sides in the politics of devolution and national resource allocations process. It was based purely on technical reasons, which were to empower the federating units to monitor their own social development and contribute objective data to improve the quality of discourse on the resource distribution.

The World Bank in Pakistan and the Ministry of Finance have advocated for one centrally administered instrument, such as Core Welfare Indicator Questionnaire (CWIQ) for monitoring of the poverty in Pakistan. The rationale for this position is also quite obvious, since it allows for a more uniform and comparable set of data across the provinces and a better construction of the long term trends. This paper argues that MICS and CWIQ are not competitive but complementary. While CWIQ concentrates on intermediate poverty indicators, MICS looks more comprehensively at the impact of PRS measures. CWIQ is an annual feature and is centralized, while MICS should only be repeated at five year intervals to capture the change in social outcomes at the provincial level. Without commenting on the legitimacy or superiority of one argument over the other, it is safe to conclude that statistical information seems to have improved the quality of political debate in Pakistan. This is a very positive sign and points to a growing and healthy tradition.

In addition to engendering an informed debate on policy issues, one of the most important contributions of the current round of MICS is that it has created a sample design for the first time in the country that can cater to largest possible national surveys, such as CWIQ, with dis-aggregation at the three levels of governance (see table 2). In the three provinces, for the first time in Pakistan, MICS is providing data on municipal level.

CONCLUSIONS AND LESSONS LEARNED

The comparison of 1995-1996 MICS with the 2001-2004 round shows that political stability and performance of a government is an important determinant of the use, relevance, acceptability, and in some cases, even the statistical validity of a survey (table 2). Some of the more important lessons are:

1. MICS should not be undertaken without the full participation and ownership of the host government. If this is done, risks must be carefully studied and understood. Some issues that could come up are; low quality data and analysis; lack of use of the survey by the public sector and challenge to its validity.

2. While it is more difficult to manage, involvement of a large number of stakeholders including the private sector, the non profit sector, public sector and beneficiaries, creates multiple foci of ownership. This is important in countries where political changes may lead to changes in decision making process or a reversal of stated political positions. Creation of a wider ownership hedges against claims of technical shortcoming to discredit the survey if it does not fit into the political agenda of a new govern.

3. While good quality data collection, rigorous tests of statistical validity are very important for an MICS to contribute to measurement of social development; it is critical to study socio economic and political trends in a country before embarking on the exercise.

4. Intensive pre survey advocacy and its contextualization in the policy and decision making process, which creates high degree of ownership in the government, makes MICS a much more useful tool for social change towards disparity reduction.

5. MICS should be socially marketed as a five -year poverty reduction impact measuring tool not in competition with yearly or annual social surveys such as PIHS or CWIQ. Taking this position will enable a more productive collaboration with BWIs, not only on poverty monitoring but policy analysis and feedback.

6. The ultimate users of information are the people and the public sector in any country. All care must be taken that public institutions guide the conduct and proceedings of the survey. In case of dis-aggregation of the data to lower geographic levels, corresponding public sector managers should be involved to ensure ownership at all levels.

7. The strength of MICS as a tool that can be modified to fit the needs of a host government should be fully exploited. This could involve for instance inclusion of impact indicators for poverty reduction or other economic indicators.

8. Capacity building prospects of MICS can be highly enhanced if the genuine partnerships can be fostered between different private and public institutions, which may have different absorption capacities for technical knowledge. A consortium of institutions is more likely to retain more technical expertise than focusing on a single institutions or creation of a specific one.

9. Awareness of political use of information must be gathered before the survey is embarked upon. This must be balanced with the long term interest of UNICEF and a host government. Unintended political outcomes should be fully understood and used to the advantage of the children and women.

Table 1. Comparison of PFC Criteria between Provinces and Relevance of MICS

PFC Criteria	Punjab	Sindh	NWFP	Balochistan
Population	67%	50%	50%	50%
Backwardness*	33%	30%	25%	
Underdevelopment				
Scheme		10%		
Backlog				
Equalization		10%		
Area				50%
Infrastructure			25%	
backlog				
Total	100	100	100	100

Source: Notifications of Planning and Development Departments.

Graph 1. <5MR Trends: Balochistan (Red) & Punjab (Blue) Comparison

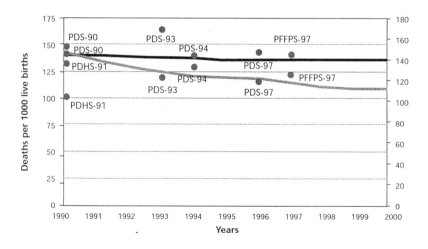

Table 2. Features of MICS 1995-96 and MICS 2001 -04: A Comparison

MICS 1995-96	MICS 2001-04
Unstable political conditions and economic conditions	Stable political conditions and economic conditions
Non functioning of institutions that use information for decision making	Institutions that use information for decision making are functional e.g. NFC
No request from high level policy makers	Requested by high level policy makers in the provinces
National and provincial dis-aggregation, but no provincial involvement in the survey	National and provincial and district level dis-aggregation available. Both provincial and districts involvement in the survey
Commissioned to the private sector with no involvement of civil society	Commissioned to a consortium of institutions that include private, non profit civil society and public sector.
Weak monitoring leading to allegations of fictitious filling of questionnaires.	Two tier monitoring instituted to ensure full compliance to quality procedures.
Weak capacity building component	Strong capacity building component.
Errors in sampling frames	No errors in sampling frames.
No involvement of the districts	High level interest from the districts
Main client perceived to be UNICEF	Main client by claim are the Provincial Planning and Development Departments and Poverty Reduction units
Total sample 14,596, nationally and provincially representative	Total sample 78,862, representative at provincial and district levels
No Poverty Module	Comprehensive Poverty Module added
Total cost approximately: $110,000	Total cost approximately: $ 1.5 million
No use in resource distribution or PRS	Relevant to NFC and PFC proceedings and PPRSPS

Graph 2. Nutrition Trends (underweight, children under 5)

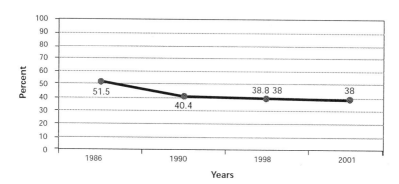

NOTES

[1] (*Daily Times Pakistan*, 2003: Going back to the Durand Line) Military strategists believe that Pakistan lacks width in its territory making it prone to be cut into two halves in case of war with India. See quotation in bibliography for more detail. "Pakistan's Taliban policy was linked by its military strategists to the doctrine of Strategic Depth vis -à-vis India, compensating for the lack of width of its own territory in case there was a war with India. Pursuing strategic depth, Pakistan backed Mullah Umar's Taliban against the Northern Alliance", dated April 8, 2004, p. 3.

[2] World Bank (2002) Pakistan's defense expenditures have been unusually high (4% of GDP). Combined with debt servicing, it leaves little for social development.

[3] (CRPRID 2003) About 55 percent of the 10+ years of age population is illiterate under a criterion of literacy which is not even "Basic" under the UNESCO definition of literacy. At even this "sub-basic" level 80 million citizens are illiterate. If "Functional Literacy" were (as it should be for participation in the affairs of a modern state in the 21st century) the criterion, then the illiterate population would be over 100 million. (Presentation made at UNICEF Pakistan, 2003).

[4] Hussein, A. (2003). Poverty in Pakistan has risen from a low of 26.6% in late 1992 -93 to 32.2% in 1999.

[5] 6 million children are out of school (State Bank of Pakistan, 2004). The State of Pakistan's Economy - Second Quarterly Report 2003-2004, p. 126.

[6] (UNICEF 2003) Rural IMR in Pakistan is 88 as compared to an urban IMR of 65. Balochistan still has the highest under-five MR among all the provinces. At 142 it compares unfavorably with NWFP at only 85 and the national at 103, (Situation Analysis Update, p. 1, Unpublished).

[7] (UNICEF: 2002) Rate of fall in under-five mortality has lagged behind in Balochistan giving rise to a widening gap between Punjab and Balochistan (see graph 1). (World

Bank: 2003, p. vi) There is evidence to indicate worsening rich and poor gap in primary enrolment. See also graph 2.

[8] (CRPRID 2003) On example of gender -gap is the fact that the Balochistan female population has a literacy rate of 9 percent while Punjab/Sindh/N.W.F.P male has a literacy rate of 72 percent. (Presentation made at Unicef 2003).

[9] (UNDP, 1999) Incidence of poverty in Punjab is 35 as compared to 47 in NWFP World Bank 2002, urban and rural poverty gap has risen from 5% in 1986/97 to almost 10% in 1993/94): (A profile of Poverty in Pakistan, p. 9).

[10] (Richard, S., Rose, L. 1991) For an excellent and dispassionate discussion on the breaking away of East Pakistan into Bangladesh. This still seen by many political experts as the failure to exercise true federal spirit of the constitution. For an excellent and dispassionate discussion on this see.

[11] At its peak now, as the sixth NFC award has been delayed. It has major implications for provincial resource availability and the annual budgeting process for all the federating units. All major newspapers have featured articles and almost daily updates of the NFC proceedings. See as Annex E.

[12] <http://www.pakistan.gov.pk/law-ivision/publications/constitution>. [PDF] For full text of the Constitution of Pakistan 1973.

[13] The Federal Bureau of Statistics (FBS) is the sole custodian of sampling frames and sample design in the country. The sampling frames are shared with the provinces on need basis, which are unable to conduct their own surveys due to lack of access to this information. The government has indicated its intention to accord FBS more autonomy.

[14] (*Daily Dawn*-Internet Edition 26 March) On the question of the sharing of resources among the provinces, the member said the meeting was in favor of a 'multi-factor approach' instead of a 'population-alone' basis in view of strong position taken by the three smaller provinces, although Punjab had still not made any commitment to give up its position on the matter. The meeting seemed converging on the principle that weight age for revenue, poverty and area would be so formulated that it would not reduce the existing share of any province so that a notional formula could be converted into a multi-factor formula with consensus, creating a win-win situation for all the provinces as well as for the federation.

[15] Ahmad, N. Wasti, S. (2000, p. 213): "Backwardness and poverty should be explicitly incorporated in the allocation of shared transfers, and they should be more comprehensively measured through an index that uses multiple indicators. These may be broadly categorized as socioeconomic and demographic indicators related to income and wealth, housing, transport and communication, education, health, gender equality, etc. Some of the indicators used in the human development index, for example, would be relevant. We recommend that a fixed percentage (5%) fund from the divisible pool be allocated first to the backward provinces and the remaining be disbursed on the basis of a predetermined formula. An equalizing formula similar to the one used in India could be developed, and it could be improved as better data become available".

[16] Benazir Bhutto 1988-1990 and 1993-1996; Nawaz Sharif 1990-1993 and 1996-1999.

[17] Kaplan (2002, p. 2, Online edition): "More than 4,000 people were killed and more than 10,000 wounded in Karachi in communal fighting in the mid -1980s, when the city began to overflow with weapons from the Afghan war. This continued during the late 1980s and the 1990s. In the first ten months of 1998 there were 629 murders in Karachi committed by what a local magazine called "unaffiliated contract killers".

[18] <http://www.Global.secu rity.org/military/world/pakistan/politicsHtm>. "In November 1996, President Leghari dismissed the Bhutto government, charging it with corruption, mismanagement of the economy, and implication in extrajudicial killings in Karachi".

[19] MOWD (2000, p. 5): "The broad-based progress in the social sectors appeared to be hampered. The reasons for slow progress being resource constraints and an unstable security environment in the region compounded the problem. This meant that resource allocation for a number of developmental goals did not correspond with the political commitment. The interplay of these factors was further complicated because of the political uncertainty in the country during most of the period under review."

[20] CRPRID (2003, p. 35): "Human Condition Report: PIHS and HIES used the 1981 sampling frame".

[21] CRPRID (2003). For an excellent discussion on surveys and mist-governance in statistical organizations in Pakistan see CRPRID, *Human Condition Report 2003*, pp. 34-38.

[22] Most of the information in these paragraphs is based on a small survey of the MICS managers from UNICEF national staff in Pakistan country Office. This includes informal interviews with ex Planning Commission officials who were members of the Steering Committee for MICS.

[23] Both of these institutions have no mandate for national surveys nor have the technical expertise to conduct one.

[24] Fukuda-Parr (2001). An evidence-driven approach has the potential to make all relevant players more accountable with respect to their constituencies, public opinion, and the communities whose human rights are at stake.

[25] Significant among these is the reversal of foreign policy position on supporting Taliban and active pursuance of a détente with India leading to substantial lowering of regional tensions and allowing for a freeze on defense spending.

[26] Ahmad, N. Wasti S. (2000, p. 216): "The devolution plan of the Government of Pakistan involves substantial decentralization to local governments that is unprecedented in the history of the country. According to one estimate, almost PRs90 billion (equivalent to almost 3% of GDP) of expenditure will be transferred from provincial to local budgets. This will increase the total outlays of local governments to almost four times their present levels and make them almost comparable in size to the provincial governments".

[27] NRB (2002): "The Provincial Finance Commission will be established by each Province to develop the fiscal transfer mechanism. The fiscal transfer mechanism would consider various factors to come up with an equitable distribution of funds. The main factors are population, under -development, fiscal effort, revenue generation capacity, and expenditure requirement besides other. The objectives of fiscal transfers are to provide base-line levels for essential services, encourage own-source revenue efforts, encourage

spending in priority areas and promote efficient spending". <http://www.nrb.gov.pk/local_finance/index.html>.

[28] In the general elections held in October 2002, Muttahida Majlis-e-Amal (MMA) achieved landslide victories in NWFP and Balochistan and formed governments in both the provinces.

[29] A high profile policy level meeting of a consortium of donors held annually in Pakistan.

[30] Pakistan's went through a substantial debt rescheduling in early 2000-2001, which created more fiscal space for poverty reduction.

REFERENCES

ADB Country Strategy and Program 2002-2006: 2002: Pakistan: I. Development Agenda: Current Political, Macroeconomic, and Social Trends.

Ahmad, N. Wasti S, 2001: Intergovernmental Fiscal Transfers in Asia, Applied Economic Research Center, Karachi, <http://www.adb.org/Documents/ Books/ Intergovernmental_Fiscal_Transfers/>.

Center for Poverty Reduction and Income Distribution (CRPRID)-UNDP/UNOPS, 2003: Pakistan Human Condition Report.

Curtis S., Arnold, F. (1994). *An Evaluation of Pakistan DHS Survey based on Reinterview Survey*, DHS, Macro International Inc. Beltsville Drive, Calverton 20705, U.S.A.

Daily Times Pakistan (2003). Going back to the Durand Line Article dated Monday

April 5, 2004-Online Edition: <http://www.dailytimes.com.pk/default.asp?page=story_20-5-2003_pg3_1>.

DAWN-Internet Edition 26 March 2004, <http://www. dawn.com/2004/03/26/nat21.htm>.

Fukuda-Parr, S. (2001). "Indicators of Human Development and Human Rights: Overlaps, Differences...And What About the Human Development Index", *Statistical Journal of the UN Economic Commission for Europe*, vol. 18, No. 2.

Garonna, P. & Balta, E. (2002). "Measuring Human Rights: The Challenges for the Information Society", *Statistical Journal of the UN Economic Commission for Europe*, Vol. 19, No. 4.

Green, M. (2001). "What We Talk About When We Talk About Indicators: Current Approaches to Human Rights Measurement", *Human Rights Quarterly*, Vol. 23.

Hussain, A. (2003). *Pakistan National Human Development Report, Poverty, Growth and Governance*, UNDP Pakistan, New Sketch Graphics, Karachi: Oxford University Press.

<http://www.pakistan.gov.pk/law -division/publications/constitution.pdf>.

ICG (2004). "Devolution in Pakistan: Reform or Regression?", *Asia Report* N°77, 22March; online edition Islamabad/Brussels, 22 March, <http://crisisweb.org/home/index.cfm ?id=2549&l=1>.

International Monetary Fund and International Development Association (1999). "Poverty

Reduction Strategy Papers–Operational Issues", Prepared by the Staffs of the IMF and the World Bank.

IMF (2001). "Pakistan, Request for a Three-Year Arrangement Under the (PRGF)", Country Report No. 01/222, IMF.

Kaplan, R. (2000). "The Lawless Frontier", *The New Atlantic Monthly*, online edition, The Atlantic Monthly Group.

Komarecki, M. (2003). *Promoting Human Rights and Social Policies for Children and Women: The role of multiple cluster indicator survey (MICS)*. (Partly reproduced as chapter 1 of this volume).

Ministry of Finance Government of Pakistan (2003). "Accelerating Economic Growth and Reducing Poverty: The Road Ahead Pakistan Poverty Reduction Strategy Paper" (PDF Version), Poverty Reduction Strategy Paper Secretariat (<www.finance.gov.pk>).

Ministry of Health, Government of Pakistan (1995). *Multiple Indicator Cluster Survey of Pakistan 1995*, in collaboration with UNICEF and Gallup Pakistan.

Ministry of Health Government of Pakistan and World Health Organization (2004). *Monthly Polio Surveillance Bulletin*, Islamabad: National Surveillance Cell.

Ministry of Women's Development, Social Welfare and Special Education (MoWD), Government of Pakistan (2000). National Report on Follow -up to The World Summit for Children National Commission for Child Welfare and Development.

National Institute of Population Studies (NIPS) (2001). "Pakistan Reproductive Health and Family Planning Survey 2000-01". Preliminary Report.

NRB (2001). "The SBNP Local Government Ordinance 2001, National Reconstruction Bureau", Prime Minister's Secretariat-Online <http://www.nrb.gov.pk/publications/SBNP_Local_ Govt_Ordinance_2001.pdf>.

"Pakistan Reproductive Health and Family Planning Survey 2000-01 (Preliminary Report)", National Institute of Population Studies (NIPS), July 2001.

Planning Commission Government of Pakistan (2004). "Pakistan Millennium Development Goals Report", unpublished.

Planning and Development Department, Government of North-West Frontier Province (2002). "NWFP a District Based Multiple Indicator Cluster Survey 2001, A Tool for Social Change, 2001-2002". Government Of North-West Frontier Province (NWFP).

Santos-Pais, M. (1999). *The Challenge of Monitoring the Observance of the Convention on the Rights of the Child*, Helsinki: ISI Conference.

Sisson, R., Rose, L. (1991). *War and Secession: Pakistan, India, and the Creation of Bangladesh*. (ISBN: 0520076656 Amazon.com).

Social Policy Development Center (SPDC) (2000). "Social Development in Pakistan, Towards Poverty Reduction", *Annual review 2000*, SPDC-Oxford, University Press.

State Bank of Pakistan (2003). "The State of Pakistan's Economy - Second Quarterly". Report 2003-2004.

UNICEF New York, Division of Evaluation, Policy and Planning (2000). "Poverty Reduction Begins with Children", New York: UNICEF Division of Communications.

UNICEF (2002). "Situation Analysis Update for Mid Term Review GoP –UNICEF Programme of Cooperation 1999-2003". Unpublished.

UNICEF (2003). "Country Strategy Paper for GoP-UNICEF Country Programme of Cooperation 2004-2008". Unpublished.

UNDP (1999). *A Profile of Poverty in Pakistan*, Islamabad: Mabub-ul-Haq Center for Human Development.

World Bank (2002). "Pakistan Poverty Assessment: Poverty in Pakistan: Vulnerabilities, Social Gaps and Rural Dynamics, Poverty Reduction and Economic Management Sector Unit South Asia Region", Report No. 24296-PAK.

World Bank (1998). Report No. 18386-PAK: "Pakistan A Framework for Civil Service Reform in Pakistan by Poverty Reduction and Economic Management South Asia Region". Document of the World Bank, <http://www-wds.worldbank.org/servlet/ WDSContentServer/WDSP/IB/1999/09/77/000094946_99030406214674/Rendered/ INDEX/multi_page.txt>.

Conference Program and Participants

Social Policies and Human Rights for Children and Women:
Achieving and Monitoring the Millennium Development Goals

April 28-30, 2004

APRIL 28

OPENING

Welcome

Arjun Appadurai, Provost and Sr. Vice President, New School University

Michael Cohen, Director, GPIA

Kul Gautam, UNICEF, Deputy Executive Director

SESSION I

Multiple Indicator Cluster Survey (MICS): Information, Knowledge and Application in Social Policy

Chair: Elizabeth Gibbons, Chief, Global Policy, Division of Policy and Planning, UNICEF

Commentator: Sheila B. Kamerman, Compton Foundation Centennial Professor and Co-Director, Institute for Child and Family Policy, Columbia University, SSW

1. Maternal and Child Health Status in Diber Prefecture, Albania

Authors: Malik Jaffer, Karen Z. Waltensperger, Erika Lutz, Fabian Cenko, Ermira Brasha, Gazmend Koduzi, and James Ricca

Presenter: Malik Jaffer, American Red Cross

2. Urban-Rural Differences in Child Labor: How Effective Is the MICS in Informing Policies that Promote the Human Rights of Children in Urban Areas? An Example of Kenya

Presenter: Frederick Mugisha, African Population and Health Research Center, Nairobi, Kenya

3. MICS in Pakistan: A Tool for Disparity and Poverty Reduction

Presenter: Abdul Alim, UNICEF Pakistan

4. Reducing Child Poverty: A Review of Tried and Untried Policies in the Developing World

Presenter: Peter Townsend, Department of Social Policy, London School of Economics

APRIL 29

SESSION II

General Situation of Children and Women (Nutrition and Health)

Chair: Musthaque Chowdhury, BRAC, Director of the Research and Evaluation Division Bangladesh, UN Millennium Project Task Force 4 on Child Health and Maternal Health

Commentator: Marianne Fahs, Associate Professor and Director, Health Policy Research Center, Milano Graduate School of Management and Urban Policy, New School University

1. Analysis of the Disparities in Chronic Malnutrition in Children Under Five Years of Age by Wealth Income Quintile and Urban/Rural Residence

Presenter: Gina Kennedy, FAO

2. Decomposing Inequalities in Nutritional Status of Children in Kenya

Presenter: Babatunde Omilola, University of Sussex, UK

3. Multiple Indicator Surveys vs. Focused Surveys: an Example of Immunization Coverage 1991-2001

Authors: Robert Jenkins and Chandra Sekhar

Presenter: Chandra Sekhar, UNICEF India

4. *Children Living Only With Their Mothers – Are They Disadvantaged?*

Authors: Enrique Delamonica, Maureen Donahue and Alberto Minujin

Presenter: Enrique Delamonica, UNICEF, New York

SESSION III

General Situation of Children and Women (Poverty, Education and MDGs

Chair: Jean-Marc Coicaud, Acting Head, the United Nations University Office to the UN

Commentator: Jorge Balan, Senior Program Officer in Education and Scholarship, the Ford Foundation

1. *Child Work and School Attendance in Niger*

Author: Mamadou Thiam

Presenter: Albert Motivans, UNESCO Institute for Statistics

2. *Poverty, Maternal Education and the Millennium Development Goals*

Presenter: Maria Angelica Sepulveda, Center for Infancy and Family Research, Universidad Metropolitana, Venezuela

3. *Achieving the Millennium Development Goals in Indian States and Union Territories*

Presenter: Varalakshmi Nallathambi, Kanchi Mamunivar Center for Post Graduate Studies, Pondicherry, India

4. *The Relationship Between Child Poverty and Child Rights*

Authors: David Gordon, Shailen Nandy, Christina Pantazis, Simon Pemberton and Peter Townsend

Presenter: Simon Pemberton, School for Policy Studies, University of Bristol

SESSION IV

Family, Women and Children Welfare and Health Policies

*Chair:*Viviana Mangiaterra, Advisor Children and Youth, Human Development Network, the World Bank

Commentator: Meg Wirth, Mailman School of Public Health, Columbia University, UN Millennium Project Task Force 4 on Child Health and Maternal Health

1. Exclusive Breastfeeding as an Intervention to Reduce Morbidity and Improve Child Survival in Developing Countries

Authors: Seema Mihrshahi, Wendy Oddy and Jennifer K Peat

Presenter: Seema Mihrshahi, Children's Hospital Westmead NSW, Australia

2. Achieving the Millennium Development Goals: Human Rights, Reshaping of Policies and Nigeria

Author: Gloria Okemuo

Presenter: Ochiawunma Ibe Women's Education and Mothering Resource Center (WEMOREC), Lagos, Nigeria

3. Determinants of Delivery Practices in Nepal

Presenter: Nebin Lal Shrestha, Central Bureau of Statistics, Kathmandu, Nepal

SESSION V

Methodology and Dissemination

Chair: Philip Evans, Senior Social Development Advisor, UK Department for International Development (DFID), UK Mission to the UN in New York

Commentator: Gaspar Fajth, Co-ordinator of the economic and social policies program, Division of Policy and Planning, Global Policy Section, UNICEF

1. Pioneering in MICS: the Bangladesh Experience Since 1993

Authors: Naomi Ichikawa, Muhammad Shuaib, A.K.M. Abdus Salam, Fida H. Shah, and Rosella Morelli

Presenter: Naomi Ichikawa, UNICEF Bangladesh

3. Health and Development Statistics in Ghana: Policy Perspective and Context

Authors: Julius Fobil, Idei Gyebi and Mercy Ackumey

Presenter: Julius Fobil, School of Public Health, College of Health Sciences, Accra, Ghana

4. Using MICS and DHS Survey Data to Measure Child Poverty

Authors: David Gordon, Shailen Nandy, Christina Pantazis, Simon Pemberton, and Peter Townsend

Presenter: David Gordon, School for Policy Studies, University of Bristol

APRIL 30

SESSION VI

Child Labor

Chair: Martin Vaessen, Project Director, Measure DHS+, Sr.Vice President, ORC Macro

Commentator: Frans Roselaers, Director, International Programme on the Elimination of Child Labour, ILO

1. Child Labor in Bolivia, a Comparison of Estimates from MECOVI and MICS Survey Instruments

Authors: Lorenzo Guarcello and Scott Lyon

Presenter: Lorenzo Guarcello, Innocenti Research Centre

2. Analysis of Child Labor and Child Education in Bosnia and Herzegovina Using the MICS

Presenter: Olivera Simic, UNICEF Bosnia and Herzegovina

3. To Labor Against Child Labor

Presenter: Mercedita Tia, Census and Planning and Operation Division, National Statistics Office, Philippines

4. Assessment and Analysis of Education and Child Labor in India Using the Multiple Indicator Cluster Survey

Authors: Robert Jenkins and Susan Bissell

Presenter: Chandra Sekhar, UNICEF India

SESSION VII

Methodology and Dissemination

Chair: Trevor Croft, Chief, Strategic Information, Division of Policy and Planning, UNICEF

Commentator: Virginia Botelho, GPIA, The New School

1. Using MICS Findings to Improve the Human Rights of Children
Presenter: Marco Segone, UNICEF Brazil

2. Triangulating Research Methods and Practices to Promote Child Well-Being: Reflecting on Young Lives Longitudinal Childhood Poverty Project

Authors: Nicola Jones and Truan Tuan

Presenter: Nicola Jones, Save the Children UK

3. The Impact of Poverty and Inequality on Educational Outcomes: A Structural Equation Approach to Measuring Living Standards and Poverty Using MICS Data

Authors: Mark Montgomery and Paul Hewett, Population Council

Presenter: Mark Montgomery

4. The Measurement of Children Capabilities: Are MICS Adequate?

Presenter: Mario Biggeri, Department of Economics, University of Florence

SESSION VIII

Education, Gender, Equity

*Chair:*Albert Motivans, Chief, Policy and Analysis Unit, UNESCO Institute for Statistics, Montreal

Commentators: Suzanne Grant Lewis, Assistant Professor of Education, Harvard Graduate School of Education

1. How to Make Children Come First: The Process of Visualizing Children in Peru

Authors: Enrique Vasquez and Enrique Mendizábal

Presenter: Enrique Mendizabal, Bannock Consulting, London, UK

2. Gender Bias Against Female Children in India: Evidence from MICS Survey and Policy

Authors: Perianayagam Arokiasamy and Jalandhar Pradhan

Presenter: Perianayagam Arokiasamy, International Institute for Population Sciences, (IIPS), Mumbai, India

3. Universal Primary Schooling in Sub-Saharan Africa: Is Gender Equality Enough?

Authors: Cynthia Lloyd and Paul Hewett

Presenter: Paul Hewett, Population Council

SESSION IX

Rights and Policies for Children and Women

Final Discussion Panel

Chair: Elizabeth Gibbons, Chief, Global Policy, Division of Policy and Planning, UNICEF

Panelists:

Carmen Barroso, Regional Director, International Planned

Parenthood Federation, UN Millennium Project Task Force 3 on Primary Education and Gender Equality

Peter Townsend, Department of Social Policy, London School of Economics

Frederick Mugisha, Associate Research Scientist, African Population and Health Research Center, Nairobi, Kenya

Nicola Jones, International Coordinator, Save the Children UK

List of Authors

Abdul Alim is a physician with a Master's in Public Health from the University of Texas. He has more than ten years of work experience in issues related to governance in social sectors, more specifically in Programme Planning, Institutional Development, and Monitoring and Evaluation. His major interest is in social policy and planning with an emphasis on practical aspects of social service delivery. He is a member of Pakistan Medical and Dental Council and Human Rights Commission of Pakistan.

Enrique Delamonica is a policy analyst in the Division of Policy and Planning of UNICEF Headquarters, where he has been working on financing of social services, poverty reduction strategies, socioeconomic disparities, and the impact of macro-economic trends on child welfare. He holds post-graduate degrees in economics and political science from the Institute for Economic and Social Development (Argentina), The New School, and Columbia University.

Asmaa Donahue is coordinator of a regional action-research project for the Collective for Research and Training on Development-Action in Beirut. Using Egypt, Lebanon and Palestine as case studies, the project explores the role of state, NGOs and active citizens in bridging the gender gap in basic services. Field research findings will be used to develop a series of country action plans for increasing women's active citizenship and access to entitlements. Ms. Donahue is completing her M.A. in International Development from the New School University in New York.

David Gordon is Professor of Social Justice at the University of Bristol. He is also Director of the Townsend Centre for International Poverty Research and head of the Centre for the Study of Poverty and Social Justice. Professor Gordon is a member of the United Nations Expert Group on Poverty Statistics (Rio Group) and a private expert member of the European Union Working Group on Income, Poverty and Social Exclusion. He has recently been working with UNICEF and colleagues at the London School of Economics and Bristol University on measuring child poverty in the developing world.

Lorenzo Guarcello is currently a researcher at Innocenti Research Centre in Florence for an Inter-Agency research cooperation project between UNICEF, ILO and the World Bank: Developing New Strategies for Understanding Children's Work and its Impact. He holds a master's degree in Economics and Institutions for the Development of South of Italy in Salerno, Italy. He was a research assistant at C.E.I.S. (Center for the Study of Economic Development), Faculty of Economics, University of Rome "Tor Vergata". His research in the area of child labour examines the determinants of child labour and school attendance; and it also focuses on comparative studies on survey instruments. His current research interests examine the relation between orphanhood and child labour, and the effect of household chores on children's activity.

Paul C. Hewett has been working at the Population Council since 1996 after receiving his Ph.D. in Political Science from the State University of New York at Stony Brook. Dr. Hewett has specialized in the areas of survey research methodology and measurement, with a substantive research focus on issues of poverty, health, and education in sub-Saharan Africa. His recent publications with Cynthia Lloyd of the Policy Research Division have highlighted the relatively slow progress in educational participation and attainment among the countries of sub-Saharan African. He has also recently conducted research on the use of computerized self-interviewing for improving the validity and reliability of reporting on sensitive topics in surveys.

V. Jayachandran holds a Masters Degree in Demography; and Master of Philosophy and Doctor of Philosophy in Population Studies from the International Institute for Population Sciences (IIPS), Mumbai. He has the credit of working with all major large scale household Demographic and Health Surveys conducted in India since 1993, which include the Multiple Indicator Survey 2000 (MICS 2000), National Family Health Surveys (NFHS-1 & 2) and District Level Household Surveys Reproductive and Child Health (DLHS-RCH). He has specialized in evaluations, demographic estimations and data analysis. Presently, he is working as Consultant at UNICEF, India Country Office, New Delhi.

Malik Jaffer is a Senior Regional Associate for Europe, Central Asia and the Middle East at the American Red Cross. Mr. Jaffer has been with the American Red Cross since July 2001, initially building a broader program portfolio in the Middle East and Afghanistan. He has been the Operational Lead for the White House Initiative, the America's Fund for Afghan Children. Currently, he is managing a Child Survival Program in Albania and a regional food and tuberculosis program in the Balkans. Prior to his work with the American Red Cross, Mr. Jaffer served as the Country Manager for the Aga Khan Foundation in Tanzania. He also served on Tanzania's National NGO Policy Steering Committee. He has also worked as the Assistant Regional Director for Asia/Middle East with Project HOPE and served as a volunteer Orthopedic Technician at the Aga Khan University Medical Center in Pakistan. Mr. Jaffer has a master's degree in Public Health from Boston University with separate Certificates in Health Care in Developing Countries and Financing of Health Care in Developing Countries. He is currently working on an MBA in Executive Management.

Robert Jenkins has worked with UNICEF for close to nine years in Uganda, Bangladesh, and Myanmar and is currently serving as the Chief of the Strategic Planing, Monitoring and Evaluation Section of UNICEF India. Prior to joining UNICEF, he worked in Lesotho, in emergency relief work in a refugee camp on the border of Somalia and Kenya, and for a development organization based in Toronto. Robert has a Master's degree from the London School of Economics and Political Science, and is currently working on his Doctorate from the University of Bath.

Nicola Jones has a Ph.D. in Comparative Politics from the University of North Carolina at Chapel Hill. She is currently the International Coordinator of an international longitudinal study on child poverty in four countries entitled "Young Lives". The project involves a partnership between a consortium of North and South universities/research institutes and Save the Children-UK. Prior to moving to the UK in October 2003, she was based in South Korea for six years where she worked on a number of gender-related public and NGO-sector initiatives. These included consultancy work for the Ministry of Gender Equality, serving on the international relations committees for two women's rights NGOS, and coordinating an eight country Women's Studies in Asia Network.

Gina Kennedy works in the field of public health nutrition, currently focusing on issues related to nutritional status in urban areas in the context of globalizing food systems. Her work is concentrated on analyzing and addressing both under and over nutrition in urban population groups and development of strategies to address the spectrum of urban nutritional problems. She is a consultant with the Nutrition Planning, Assessment and Evaluation Service of the Food and Agriculture Organization. She holds a bachelor's degree from Georgetown University and a master's degree in Public Health from the University of Alabama.

Marina Komarecki holds a M.S. degree in International Affairs from New School University in New York. She spent several years as an Associate Producer for 60 Minutes, 48 Hours and the Evening News With Dan Rather. She also worked as a Field Producer at CNN in New York. Ms. Komarecki worked as a journalist and a radio producer in her native Yugoslavia and has been a US Correspondent for Radio B92. Her current interests are related to research in the area of child rights and social policies for children and women.

Scott Lyon has fifteen years of research and programing experience in the area of children's rights. He is currently a researcher with a joint ILO-UNICEF-World Bank research project: Understanding Children's Work (UCW). Prior to this, he led a research team analysing emerging issues affecting the rights of children in the Southern Mediterranean region. Mr. Lyon spent seven years in Jordan where he served as a Programme Officer in the UNICEF Regional Office for the Middle East and North Africa.

Enrique Mendizabal is currently a research analyst at the Overseas Development Institute in London. He holds an M.S. degree in Social Policy and Planning for Developing Countries from the London School of Economics (2003). In Peru, he has carried out PRA studies with vulnerable groups (children, victims of domestic violence, and people with disabilities). More recently, he has specialized in the theoretical and practical use of the Sustainable Livelihoods Approach, applying it to the Peruvian coca producers and the border region between Malawi and Mozambique. He has published a book on public expenditure on children and child welfare in Peru during the 1990s, a paper on social protection and pension reform in Latin America (UNDP 2001), a chapter in a book on philanthropic and voluntary organizations in Peru, and various articles in specialized magazines including an upcoming piece in Harvard University's Latin American Review (ReVista).

Seema Mihrshahi is a Ph.D. student in International Health from Sydney, Australia. Her proposed thesis title is "Effectiveness of Exclusive Breastfeeding as an Intervention to Prevent Child Morbidity and Improve Child Survival in Developing Countries". She completed a Master's of Public Health from the University of Sydney. In 2001, she participated in an Australian Youth Ambassadors Project at the Ministry of Public Health in Thailand. Since 1997, she has been responsible for coordinating the Childhood Asthma Prevention Study, an internationally recognised randomised clinical trial that is testing two interventions for the primary prevention of asthma in children. She has published ten peer reviewed journal articles of which she is the primary author on eight. In 2003, she received the Young Investigators Award at the Children's Hospital Westmead Annual Meeting for her contribution to clinical research.

Alberto Minujin is a Mathematician with postgraduate studies in Applied Statistics and Demography. He is Senior Programme Officer, Policy Analysis, at the Global Policy Section in the Division of Policy and Planning of UNICEF Headquarters (New York), working on social policy, poverty and human rights issues. He is the former Regional Advisor for Social Policy, Monitoring and Evaluation for Latin America and the Caribbean and Programme Coordinator of UNICEF Argentina. He was Deputy Director of the National Statistical Office of Argentina and professor of postgraduate studies of the School of Social Sciences, University of Buenos Aires. At present he is professor at the Graduate Program in International Affairs, New School University, New York. He has spent time as a visiting research fellow at the International Development Centre, Queen Elisabeth House, at the Latin American Centre, St. Anthony College, Oxford, England. He was also a visiting research fellow at the Département de la Demographie, Université de Louvain, Belgium, and researcher at the Social Science Institute, Universidad Autonoma de Mexico. He has published several research papers and books including Globalization and Human Rights (Santillana Pub Co.), The New Poor, (Ed. Planeta), Proposal for Inclusive Societies, (Santillana Pub Co.), and numerous articles and papers.

Mark Montgomery is Professor of Economics at the State University of New York, Stony Brook and Senior Associate, the Population Council. With Richard Stren, he co-chaired the U.S. National Academy of Sciences Panel on Urban Population Dynamics from 1999 to 2003, which focused on issues of health, reproductive health, poverty, and governance in the cities of developing countries. The panel's report, Cities Transformed: Demographic Change and Its Implications in the Developing World, was published by the National Academies Press in October 2003. He has written extensively on demographic issues in developing countries, with recent emphasis on the measurement of living standards with survey data, the linkages between fertility and children's schooling, social models of risk perception, and the role of social networks and social learning in demographic behavior.

Frederick Mugisha is an Associate Research Scientist at African Population and Health Research Center based in Nairobi, Kenya. The African Population and Health Research Center (APHRC) is a non-profit, non-governmental international organization committed to conducting high quality, policy relevant research on the population and health-related issues facing sub-Saharan Africa in the next century. He joined APHRC in 2002 after completing his doctoral studies at the University of Heidelberg, Germany. Before his doctoral studies, Dr. Mugisha worked with the Global Program on evidence for health policy at the World Health Organization headquarters in Geneva and with the Medical Research Council (UK) program on HIV/AIDS in Uganda, primarily on the Masaka IEC/STD treatment trial. Dr Mugisha's research centers on urban poverty and health. He is currently involved in a longitudinal research project on urban poverty and health in the informal settlements of Nairobi, Kenya, among other projects.

Shailen Nandy is a post-graduate researcher in the School for Policy Studies at the University of Bristol. His research interests encompass all aspects of international development, particularly health and anti-poverty policy issues.

Christina Pantazis is a research fellow in the School for Policy Studies at the University of Bristol. Her research interests include: Crime, social harm, and criminalisation; Poverty, social exclusion and inequality.

Simon Pemberton is an ESRC Post-Doctoral Fellow at the University of Bristol, UK. His main interests lie in the areas of State and Corporate Harms. Consequently, his research to date has encompassed a number of diverse areas: poverty, human rights, deaths arising from state custody, the UK minimum wage, deaths at work, and deaths from pollution.

Marco Segone holds an M.S. degree in Political Science. He worked in Bangladesh, Pakistan, Thailand, Uganda and Albania in integrated development projects. In 1996 he joined UNICEF working for the Regional UNICEF Office for Latin America and the Caribbean. From 1999 to 2001 he worked as Monitoring and Evaluation officer for UNICEF Niger, where he founded and coordinated for two years the Niger M&E Network. He is now the UNICEF Monitoring and Evaluation Officer for Brazil, where he founded and has been coordinating the Brazilian Evaluation Network since 2002. In 2003 he was elected Vice President of the International Organization for Cooperation in Evaluation (IOCE).

Chandra Sekhar is working as Monitoring and Evaluation Officer at UNICEF, New Delhi, looking after the planning, monitoring and evaluation components of the India Country Programme of Cooperation. He joined UNICEF in 1998 and prior to that worked in the Indian Council of Medical Research for twelve years in the area of medical statistics. He has experience in the monitoring of various multi-centric projects of national relevance with a strong support in the form of preparation study design, sampling methodology, and conducting large-scale surveys. He has experience in providing programmatic information by carrying out various studies, surveys, and data analysis to measure the outcomes, assess trends, and make available the results by maintaining and updating databases on children and women. He holds a Ph.D. in Statistics and Master's degree in Statistics and Economics.

Mamadou Thiam is a statistician at the UNESCO Institute for Statistics (UIS) where he works on education indicators from household surveys. He has previously worked as a sampling statistician for the Demographic and Health Surveys (DHS) project. He also worked as a Data Analyst at the Mayo Clinic in Rochester, Minnesota where he provided statistical and computational support to a wide variety of medical research studies. M. Thiam holds a Master's degree in statistics from the University of Maryland.

Enrique Vásquez is an Economist from Universidad del Pacífco (Lima, Peru). He holds an M.S. degree in Public Policy and a Ph.D. in Politics from Oxford University (United Kingdom). After his postgraduate studies he worked as an Economics advisor at the Ministry of Presidency in Peru in 1995 and then he was appointed a C.E.O of the Food Security Governmental Program in 1996. In 1997 Dr. Vásquez joined the Department of Economics at Universidad del Pacífico. He has published *Cómo reducir la pobreza e inequidad en América Latina, Los desafíos de la lucha contra la pobreza extrema en el Perú, Estrategias del Poder, Gerencia Social, El ataque a la pobreza: un enfoque de mercado, Buscando el Bienestar de los pobres ¿Cuán lejos estamos?* among others. At present, Dr. Vásquez is a Senior Researcher at Universidad del Pacífico and a Consultant of Save The Children Sweden, World Bank, UNICEF, InterAmerican Development Bank, and Swiss Cooperation, among other international organizations.

Peter Townsend is Centennial Professor of International Social Policy in the London School of Economics, and he is Emeritus Professor of Social Policy in the University of Bristol. In 2002 he was the Acting Director of the Centre for the Study of Human Rights at LSE. He has Honorary Doctorates from the University of Essex, 1991, the University of Teesside, 1994, the Open University, 1995, the University of Edinburgh, 1996, the University of Lincolnshire and Humberside, 1997, the University of York 2000, and the University of Stirling 2002. In 1999 he was elected a founder Academician of the new Academy of Learned Societies for the Social Sciences (AcSS). Since 1990 his publications include six books based on new research: The International Analysis of Poverty (1993), A Poor Future (1996), Poverty and Social Exclusion in Britain (with other authors, 2000), Breadline Europe: The Measurement of Poverty (co-editor), 2001, World Poverty: New Policies to Defeat an Old Enemy (co-editor), 2002, and Child Poverty in the Developing World (with other authors, 2003). During 1960-1990 he served in various capacities for UNESCO, WHO and ILO. He was consultant to the UN in 1993-95 during the preparations for, and at, the World Summit for Social Development at Copenhagen in March 1995; and was a member of a UNDP Management Development Programme mission to the Republic of Georgia in 1994. He is currently a member of a UNICEF research team [2000-].